AUSTRALIA'S HARDEST
PRISON

Also by James Phelps

Australia's Most Murderous Prison:
Behind the Walls of Goulburn Jail

Australia's Toughest Prisons: Inmates (August 2016)

AUSTRALIA'S HARDEST
PRISON
INSIDE THE WALLS OF
LONG BAY JAIL

JAMES PHELPS

EBURY
PRESS

An Ebury Press book
Published by Random House Australia Pty Ltd
Level 3, 100 Pacific Highway, North Sydney NSW 2060
www.penguin.com.au

Penguin
Random House
Australia

First published by Ebury Press in 2014
This edition published in 2016

Addresses for companies within the Random House Group can be found at
www.randomhouse.com.au/offices.

National Library of Australia
Cataloguing-in-Publication Entry

Phelps, James
Australia's hardest prison: inside the walls of Long Bay Jail/James Phelps

ISBN 978 0 14378 079 3 (paperback)

Long Bay Correctional Centre
Prisons – New South Wales – Long Bay
Correctional personnel – New South Wales – Anecdotes
Prisoners – New South Wales – Anecdotes

365.9944

Cover design and image by Luke Causby/Blue Cork
Internal design and typesetting by Midland Typesetters, Australia
Printed in Australia by Griffin Press, an accredited ISO AS/NZS 14001:2004
Environmental Management System printer

Random House Australia uses papers that are natural, renewable and recyclable
products and made from wood grown in sustainable forests. The logging
and manufacturing processes are expected to conform to the environmental
regulations of the country of origin.

*This book is dedicated to John Mewburn,
Geoffrey Pearce and every man and woman who
has ever served in the Department of Corrective
Services. Your bravery is finally noted.*

*And to Peter and Kerry Phelps. Thank you for
giving me the upbringing most of the people
you will meet in the following pages never
had. This book would not have been possible
had you not loved, guided and sometimes
smacked me on the bum.*

Contents

1.	Welcome to Long Bay	1
2.	Haunting	4
3.	Arriving	18
4.	Surviving	38
5.	Enforcing	57
6.	Raping	75
7.	Rooting	89
8.	Drinking and Gaming	101
9.	Injecting	110
10.	Protecting	132
11.	Murdering	155
12.	Cutting	177
13.	Shooting	197
14.	Rioting	208
15.	Escaping	230
16.	Failing	277
17.	Ganging	290
18.	Guarding	301
	Select Bibliography	319
	Acknowledgements	322

1

WELCOME TO LONG BAY

Keep an Eye Out

'You have to be violent.'

Former Long Bay inmate Graham 'Abo' Henry

Graham 'Abo' Henry entered the shower block: eight separate cubicles behind a brick wall at the end of 13 Wing. First he heard the muffled screams and then he saw the blood.

'Four Aboriginal blokes were at this guy in the shower,' said Henry. 'And they were flogging the shit out of him. There were no knives, no weapons, but there were plenty of fists, elbows and knees.'

Henry walked past the blood and the screams, and found an empty shower. He turned on the hot water and began to wash. He pretended not to hear the slapping, smacking and smashing; the bone breaking and the blood spilling.

He whistled as he soaped his face. After all, it was just another day at Long Bay.

'Mate, I have seen blokes in there get raped, murdered, bashed and burned,' Henry continued. 'It all goes on. Long Bay is a place that should have been condemned. It was a fucking tough place when I was in there, and to survive you had to be tough too.'

Seeing a bloke get bashed in the shower was nothing, as far as this career criminal was concerned.

'Who's got soap?' someone yelled amidst the action.

'Right-o,' Henry said. 'Coming at ya.' He grabbed the hefty block of Sunlight, recently pulled from its wrapper, and tossed the soap over the tile wall that separated his shower from the next. The soap sailed off into the rising steam.

'It was a shit throw,' Henry recounted. 'And it hit one of the blokes who was throwing punches flush in the head.'

Henry quickly grabbed his towel and walked out.

'Next thing my mate is walking out with claret all over his face,' Henry said. 'They accused him of throwing the soap and punched the shit out of him.'

Abo Henry, an infamous armed robber and street thug, looked at his mate. 'We'll get the cunts in the yard,' he snapped. 'We ain't nothing in here if we don't square it up.'

So Henry found the bashers in the yard. There were four of them, and they were ready to fight.

'I stepped into the first bloke,' Henry said. 'And I pulled out his eye. I plucked it straight from his skull and left it dangling down his face.'

The rest of the men backed away.

'You are fucking mad,' one said before walking off with the rest of the group, leaving their mate, now a bloodied half-blind mess, on the ground.

'That's the thing in jail,' Henry said. 'You have to be violent. You have to do it because you have to stand out. If you don't stand out, then they'll step on you. You need to scare them so that they shit themselves.

'Me and my mate used to electric-shock them in the balls. He had an electrical cord he'd pulled out of a toaster and he'd hold the end, while I grabbed the bloke we were after and throw him into the cell. Then we'd jam the wires into the guy's nuts and watch him scream.'

There are only three ways to survive in Long Bay Jail:
1. Fight.
2. Ask for protection or pay for it.
3. Say nothing and do whatever they ask.

But as you will soon find out, nothing in this place is guaranteed . . .

2

HAUNTING

Ghosts and Gallows

'There's nothing freakier than being alone in those towers at night.'
Former Long Bay prison officer (PO) Paul Rush

Click!

He unclenched his teeth as he pulled the gun away from his face. The barrel, which had been tightly pressed against his temple, left a rising red welt.

This place was driving him mad. He could no longer take the silence, the dark, and that constant feeling of being watched. There were no other guards, no inmates, no cameras. But he wasn't alone. He was *never* alone. Someone, or something, was watching. They were *always* watching.

The trigger smashed on an empty chamber. But there

was no bullet exploding through brain and bone. This time it was just wind kissing his face. He lowered the gun, spun the chamber and pressed the steel back against his head. The solitary bullet waited patiently . . .

Click!

'What the fuck are you doing?' screamed the guard as he burst through the door.

The guard with the gun shrugged. 'I don't know,' he said, seemingly lost.

The ghostly game of Russian roulette was stopped just in time. After ten minutes of silence from his colleague up in 7 Tower, the guard knew something was wrong.

'Many guys lose it up there,' said former Long Bay PO Paul Rush. '7 Tower is supposed to be haunted. 9 Tower and 10 Tower, too. Guards have said they've been tapped on the back, even though they're on their own. And all of us have heard the noises. There's nothing freakier than being alone in those towers at night; guards up there have called down and requested to be taken out. One night a guy lost it and ended up pointing the gun at his head and shooting. I didn't believe it until I saw the report. But I should have, because many who have worked there at night become unhinged.'

This guard did not fire a bullet from his gun, but several have 'accidentally' discharged their firearms while in the tower. One man recently shot himself in the thigh, while another sent a bullet ricocheting off a window and into a wall. Were they simply mishaps or something more?

Ghosts don't exist. Or do they?

*

The inmate confronted the guard at muster, when prisoners were asked to line up for roll call.

'There's something wrong with that cell,' he said. 'I can't sleep in there. I keep hearing noises and it's freezing all the time.'

The guard glanced back. 'Bloody oath, there is something wrong with that cell,' he remarked deadpan. 'You're in what used to be death row. You live in a "condemned cell", so have fun with the ghosts.'

The inmate went white. He'd seen the welded iron outside his cell – No. 47 in 4 Wing – but never realised why it was there. Until now.

'That's the trapdoor,' explained retired guard Dave Farrell, 'where the gallows used to be. You can still see the wooden beam above and the iron doors below.'

Cells 47 and 48 were the final stop for the nine prisoners executed in Long Bay Jail. And according to both guards and prisoners, these cells are haunted by those who had their necks snapped by the hangman's noose.

Whack!

1917. The trapdoor snapped open, the steel swinging as the body dropped through the floor. Long Bay claimed her first kill eight years after she opened as a women's reformatory in 1909. NSW government architect Walter Liberty Vernon never imagined the prison he designed would become a place of death and horror. His Federation Gothic jail, complete with royal coat of arms and portcullis gate, was to be the most humane and comforting prison in history, as per the orders of Captain Frederick Neitenstein. Long Bay was to be Neitenstein's legacy – the NSW Inspector-General of Prisons was going to end brutal penal punishment and turn prisoners into model citizens, with this building to spark international reform. There would be larger cells and electric lighting, and hygienic measures to be taken. There would be work, and rehabilitation programs to help facilitate life after prison. The 'petty' or young offenders who were sent to Australia's first purpose-built dual institution for men and women would return to society and never offend again.

James Wilson would not offend again – but not because of the hot water delivered to his shower from the boiler room, or the on-site electrical generator that lit up his spacious 3.96 × 2.13-metre cell, or from the never-before-seen back-to-back cells, complete with verandahs. No, the hood pulled over his head and the rope around his neck would end his life of crime.

The man who murdered George Pappageorgi in Haymarket shivered as Reverend Arthur Morris asked him for his final words. At three seconds past nine on 31 May 1917, the trapdoor sprang open and the condemned man shot from the scaffold.

Wilson could be one of the many ghosts that haunt Australia's most notorious prison. But let's start with those who were killed outside those cold, noisy cells No. 47 and No. 48 in 4 Wing, in the male penitentiary, by way of execution.

Built directly next to the sandstone-dressed 'art nouveau' women's reformatory in 1914, this 352-cell jail that finally formed the Long Bay dual institution housed petty thieves and drunkards, who had caused Darlinghurst Jail to overflow. The male penitentiary was built on 'bold sand hills, with rocks and gullies and a wealth of wildflowers' and 'placed on a sandstone ridge to take the [ocean] views'. An execution chamber was not in the architectural blueprint or ever discussed by the prison's founders.

The lump of wood and an iron trapdoor were hastily, and cheaply, introduced when this vision of reform became New South Wales' worst and most feared prison. So was the rope that strangled the life from James Wilson, Christian William Benzing (executed on 16 June 1917, for raping and murdering an 11-year-old girl), Edward Williams (executed on 29 April 1924, for murdering his three young children), William George Gordon Simpson (executed on 10 December 1924, for murdering Guy Chalmers Clift and Police Constable James Flynn), William Cyril Moxley (executed on 17 August 1932, for the murder of Dorothy Ruth Denzel and Frank Barnby Wilkinson), Edwin John Hickey (executed on 14 May 1936, for murdering Montague Henwood), James Leighton Massey (executed on 15 June 1936, for murdering Norman Samuel McLaren Stead), Alfred Spicer (executed on 26 May 1938, for the rape and murder of a child), John Trevor Kelly (executed on 24 August 1939, for murdering Marjorie Constance Sommerlad).

And that rope is the reason one of these men went on to become the Night Strangler of 7 Tower.

*

The crisp night air kept the guard awake as he paced up and down the catwalk; he had seen nothing but blackness since the last cell light switched off. And that was more than three hours ago. He walked back to the warmth of the tower, the door closing behind him and shutting out the cold.

He sat down, the comfort of the chair easing the ache in his back.

Zzzzzzzzz.

Soon he was asleep, just like the rest of the prison.

Suddenly he awoke, his shoulders exploding into the back of his chair. It was like a bolt of lightning had ripped through his body, the painful jolt shocking his eyelids open.

He wanted to scream but he couldn't.

'Help!' a painful rasp, whisper-quiet, was all he could get out.

Help . . .

He was no longer alone.

'I was being choked,' explained the guard, who asked to remain anonymous. 'One minute I was sleeping, and the next I couldn't breathe. I felt like I was being strangled. I was being pushed into the back of the chair but nothing was there – nothing I could see anyway. And that's when I realised it was a ghost. I thought I was going to pass out, if not from the hands around my neck, then from the fear. I was terrified. And then it stopped. I jumped from the chair and bolted down the stairs and back into the jail. I refused to work in that tower again, and I've never been back since.'

7 Tower is haunted. Ask anyone who's worked there.

'The whole jail is weird because of the history,' attested another guard. 'But the towers are especially scary because you are all alone and you know what lies beneath. Blokes freak out around there, and we've had stories from guards about feeling strangled.

'At the base of 7 Tower is where all the executed prisoners were buried, where the old Long Bay cemetery is. Even though there's nothing official to mark it, we all know it's there. There are bodies right under the tower inside the jail. I don't know how many – I don't think anyone does. They weren't real good at keeping records back then, and I think you'll find that some of the people buried there might've died in suspicious circumstances. It's a veggie patch now. They're all under a veggie garden and it's freaky as shit.'

Infamous Sydney crook Frederick 'Chow' Hayes, the most feared gunman and gangster of his generation, was the first to publicly speak about Long Bay's cemetery. He was on remand in Long Bay when Moxley was executed in 1932.

'If no one claimed the body, it was buried in the prison,' Hayes said. 'And that was the case when William Cyril Moxley was hanged.'

Hayes would have ended up alongside him, had the death sentence not been abolished while he was living in Long Bay's death row.

Oh, what would Neitenstein have thought if he had been alive. His vision of a place for criminal reformation had become a dumping ground. The petty offenders were soon tossed out and the foulest offenders in New South Wales were sent to rot in this towering prison, which was conveniently remote from Sydney but commutable by both road and tram. The crowded Darlinghurst Jail was soon closed, the murderers, rapists and thieves sent to Malabar on a specially made 'prison carriage', which was connected to the public tram. Immediately notorious, the prison had a new name: Long Bay.

According to the 1997 Department of Corrective Services report on Long Bay's conservation plan:

It has been the centre of the prison system for over 80 years and became the largest and best known of the new reformatory prisons in Australia.

It is the only complex in Australia to be master-planned with separate prisons for men and women, including separate transport systems (tram and road), staff housing, chapel, boiler house and electrical power generation. The former women's jail was the first separate purpose-designed women's jail in NSW and the last 19th century radial prison. It was the first jail in NSW for petty offenders and of rare back to back design.

Long Bay would go on to cage Australia's most infamous killers and criminals. Bitter Razor Gang rivals Tilly Devine and Kate Leigh, two very prominent members of the Sydney underworld, terrorised the women's reformatory in the 1930s and made the female-only institution as bloody as the building next door – the men's jail that would become New South Wales' most violent reception and remand prison.

No jail can boast a line-up like this: Darcy Dugan, Chow Hayes, Archie 'Mad Dog' McCafferty, Ivan Milat, Bilal Skaf, Rene Rivkin, Rodney Adler, Neddy Smith, Graham 'Abo' Henry, Danny Karam, Michael Kanaan, Lennie McPherson, Tony Lanigan, Anthony Stewart, The Running Man, Tom Domican, John Elias, The Cobby Killers, Sam and Michael Ibrahim, Maddison Hall, The Granny Killer, Ian Hall Saxon, Raymond John Denning and Harry M Miller. You will soon meet many of them . . .

It's not only the ghosts of inmates that haunt Long Bay.

'I was working in a really old area now called MSPC2 (Metropolitan Special Purpose Centre 2),' said a guard. 'It was the original remand section, before the MRRC (Metropolitan Remand and Reception Centre). I was doing a perimeter check and I came up around the tower and looked all the way down to the other end of the jail.'

That's when the guard stopped; he was stunned and silent.

'I saw something,' the guard said. 'It was the size of a person and it was mostly blue. The exact same blue as the colour of an officer's shirt, and it was up in the catwalk, standing exactly like an officer keeping watch.'

Maybe it was just another officer, patrolling the grounds?

'No, that tower had been abandoned a long time ago,' the guard continued. 'It wasn't human. As I focused on it, it dashed across the catwalk and into the tower, never allowing me to get a proper view. I was with another guard at the time and I turned around and looked straight at him and said: "Did you see that?" And he said: "No. I saw you looking up there and you were terrified. There was no way I was looking at whatever it was."

'Long Bay is haunted, for sure. It's not that it's just old or that people have died there. I think it's because of the amount of troubled people this place has seen. A lot of these people were mental patients, or the worst and most fucked-up people around. No other place has seen so many tortured souls.'

Harold Maclean, Comptroller General of Prisons, was the first to float the idea of a new Sydney jail in 1870. He formally recommended a new penitentiary 'to house drunkards and petty offenders' be built in 1888 after the vacant Cockatoo Island was reclaimed to house 'habitual vagrants and petty offenders', as reported by historian Terry Cass, whose research has provided much of the historical information in this chapter. The recommendation remained just that until Neitenstein began campaigning for a 'modern and humane' prison for women and a first-time offenders jail for men and minor criminals. A report stating 135 women were sharing a single ward at Cockatoo Island helped his cause.

So architect Walter Vernon submitted his first plans in 1899 to the Parliamentary Standing Committee on Public Work, with Randwick as the chosen site for the prison.

The site was rejected and moved 12 kilometres south of Sydney to a raised plot of land; the grass separated from the tumbling ocean by a series of towering cliffs.

The new site, and the revolutionary prison, was eventually approved and the first brick of the soon-to-be criminal's hell was laid in 1901. The female prison was given priority and the 276-cell 'modern and humane' jail was opened in 1909.

It is the grandest, oldest and most intimidating of the Long Bay jails, which haphazardly and quickly sprang from the rolling cliff-side green as the prison population exploded and the quick-fix pick and shovel were taken to the grass. The male jail, a seemingly rushed and inferior imitation of the grand Victorian Gothic next door, opened in 1914. Several jails followed: a building of 220 cells called the Additional Accommodation for Prisoners in 1962; the state's first purpose-built remand centre with a housing capacity of 224 inmates in 1967; the infamous supermax called Katingal; a state-of-the-art maximum hospital and a 'secure' jail used to hide informants whose names were deleted from the system and replaced by numbers.

'Long Bay is made up of a number of separate jails,' said former prison governor Michael Vita.

'Basically you have the two original jails (the women's reformatory built in 1909 and the men's penitentiary built in 1914) and then a series of other jails that were added over the years as the Long Bay complex grew. Each jail in the prison has had a number of names and purposes over the years. The women's prison became a men's maximum prison, then a remand prison and eventually the Central Industrial Prison (CIP).'

The oldest, most important, and certainly the most haunted, jails in Long Bay are the former women's reformatory and the former men's penitentiary. The two buildings have housed and 'killed' some of Australia's worst criminals. The women's reformatory features a medieval gatehouse, dressed sandstone walls and four two-storey wings around a circular yard in the centre of the yard. There are five one-storey buildings in between the wings. Three of the wings are identical (7 Wing, 9 Wing and 10 Wing), each with 72 cells: 36 up-and-down cells on one side of the gallery and another 36 on the other.

'It's just like what you see in the old prison movies,' said a former inmate. 'There are two floors with cells stacked side by side and directly above. There's a big walkway and you look across at exactly the same thing on the other side. Each cell has the old iron bars and there's nothing in there but concrete and a shitty bed.'

Originally called Cell Ranges 2, 3 and 4, there is a semi-circular one-level bathroom at the end of each wing. The wing walls are made of English bond with chunky sandstone dressings around the windows.

The other two-storey wing, originally called Cell Range 1, has 120 cells in rows of 30. The wing became the Special Care Unit in 1979.

The one-storey buildings in between were originally the laundry, the kitchen and a block of punishment cells. Other buildings surround the wings: a workshop, a hospital and a wardens' quarter. And they are all contained by a 466-metre wall made from English bond: 4.57 metres high and almost half a metre thick.

The first Long Bay prison became a white elephant. In 1922 only an average of 42 of the 276 cells were occupied. The women of New South Wales weren't bad enough for the Bay.

Meanwhile, the men's penitentiary, finally opened in 1914, was bursting at the seams. With 70 percent of the state's receptions sent to this now-maximum-security moshpit, up to four inmates were housed in a single cell. The prison, which was only built to incarcerate drunkards and petty thieves serving no more than a three-month sentence, had become the biggest prison in New South Wales. The men's penitentiary, which became the Metropolitan Reception Centre, did not have the finely crafted gatehouse nor the sandstone dressing of the prison next door. Compared to the women's reformatory, this jail was brutally plain, hard and cold. Perfect, really, for what it would become.

During the 15 years it took to build the six two-storey cell wings, with 21 yards, Neitenstein had retired and the hastily added gallows and the cheaper-more-conventional-than-originally-planned building indicated that this was no longer to be the minimum security solution to Darlinghurst. As soon as the institution was opened, 'Darlo' was shut, as were several smaller NSW jails, and the most notorious crooks were sent to Long Bay from central Sydney on a tram.

The prison had 352 cells in the six two-storey wings. Four of the six wings were back to back, an experimental design touted as a world-first, even though it wasn't. There was also a debtor's prison, a workshop, a hospital, an observation ward and a sterile zone. And three highly undesired 'punishment cells'. The cells led directly out to a yard, with a top landing surrounded by a caged balcony. There were 17 cells in each row and 68 in a wing. Soon that was not enough, and the men took over two wings of the women's jail, and eventually, in 1957, the whole lot. The two jails were combined and called the State Penitentiary.

But without the inmates, Long Bay is just an old brick building with bars. It's the prisoners who have made this patch of land the worst address in Sydney. Let's go and meet them: the murderers and the murdered, the rapists and the rooters, the enforcers and the survivors, the paedophiles, the Dogs, the ones who have escaped and the others who have failed.

This is Long Bay Jail – Australia's hardest prison.

3

ARRIVING

Sugar and Spite

'This is Long Bay, mate. Shut up and don't say a word.'
Former Long Bay inmate John Elias

A crooked walking stick rests against the wall of a South Sydney home; the wood bruised, chipped and stained with time. A stark reminder of the consequences of Long Bay's brutality.

Jamie Partlic, 47, soon has the stick in his hand. His skinny silhouette moves from the shadows and towards the afternoon light. His stick is the only thing keeping his frail frame, a skeleton covered in flesh, from falling to the floor.

'What do you want?' he fires in a voice 80 grit sandpaper rough. 'How did you find me here?' His wispy long hair falls to cover the deep red scars on his face.

'I want to know how it happened, what provoked it and what you think of the place that took away everything but your life.'

He edges back towards the dark. 'Can you get the last 27 years of my life back?' he asks, his walking stick shuddering high to form a pointless defence. '*Can you*?' he screams.

Of course not.

But we can finally reveal how life at Long Bay changed Partlic's life forever . . .

The vehicle stopped and the 19-year-old aspiring computer technician stepped out. He was dwarfed by the towering sandstone: almost 5 metres high and topped with clumps of skin-ripping barbwire. The late afternoon sun blazed against the 500-million-year-old rock, dug from a Pyrmont quarry and fashioned into a 286-metre wall. Inside were murderers, rapists and thieves – more monsters than men.

Partlic did not fear the Long Bay beasts. In fact, he never thought he would see the insides of a cell.

The teenager from Cronulla reached into his pocket and pulled out a freshly folded piece of paper. He handed it to the cashier.

'Sorry, we don't take cheques,' was the response. 'It's Friday afternoon and we only take cash.'

Partlic fumed.

'What?' he screamed. 'You have to be joking. It's fucking money!'

'Sorry,' the cashier replied. 'Nothing I can do.'

Partlic snatched back the cheque, his palm furiously reducing it to a marble-sized mess.

It was just an hour ago that he believed this piece of paper would be his last-minute saviour. He'd hugged his brother Frank and thanked him for the $1197 loan, before neatly folding the cheque and tucking it into his pocket.

Now his brother's generosity was nothing more than a crumpled piece of paper. He turned to the wall and his anger morphed into fear.

He would soon be with the monsters.

His crime? Unpaid fines. His sentence? Four days inside the Long Bay Correctional Centre, Australia's hardest prison. His punishment? Four months in a coma and a life of pain.

'Balls up,' screamed the guard. 'Spread them open.'

Partlic looked down at the cold concrete ground as his anus was inspected. He had given all his belongings – his clothes, his useless cheque and his dignity – to a Long Bay prison guard sitting behind a counter.

Arse in the air, he ignored the prisoners to his left and right. He hoped they were fine defaulters too. But he feared they were rapists . . . prayed they were not murderers.

The kettle whistled and Partlic turned away from his new friend. He poured the water over the instant blend, the polystyrene cup filling with boiling brown. He was feeling better. Locked away in his cell, the night had been incident-free.

Door shut, he couldn't get out, but no one could get in. He was woken for muster, his name checked off and breakfast served: fresh eggs on toast. No one said a word.

Maybe this was easier than paying back Frank?

Partlic had met a man before making his coffee. A fellow low-risk inmate had said 'G'day', and they'd joked about their predicament before deciding on a warm drink. They'd walked from the yard to the makeshift kitchen, unaware of the lurking danger – a thug called 'Casper', especially violent on this day, drunk on Long Bay prison brew.

Gary Donald Stokes, better known by heavies, hardened and influential criminals, as 'Casper', barged his way through the misfits. He looked like a bloke desperate for coffee. But he wasn't. No, he was only craving trouble. A tall, thickset man of 33, he grunted at the skinny teenager.

'Give me some sugar,' he said.

Casper, who was serving 18 years for stomping on the head of a man following a drug argument in Newcastle, laughed as he nudged his goateed mate, Darren Dilford, who was in for break and enter.

Partlic grabbed the container and handed it to Casper. 'No sugar,' he said. 'Just coffee.'

How could Partlic, after one day in jail, know that sugar was prison code for homosexual sex?

But Casper didn't care. He didn't want to fuck this kid. He just wanted to fuck him up.

'I think we have a smartarse here,' Dilford said, blood still hot after a session on the punching bag with his big mate.

Casper nodded.

Bang!

Partlic's tiny frame was sent crashing to the ground by the thunderous hit. Casper was a fighter, a man who had spent his life throwing hooks, uppercuts, jabs and crosses, hitting jaws, ribs, kidneys and faces.

Partlic had never been punched before. The huge right thrown straight from Casper's meaty shoulders knocked him out cold. His head bounced on the concrete, his limp body unable to mount a defence against the hard prison floor. Surely that was enough? Big Casper had proved his point?

Whack!

Partlic's bloodied face was slammed into a fire hydrant, his skull collapsing as it collided with metal. The sound of breaking bone sickened onlookers. Even hardened criminals looked away.

But Stokes wasn't finished. He picked up the teenager and speared him headfirst into the ground. Witnesses thought Partlic was dead, the teenager not moving an inch once his feet, arms and then torso followed his head into the ground.

Thud!

Casper's foot smashed into Partlic's chest, forcing the boy's body to show momentary signs of life – his chest heaved and blood spewed from his mouth. Red pooled on the prison cement as his skin turned white. There were no screams, no yells, not even when Partlic's flesh was then burned by a scorching cigarette. Partlic could not feel a thing; he was brain dead.

James Partlic, the 19-year-old fine defaulter, walked into

Long Bay Jail on 7 November 1987, and was carried out a vegetable the very next day.

It has been 27 years since the attack but Partlic cannot look in the mirror without being reminded of his gruelling ordeal. Doctors said he was lucky to live. He uses his walking stick regularly to keep his body upright.

'He spent eight months in Prince Henry Hospital,' said his mother, Manyana.

'At first we didn't expect him to live. They had to pop and drain fluid from his lungs to stop him from drowning. They operated on his brain, and he had huge damages everywhere: his legs, arms, head and chest. He spent four months in a coma, and he was a shadow of my boy when he woke up.'

Gary Donald 'Casper' Stokes was sentenced to a maximum penalty of life imprisonment after being found guilty of maliciously inflicting grievous bodily harm with intent to cause grievous bodily harm. His minimum sentence was 18 years. Dilford, the co-accused, was given a minimum of seven years, which was overturned on appeal. Prison officials were forced to explain how a violent offender gained access to the low-security fine defaulters' yard, where the attack occurred. The responses shocked both the District Court judge and the public, prompting widespread prison reform.

'They just opened the door and walked right through,' said a witness in the case.

'The [grille] door [which separates 6 Wing from the fine yards] is left open all the time. Prisoners come and go as they please.'

It also emerged that Casper was a prison 'sweeper', an influential inmate who had special privileges, including access to the fines yard.

Partlic would be the last fine defaulter to spend a night in jail. The attack outraged the state, the NSW government swiftly acting to abolish jail terms for those who failed to pay fines for minor offences. Offenders would now have their licence cancelled or their car registration revoked.

'It was a terrible incident that not only changed the law but also how we viewed other low-classification prisoners,' said former Long Bay Jail governor Michael Vita. 'They reviewed and changed the penalties for fine defaulters. We also had a good look at what access prisoners had in terms of where we were putting vulnerable offenders. We used to be careful where we put people, but as hard as we tried we couldn't guarantee their safety. One-out cells were rare and at the end of the day if we had a vacancy we just had to use it. Some offenders were very scared, and rightly so. Looking back now, I can say we made some big calls putting people in with other people. Many walked in and found their roommate was a hardened crim who'd say, "Don't come in here, cunt." Partlic helped change some of that.'

But for Partlic, there was no silver lining to his bashing. Left with brain damage, he wears a stack-hat to places like Harold Park to watch the trots, doing his best to live a normal life. But he is unable to work and finds socialising difficult. And those scars? They'll never go away.

'I can't remember any of it,' Partlic says. 'It was so long ago. I can't do anything but leave it in the past. I'm as well as I can be and I do what I can.'

But Partlic is far from well. He suffers from psychotic episodes and is growing increasingly paranoid. He rarely leaves his house and has become estranged from his family.

'You can't have a conversation with him anymore,' said a close family member. 'After five minutes he just snaps. He's become really bad over the last few years and doesn't know who he is in the head. He has broken our hearts and there's nothing we can do for him now. And it's all thanks to Long Bay.'

Partlic's only consolation is that he lived.

Green Dunlop Volleys

'You'll end up in Long Bay and you'll be fucked, bashed or murdered, and maybe all three.'
Former detective-sergeant Roger Rogerson

John Elias looked at the towering walls as the bus stopped. He no longer felt brave. He had sucked it up when they'd cuffed him, kept his head held high as the two beefy guards shoved him into the wheeled cage, and ignored the criminals threatening him as the bus had hurtled towards the jail. But now, cuffs not feeling tight enough, the other inmates suddenly silent, the future rugby league player prayed for the driver to put the bus into reverse.

'I shat myself,' Elias said, thinking back to that day. 'I was in a van with a load of prisoners and I never said a word. I looked at the jail and was just terrified. I'd been to boys' homes before, but I never expected a real jail to be like this. The first thing I noticed after the walls was the smell. The place just fucking stank. I can't describe it, but it was just wrong.

'I was only 16 and two months. The cops charged me with assaulting a bus driver and I was already on previous assault charges. They said it was attempted murder. Still, I thought I was going to be locked up in a boys' home. But here I was at the gates of Long Bay, the scariest prison of them all.'

Elias had been told all about Long Bay and until now thought they were merely stories of fiction. Former detective-sergeant Roger Rogerson, who was extensively interviewed for this book just two months before he was charged with murdering drug dealer Jamie Gao, would try to scare boys like Elias from committing further crime using the infamous institution as a reason.

'With kids you would always tell them that this was their last shot before they end up in Long Bay,' said the one-time NSW Police Officer of the Year.

'It was a bloody scary threat because Long Bay was legendary mean. It struck fear into the heart of even the most hardened crim, let alone a boy. We told them they would end up being fucked, bashed or murdered in Long Bay, or maybe all three. The real scare in going to Long Bay was that you would never get out. Long Bay was the jail everyone feared. And for good reason.'

*

Crack!

Elias jumped as the cage snapped shut behind him. The metal-on-metal slap did nothing to lighten his mood. Sitting silently on the bus with other crims, he was now locked in what was known as the 'Birdcage'.

Brrruuhtttt!

The next gate sounded like the growling belly of a beast as the iron scraped against the concrete ground. Elias looked to the floor as the opening gate grunted and groaned, keeping his eyes firmly focused on the carpet until the moaning stopped; the beast seemingly satisfied for now. He didn't want to get off the bus but soon Elias was being pushed right into the imaginary monster's mouth. The Punchbowl misfit puffed his chest and flexed his arms in a bid to look big as he walked through the gates of hell. He only weighed 70 kilos, but with his muscles pushed out he looked heavier. Elias had already let his tightknit curls grow into an afro so that he could look taller. But when he was told to stand in a line, completely naked, nothing could stop him from feeling absolutely vulnerable, alone and terrified.

Elias looked to the other inductees. *Maybe they're scared too?* he thought to himself.

Maybe I'm not a sissy?

The fear he saw in their eyes did not give him the comfort he'd been desperately seeking.

'I walked into reception and it was just a giant steel cage,' Elias said. 'They made me bend over, then looked up my arse and pulled at my hair, checking to see if I had drugs or a hidden weapon. They did all the things you hoped they wouldn't do but knew they would.'

Elias' clothes, wallet, keys and shoes were locked away in a cupboard. He was handed a bag; the things inside were now all he owned.

'I got a pillowslip with a bullshit bar of White Ox soap,' Elias said. 'I got toothpaste, and a toothbrush and clothes. I got shorts, a shirt, a jumper and they were all green. They also gave me a pair of Dunlop Volleys, not the blue-and-white kind – they were the green ones, of course.'

Elias' terror subsided, if only for a moment, when a guard showed him some form of kindness as he entered the remand centre.

'PO Mercer, who is actually the father of [ironman athletes] Dean and Darren Mercer, couldn't believe how young I was,' Elias said. 'There was nothing he could do about me being there, but he was good enough to put me in my own cell, what they called one-out.'

Elias was relieved at knowing he wouldn't have to contend with a cellmate trying to rape him in his sleep. But his assumption was wrong – not because he would be raped, but because he wouldn't sleep.

'I was taken to my cell after they made us shower in the bathrooms at the end of the wing,' Elias said. 'I got a [prison ID] card and was marched down the wing. It was just like you see in the movies; there were iron bars and rows of cells stacked beside and on top of each other. There were 80 upstairs and 80 down, so 160 cells all up in the wing.

'I walked into my cell and couldn't believe that anybody could live there. The bed wasn't a bed, just a piece of foam pretending to be a mattress. The window was just a hole in the wall with steel bars. I'd noticed that other inmates had covered theirs with pieces of cardboard. There was a big green thing hanging on the wall. I asked the guard what it was, and he told me that's where I had to put my clothes. I was on the top landing.

'He shut the door, and I just sat there trying to comprehend where I was and how I'd gotten here. I'd seen cunts shooting up hammer, spewing, and I'd only been there five minutes. It was horrible. I hadn't been classified yet because I was awaiting trial. And the worst thing about the remand centre was that there could have been anyone in there – murderers, rapists and serial killers. They could be here for years until their trial finished and then they would be sent to max.'

PO Michael Vita could see it in the prisoners' eyes: the fear, the terror and the 'How the fuck did I end up here?'

'Some were very scared when they came in,' Vita said. 'We'd give them their pillow and sheets, their towel, their toothbrush, toothpaste and toilet paper. We would have their cell card made up and it would say, for instance, No. 72. Then we would send them on their way.'

The only advice Vita and the other screws would give the 'fresh meat' newcomers was: 'Make sure you make it to muster'.

'Five minutes later they'd come back, saying, "Boss, I need another room,"' Vita continued. 'We'd ask them why, and they'd say it was because they were scared of the bloke they were with. All we could say was, "Mate, you're in jail, bad luck." I think about it now and I wonder how I would've liked it; walking into a tiny room and seeing some hardened crim who didn't want me there.

'When I joined in 1978, you had double bunks and shit-tubs. There was no plumbing and prisoners would have to shit in a bucket. Eventually we had to put in plumbing because the deranged crooks would throw shit everywhere. That's where the old saying "shit-canned" comes from. In institutional settings, there's mad and there's bad. But they all come in on a truck and it's up to us to work it out.'

Each load of receptions – new prisoners coming into the jail – is the same. At least to the guards who unload them twice a day, every day.

'The receptions all come in on a truck,' said Vita. 'After coming past the gates, the truck goes into the Birdcage, which is basically a big loading area. Each of the jails in Long Bay has a big set of gates. The truck would come in the first gate, stop and wait for it to be locked and then move through to the second set after they've been opened. The vehicle would then make a left before stopping at a yellow line. And that's where the crims would get off.'

And that's when they got scared. When the clothes came off, and the rubber gloves went on.

'They would be checked off on a warrant first,' Vita said. 'We'd look at their tattoos and identification marks and compare them to the papers. Then we'd give them an initial search before inviting them into the reception room. The prisoners would walk up to the desk and check in their valuables with the prison guards.'

Then came the dreaded search.

'"Bend over, open your mouth, and spread your cheeks," is what we would say,' said Vita. 'Followed by "Open, show me, spin around, and bend over." Their balls would go up and they would spread their arse open. They'd be given their green prison garb, and their cream pillowslip filled with the things they need inside, plus a cup, and a plastic knife and fork. They would then have a shower before going to the reception section of the wing that they'd been assigned.'

Men, even the toughest of the tough, broke down.

'Plenty of guys were terrified,' said Vita. 'Some so much so that they would try to kill themselves and we'd have to put them in observation rooms. We had one or two "dry" cells, which had absolutely nothing in them – not even a toilet. Jails were not nice places. If you didn't overcome your fears quickly, you wouldn't survive. Reception was just the beginning. Those people did not last very long in the wing. Even in the 70s, we tried to look after them and safety was an issue. We did our best to separate the weak from the strong and they would end up in the hospital under supervision. But unfortunately for them, they couldn't do their whole sentence there, and they'd eventually have to bite the bullet and confront their fears in gen pop [general population].'

Ian Mathie went through reception twice. Now a reformed standover man all tattoos, muscles and fearsome, he recalled being a terrified teen at Long Bay.

'I was 18 and three months when I went to Penrith Court,' said Mathie. 'I'd done some car thefts and things like that and I thought nothing of it. All of sudden the judge said to me, "You are going to Long Bay." I perked up a bit when he said that.

'All I remember of the trips to reception was that it was a fucking long way. I was caged up with other criminals and I suppose I was scared. I can remember getting to the jail. I walked straight in and they stripped me down, hosed me off, the whole deal – just like you see in the movies. Then I was given a dirty pair of green pants, a green shirt, white undies, and white socks. Then they slapped a pair of Dunlop Volleys in my hand. The second time it was all the same, except they gave me a pair KT46s instead. Then I was taken to my cell and I got this scratchy old grey blanket, which was as hard as fucking nails, and a pillowcase to match.

'My first cell was four-out. And I was shitting bricks. The thing back then [early 80s] was that everyone took pride in the way they looked. That was the era. Everyone was clean-shaven, and they brushed their hair. There were no tats or beards, like these days, to give it away. It was shit because you had no idea who was dangerous and who wasn't.'

Mathie, like every other Long Bay reception inductee, would soon find out . . .

Worry Beads

'Maybe he was really sick before he got to Long Bay. Or maybe it was Long Bay that made him sick.'
Current Long Bay guard

The 59-year-old placed the neatly folded $100 bills on the table.

'He must have slapped down around $2000,' said the guard who'd been there at the man's arrival. 'I'd never seen so much cash in the prison.'

Long Bay's newest prisoner put his 'pocket change' on the counter and shrugged. 'That's all I have,' he said. 'You don't have to search me, do you?'

The guard looked back at the disgraced millionaire. 'Mr Rivkin,' he said, 'please put those beads you are holding onto the counter and then we are going to search you. That is the procedure for every prisoner and we do not make exceptions. Do you understand?'

Rene Rivkin, the bearded, cigar-smoking investment guru, sentenced to nine months of periodic detention after being convicted of insider trading, wrapped his trademark gold worry beads around his hand and made a fist so tight his knuckles turned white.

'You cannot take these,' he said. 'You must not take these.'

The guard regarded him sternly. This time he was not polite. 'Hand them over now,' he said. 'And take off those compression socks too.'

Rivkin's hands suddenly moved to his head. 'Oh . . .' he muttered. 'Oh, I don't feel so well. What's happening?

My head...' Rivkin dropped to the ground, mysteriously and suddenly. The medical staff, on standby and plentiful, rushed to his aid.

'Mr Rivkin,' one said. 'Are you okay?'

The stockmarket guru who'd made a fortune out of selling the 'Rivkin Report' to Australian mums and dads didn't respond.

The guard tried to prevent the laughter rising from his throat but he couldn't.

'A-HA-HA-HA-A!'

Then another guard laughed, but this time much louder.

'AH-HA-HA-HA-HA-A!'

Soon the hospital was in hysterics; even the 'unconscious' Rivkin tried to restrain a faint smile from playing on his lips.

'We might have believed him if he hadn't broken his fall with his arm,' said the former officer who'd been there that day. 'He was like, "Oh, I'm passing out" as he went down before putting both his hands out and softly placing himself on the floor. He just went down to the ground and pretended he was asleep.'

Rivkin had avoided prison for seven months after 'collapsing' in Silverwater Jail while serving the first day of his nine-month sentence.

'And here he was trying it on again,' said the guard. 'It was bloody hilarious.'

But not even his high-priced lawyers and his 'medical complaints' could get the controversial Eastern Suburbs celebrity out of this one.

Former NSW Corrective Services commissioner Ron

Woodham demanded that Rivkin resume his sentence on 6 February 2004 after altering his court order to allow him to serve his periodic detention in the Long Bay prison hospital.

No medical certificate was going to keep Rivkin in his $2 million Point Piper apartment. Here in Long Bay he would receive treatment for whatever illness his army of private doctors could throw up: brain tumors, gall bladder infections and deep vein thrombosis. The prison hospital even assigned him personal psychologists to treat his severe depression and suicidal tendencies.

Rivkin abandoned his rich, extravagant evasion efforts 244 days after collapsing in Silverwater Jail, checking himself out of a private psychiatric clinic in Sydney's east to resume the rest of his nine-month periodic detention sentence.

Rivkin was reported to have arrived at Long Bay in the back of an ambulance – but according to guards he did not.

'He arrived in a soft-top Bentley, top down,' said a guard. 'He was taken straight into the prison by his driver. Somehow he'd got permission to be delivered to the hospital's front door. He had an escort and everything.'

'I'm Rene Rivkin,' the multi-millionaire said to the guard as he arrived at the front entrance.

The guard nodded. 'And who is that?' he asked, pointing at the man standing next to Rivkin, bag in hand.

'Oh, that's my bodyguard,' Rivkin said. 'He's coming in with me.'

'Like fuck he is,' the guard fumed.

The driver/bodyguard was sent on his way and Rivkin became just another Long Bay reception.

'Rivkin was taken in and told he was going to be searched,' said a guard years later, recalling the moment. 'He said, "What do you mean? I never agreed to a strip search." And that's when he put his hands on the ground and pretended to faint. They waited until he realised it wouldn't work before giving him his greens and some slippers.

'I still can't believe they let him drive up to the gate with his security guard. They brought in special security to search him because they weren't prepared to let just anyone do it. They didn't want him freaking out and it disgusts me that he got special treatment because of who he was.'

Rivkin spent 76 nights in Long Bay Jail. Several guards claim he received preferential treatment while locked away in the Malabar complex.

'It started when he was allowed to be driven into the jail by his bodyguard,' said a current prison officer. 'He also presented himself early and left early.'

Rivkin was released from his first weekend of periodic detention at 12.30pm on 8 February 2004.

'He arrived early,' said a prison spokesperson at the time. 'And he would have completed the required number of hours by 12.20pm.'

He was told not to turn up early again.

'You can't just turn up whenever you want,' said the spokesperson.

But apparently Rivkin did what he wanted when he wanted, with the infamous stockbroker permitted to expedite his sentence by serving his final 15 days in a single stretch.

He jumped into a heavily tinted 4WD on 7 October 2004, wearing gold sunglasses, after serving 77 nights behind bars. Several guards have made unsubstantiated claims that he used his money to acquire privileges in jail. A current guard refused to talk about corruption but said Rivkin was on good terms with most prison officers.

'He was just another crim as far as I was concerned,' said the guard. 'He was locked up just like the rest of them. But I saw a lot of officers change while he was in there. They would go and sit in his cell and talk with him. I have no proof, but it was pretty obvious why they were doing it – they were getting their free investment advice. In return, they gave Rene a little bit more leniency with what he could have in his cell and what he could do.

'I have no problem with the fact that he was put in the hospital because lots of non-high-profile prisoners are, even when they aren't sick. It's used as a place of protection at times and Rivkin needed protection because he would have been stood over and maybe killed in any other jail.'

Rivkin was found dead on 1 May 2005 – 207 days after he was released from Long Bay. He took his own life. It was later revealed he spent his final days crying in a dark bedroom.

'Maybe he was really sick before he got to Long Bay,' said a guard. 'Or maybe it was Long Bay that made him sick.'

4

SURVIVING

Paying?

'I got seven years for stealing $120,000 from Centrelink. He got two-and-a-half for stealing $2 million from pensioners. Where's the justice in that?'
Long Bay inmate

The sweeper approached the cell, struggling to wipe the smile from his face.

This should be interesting, he thought.

The convicted drug dealer and Long Bay veteran hadn't met many like this.

In fact, no one had.

He walked into the open cage, his grin disappearing. He would not have gone near the cell to approach the millionaire-cum-inmate sitting on the edge of the bed, had the order not come from the screw. ('Look after him,' he'd said.)

Long Bay's most unlikely prisoner was shaking.

'How you holding up?' the inmate said to Rodney Adler.

'Not good,' Adler replied. 'To be completely honest, I'm terrified.'

The sweeper laughed inside. This bloke had every reason to be. *They'll eat him alive*, he thought.

That suspicion was only reinforced when the next question came.

'How's your family coping?' the sweeper asked.

'Not good,' Adler said, seemingly on the verge of tears. 'We've had to sell the house.'

'How much did you get for it?'

'$16 million. Yeah, it's been tough. We've had to downsize. Lindy isn't taking it well.'

'That's not good, mate,' the sweeper said. 'Same thing happened to me. I had a house worth about $1 million in Ashfield and the Crime Commission seized it. But they left enough for my wife to get a decent three-bedroom joint up on the coast. What did you end up with?'

'Oh,' Adler said. 'We had to get a place in the Eastern Suburbs.'

'Yeah?' the sweeper said. 'How much is that one worth?'

'Six million,' Adler replied.

The veteran inmate felt like smacking him in the face. But he couldn't; he'd been told to look after the bloke.

'I just said to him I'd tell him something that might save his life,' said the now former inmate, who asked to remain unnamed. 'I told him that doing it tough in here means not being able to feed your kids. It's not fucking having to downsize to a $6 million house. I told him never to speak about money again and he might be safe.'

Rodney Stephen Adler knew his stay in prison would not be comfortable. Given his crimes, and the amount of press they had received, he knew he was a marked man.

'I was always going to be a target,' Adler said. 'People approached me before I even got into jail and said I'd need protection. They offered to protect me in return for money. I knew I was going to have a hard time inside, thanks to the media, who didn't leave me alone and kept on hounding me and writing articles about me. I am not a physical man. If I hit someone they would laugh at me like I was tickling them. If they hit me, I would be in hospital for three months. I knew I'd have to use my brain inside to survive.'

Adler's fall from grace was swift. Just six years after being appointed a Member of the Order of Australia for services to the insurance industry and philanthropy, he was sentenced to a maximum of four-and-a-half-years in prison after pleading guilty to four criminal charges. Adler was appointed Chief Executive of FAI Insurances, following the death of his father, Larry Adler, who founded the high-flying insurance company in 1960.

Before his imprisonment, Rodney Adler appeared to have everything: the money, the address, the designer suits and a loving family. But his world came crashing down in 2005, when he was advised to plead guilty to two counts of disseminating information knowing it was false, obtaining money by false or misleading statements, being intentionally dishonest and failing to discharge his duty as a director in good faith.

Rodney's life as a high flyer became a distant memory when he arrived at Long Bay Jail. He was taken to reception, stripped naked and told to bend over.

'I got the prison greens and the search,' Adler said. 'All of that. A lot of people find the strip-search humiliating. I didn't like it, but I didn't find it was that bad. It wasn't as humiliating as you would think. You have to understand I was a white-collar criminal with a high profile. I don't do drugs, I am not violent, and I don't smoke. Most of the officers looked at me like I was a freak show. I was a square peg in a round hole. They'd read about me and I was a curiosity. They didn't treat me well, they didn't give me special treatment, but there were no drugs to find up my arse, if I can put it that way. They knew that.'

But Adler, at 6 feet 2 inches (1.88 metres) tall, was treated differently. The rich kid from the Eastern Suburbs could not fight. He had never thrown a punch, or been punched. He was kept from other prisoners on the bus.

'I was always on my own and I was even strip-searched alone,' Adler said. 'They were nervous that I'd be bashed. The first one-and-a-half years, I was always in a single compartment in the truck. The trucks can take a lot of people, but there are many compartments. There are compartments for one, for two, for four and so on. I was always in a compartment for one.

41

'But there were people around me when I went to Long Bay. I could hear them breathing, talking, crying and screaming. I was scared. No doubt about that. None at all.'

Not many felt sorry for Adler, especially the beasts of Long Bay. To them he was just a rich man who had ripped off mums and dads. Following an initial stint at the Metropolitan Remand and Reception Centre, he was transferred to Long Bay. The guards were concerned for his safety and decided to lock him in protection, putting him alongside sex offenders, and those who were at risk of being beaten.

Adler was furious when the guards told him he would be sharing a wing with convicted paedophiles. He wanted to take his chances with the murderers and thieves.

'It doesn't matter what I do, I always want to be the best that I can,' Adler said. 'Even though I was in the jail environment, I didn't want to be put in the Dog [police informant] yard. I didn't want to be a lesser jail citizen. I wanted to be a full jail citizen, if I can put it that way. If you are in protection, you are a Dog, and your reputation is nothing. You are a Dog if you are either a paedophile or you have informed on someone to police. I wasn't a Dog. In the jail hierarchy, if you are not in the main population, then you are a second-class citizen. I didn't want to be a second-class citizen in a secondary institution. My own personal pride, and whatever dignity I had left, I wanted to keep.'

Despite his pleas, Adler was put in a cell next to a sex fiend. He was told it was only temporary, and for his good, but he counts those three-and-a-half weeks as among the worst of his sentence.

'They ended up sending me down to a sex offender unit. And I was quite concerned about going down there. When you're a sex offender and you want to get out on bail, you have to do a sex offenders' course. Long Bay is one of the jails that offered this course, which lasted about nine months. You had to go every day to this course, and part of what you had to do was to tell them what you did, how you did it, and you had to tell them in graphic detail. You had to keep a diary. You had to take note of every time you masturbated, every time you had a sexual thought, every time you had an urge. It was part of the recovery process.'

Adler was not a sexual offender. He didn't have to do the course. But he was confronted by child rapists talking about sex and their horrible crimes.

'What actually happened was when you're at the lunch table, everyone was always talking about what they did to certain people. There were only three non-sex-offenders in the unit. Some of those stories I heard were horrendous. It was disgusting what these people did to other human beings. It just wasn't a nice place to be. Obviously being in jail was a punishment, and jails aren't supposed to be nice places. But you don't want to be surrounded by people who have done things to other human beings that are that deplorable. I didn't want to hear the stories and I did not want to be associated with these sexual predators. I knew it was going to be temporary, but you don't know what temporary can mean in jail. It could be three weeks or four months.'

Adler was locked up in the sex offender wing for almost four weeks. He was moved to the minimum security

Kirkconnell Correctional Centre in 2005 before being transferred to Bathurst Correctional Centre, a maximum security
prison, after it was alleged he was attempting to restart his
business from inside the jail. Following his stint in protection
at Long Bay, Adler successfully asked to be put into general
population.

'I decided I would not go into protection before I even
pleaded guilty to the charges,' Adler said. 'I did a lot of
research. I made it my mission to meet a number of people
who had been in jail so I could ask them how to act and what
I should expect. I was scared, I was really scared and I didn't
know what to expect, so I tried to research it to the best
of my ability. It's like any investment, if I can put it that
way – you don't know how well you're going to go, but the
more research you do the better your chances. And the more
you know about the investment, the safer you feel. This was
really just another type of investment. Obviously a little more
serious, but I researched it as much as I could and I came
to the conclusion that the risk for me personally was a little
bit more dangerous in the main population. But I felt that
for my family and my long-term sanity, I would be better in
main population.'

Adler said visiting conditions played a role in his bold
decision to take his chances with some of Australia's hardest
men.

'The other reason I did it is I have a family, a very close
family, and I wanted to get as many visits as possible,' Adler
said. 'The thing about being in main population is the
visiting area is much better. The people my family would

meet in the protection area are much worse than the people my family would meet in the general population area.

'The only thing I thought about was my family when I was in jail. I wanted to see them as often as possible and I also wanted them to have the best possible environment to see me in. I didn't want them exposed to people who committed these shocking sex crimes.'

Now comes the part of Adler's story that is not so clear. According to both guards and prisoners, Adler ensured his safety in general population by paying prisoners for protection.

'He was locked in his cell when he arrived at Bathurst by a couple of Lebanese guys, and one produced a mobile phone,' said an inmate who served time with Adler.

'He was given the phone and told to arrange for $2000 to be put into an account, or he wouldn't be walking out of the cell. He was then told to make sure another $2000 was paid into the same account every week. Every Lebo in Bathurst was running around in a new tracksuit by the time Adler left. He then paid a Polynesian gang for protection when he was moved, but it was a lesser amount.'

'He told me he looked at it just like business,' said another inmate. 'He said he paid people on the outside far bigger amounts for services that were far less important. He didn't see an issue with it.'

Adler is adamant he never paid for protection.

'Everybody tried to get protection money from me, but I never did it and I never paid,' Adler said. 'Though I had some very unpleasant experiences when I did say no.

45

The Lebanese fundamentally control the NSW jails. And I must say my experience with the Lebanese was pretty good. I am Jewish, and being in with the Lebanese, the Muslim Lebanese in particular, wasn't very easy. But my experiences with them weren't so bad. Once you sit down and have a talk with them, and approach it properly, I got pretty friendly with a few of them. A number of them were pretty good to me.'

Adler said he was threatened after refusing to pay for his protection.

'When you refuse protection payment they don't say, "Thanks very much it was nice talking to you,"' Adler said. 'They grab you and throw you against the wall; they threaten you and they threaten your family. It's not an MBA-type conversation. But they speak shit in jail. None of what they say or threaten is true.

'They got ugly. The threats were made against my family and there were suggestions that someone would visit the cell and hurt me or go to my house and hurt my family. In jail a lot of people tried it on, but mostly they were plastic gangsters: they talk shit and don't follow through. You just had to be tough. You had to stand your ground.

'I figured at the end of the day they are all just guys. Although we all did bad things to get to jail, they are just guys who have made mistakes or done something wrong, and if you approach them the right way and treat them with respect, most of them treat you with respect back.'

Regardless of whether or not Adler paid protection, he survived. And the fact that he refused to be put into official protection by the system can only be described as brave, especially given the violence he witnessed during his time inside.

'I was in the yard and all of a sudden I heard some commotion,' Adler said. 'And then a fight started. It happened so quick. That's the surprising thing about these fights. By the time it starts to the time the officer presses the alarm, it's all over and the damage is done. Ten seconds is all the time it takes for someone to get seriously hurt. I turned around and one guy was smashing into the other guy. He pulverised him in five seconds flat. He broke his nose and pulled out his eye socket. He kicked him that many times in the ribs that he had four or five broken when he was done. His lips were cut and bleeding and he was on the ground. Out. It took five seconds to do that much damage. I looked at it and I thought, *wow*. The damage that guy sustained in five seconds was quite unbelievable. He was in hospital for two-and-a-half months. They had to wire his jaw, he had stitches everywhere, and it took just five seconds.

'I was lucky to avoid anything like that, and I think it's because I was honest with them. That's my advice to people going in. Nothing pisses an inmate off more than lying to them. They will belt the shit out of you. If some guy thinks you're lying, they'd smash you in the face. They will say, "Bang!" They won't discuss it. They'd say, "You fucking putrid cunt", and punch you in the face.

'It's as simple as that.'

Sweeping

'The sweeper knows there will be retribution if they do the wrong thing.'
Former Long Bay PO Grant Turner

Graham 'Abo' Henry boldly, and suddenly, stepped out of line. The inmates' eyes lit up as they stared at the man crazy enough to step out of the military-precise muster.

He's fucking mad, they thought. *He'll get bashed.*

Henry slowly walked across the yard and towards the guard. The boss of the wing looked up from his roll-call clipboard.

'What are you doing, Abo?' he said. 'Get back in line.'

There would have been no questions asked had it been anyone other than Henry. The guard would have charged, crash-tackled and cuffed the insubordinate.

But Henry was the 'sweeper', the only man who could keep the 180 inmates from also jumping out of line and maybe taking the officer, and his solitary baton, on.

'When you run a wing, you pick the most feared criminal and make him your sweeper,' said former PO Grant Turner. 'You need a tough bastard with a reputation. He has to be someone the other prisoners won't mess with. He also has to know about everyone and everything that happens in the wing. You tell him that he is in charge, and you give him concessions in return. Tough guys like Neddy Smith become your sweepers and they eliminate trouble and carry out your orders in return for things like TVs, extra visits and unlocked cells. They also pass on information about things the inmates are getting up to.'

Henry, the sweeper, didn't even answer the guard. He walked straight up to him and used the muster – the prison roll call – to issue a threat to the prisoners.

'Do you want to have to deal with him?' Henry roared at the inmates, looking to the guard first. 'Or me?'

The guard's mouth was wide open, clipboard shaking at his knees.

'I was head sweeper of 13 Wing in the remand centre,' Henry said. 'One day I stepped out of the muster line and pointed at the guard. He was a huge fat prick and a cunt of a thing. He'd been running around, badmouthing a prisoner he didn't like. The prisoner who he'd been shitcanning was harmless, a real intelligent bloke who was actually a prince back in Sri Lanka. The guard had been telling everyone that he was a Dog because he spoke like he had a plum up his arse. But the bloke wasn't a Dog; just educated and polite. But because of the shit the guard was spreading, this Sri Lankan bloke was going to get knocked in the yard for nothing.'

Finally, the guard stepped back into the huge shadow cast by the tattooed sweeper.

'Right,' Henry said, 'this prick has been giving Asoko a hard time.' He glared at the guard cowering behind him. 'And Asoko tells me you've been giving him a hard time too because of what he has said. Now you better pick who you want to be with – it's him or me. If anyone touches this cunt because this big lump of lard tells you to, then you'll have to deal with me. Any cunt who's going to belt any cunt on behalf of this screw will get the receipt from me.'

Henry never had to thrash out an invoice, with his Sri Lankan prince suddenly gaining 180 new friends, including the guard who was now telling everyone all about the 'Prince Charming' he had in his wing. For one reason or another, Henry went in to bat for the Sri Lankan, and he most likely saved his life. The first rule of survival in Long Bay is befriending the sweeper.

'Look, no one can make your life easy in a place like Long Bay,' said Henry. 'But your best bet is the sweeper. If he's proper tough, the crims won't step up to anyone he says not to touch, even though the bloke might deserve it. I've gotten blokes like Harry M Miller through. I nursed that bloke like a baby. I told him not to speak about his money because people would stand over him; I told him not to go near the junkies, and I made him walk next to me in the yard so people knew he was with me. No one touched him after that.

'But being a sweeper isn't all about just protecting the weak. You had to look after the whole wing, making sure the stores were right, that nothing was broken and you were in charge of everything that happened in the yard. Really, your job was to listen to every cunt complain and be the middle man. You would sort out all the inmates' problems, as well as those of the guards. A guard might come up to you with a new bloke and say we can't put him one-out but he's not to get raped. You would then have to take him to his cell and tell the new bloke's cellmate not to touch him or you would kill him. We did all that sort of stuff.'

So why do it? Sounds like a lot of responsibility.

'The benefits,' Henry explained. 'First of all, we got leeway. We were never locked up and could move between the jails. They would also bring you in whatever you liked . . . you know, a Chinese feed, new release videos and magazines. Grog too. That was the best bit. They'd walk it through in a hot water bottle and hand it to you. But you had to drink it straight away or it would be just horrible. If you left it for a day, it'd taste like shit, just like you were drinking rubber.'

Tabloid Terror
'In Long Bay, it's all about the smallest signs. Not being able to find the paper is a warning that could save your life.'
Former Long Bay inmate

'Did the Rabbitohs win?' shouted Mathie, as he rifled through the bin. 'Fuck the Roosters. Surely we got 'em this time.' He'd searched the entire common room and TV room for the newspaper, but nothing. And now he was elbow deep in food scraps. Still nothing.

Fuck, he suddenly realised, no longer caring about the football score.

He quickly pulled his hands from the muck, not even bothering to wipe them on his pants, turned away from the bin and walked. *Fast.* He wanted to run, but he couldn't look scared.

Finally he was back on the top landing and inside his cell. He sat on the edge of the bed and looked at the door. Oh, how he wished it were locked. He cracked his neck, pushed his shoulders back, and pulled his fingers into his palm to create a rock-hard fist.

'You always knew something was going on when all the magazines and newspapers disappeared,' Mathie said. 'You would go for a shit and look for something to read, and if nothing's there then you had to pucker up and get ready for it.

'In Long Bay, it's all about the smallest signs. Not being able to find the paper is a warning that could save your life. If you know what to look out for, you would notice something like magazines, cardboard and newspapers missing. If that happened, you knew shit was about to hit the fan.'

Perhaps this happened for completely innocuous reasons? Was an inmate ready to rampage because they didn't like the page three girl? Maybe a prisoner had collected every bit of press because they didn't want anybody to know what had happened in court?

'Fuck no,' Mathie said. 'People were arming themselves up for a big fight. They were going to riot, or brawl, or that something was about to start with the gangs. They would shove the newspapers and magazines down their pants and around their gut, and down the front of their jumpers as padding for their chests. They'd also stick them down their arses to cover their backs. For protection. From the slashes, the shivs and the stabs.'

Missing newspapers and magazines can save your life. And so can keeping clear of anybody and everybody – even your best mate on 'visiting day'.

'The yard gets so tense after the visits,' commented an inmate. 'My best advice to anyone coming in is just to sit in a corner for a couple of days after anybody has had a visit. Seriously, I have seen blokes attack their best mate for simply asking how it went. You don't know what's happened during their visit, so it's best to shut up and not say a word.

'Look at it this way: every bloke in there is doing his head in about the outside world. They keep it together, but then their missus comes to visit and asks them about money, or tells them about one of their friends who's been coming round to help.

'I was lucky, because whenever I went to jail, I didn't have a bird. Which was great, because the last thing you want is to be worried about who's fucking them, or who's telling them what. In the end, there isn't a fucking thing you can do about it, so you get filthy on the world. That's why blokes kill people for nothing, or why some guys try to escape when they only have two months left. They will risk another five years to get out because they've just had a visit from their missus and she's said something to provoke them.

'The only blokes who don't worry about that are the ones who've been given life. The ones who have been given life send their wives a dildo and a box of batteries. The rest, fuck, steer clear of them after a visit.'

Dumbbell Danger
'His skull was smashed in and blood was splattered all over the gym.'
Former Long Bay inmate

The new Long Bay inmate walked into the 10 Wing gym.

This isn't bad, he thought as he checked out the prison's equipment.

It was no Gold's Gym, but it was better than nothing. He knew this jail wasn't for the weak, but he was strong. And with the help of these machines, he would stay that way.

He sat on the bench, pulled his right arm across his shoulder and stretched his chest. He clapped his hands together, pushed his back against the vinyl and swung his feet from the ground. Then he grabbed the bar and heaved it off the bracket, slowly moving the weighty steel stack towards his chest. He paused for a moment, bar gently resting on his sternum, and mentally readied himself for the lift. He had no idea that another green-clad inmate, armed with a metal bar, was walking towards him. How could he? Flat on his back, all he could see was roof.

Whack!

His skull exploded as the bar smashed against his head.

Bang!

The next hit sent shards of bone across the room.

Crash!

The final blow tore through his jaw, the force of it splattering the entire room with saliva, blood and flesh.

Thud!

The heavy metal bar clunked to the floor, the attacker smiling as he dropped it. 'I hope she was a good fuck,' he said. Then he spat on the beaten body, and walked back into the wing.

The new inmate had made three costly mistakes. Firstly, he fucked the girlfriend of a fellow prisoner before having become a prisoner himself. Secondly, he didn't bother to find out which jail this jilted man who now wanted to kill him was in. And thirdly, he went to the gym alone.

'Bruce [name removed] was rooting the sheila of a fella who was locked up for 15 years, and his missus wasn't a bad sort. The fella found out Bruce was coming to Long Bay and was absolutely filthy with him,' said an inmate who witnessed the attack. 'The next thing you know he's into him. I thought he'd killed the new bloke for sure. His skull was smashed in and blood was splattered all over the gym. The equipment was a putrid mess. You had to be careful in the gym because it was a good place to bash people. It was rarely supervised and the weights made for good weapons.'

Phone Fight

'That fucking phone caused 90 percent of the fights.'
Long Bay inmate

The phone was also best left alone, or at least to those people standing in line, all foaming at the mouth and screaming, 'Hurry the fuck up!'

'There's only one phone in the yard and everyone is entitled to a six-minute call,' explained an inmate. 'Each day there would be about 80 blokes who'd want to use it. Three blokes would charge towards it and arrive at the same time. They'd all say they were first, but eventually they'd sort it out and form a queue and all would be okay. But then whoever the first bloke's calling wouldn't answer, so he'd stand there on the phone for ten minutes, constantly redialling. The bloke next in the line would get even more pissed off, especially because he let this guy go first, and just walk up and crack the first bloke in the back of the head. If it wasn't something like that causing trouble, then it would be someone trying to push in. And depending on who it is, others could get dragged into it, and you'd have a full-scale brawl on your hands. That fucking phone caused 90 percent of the fights.'

5

ENFORCING

Neddy

'Ned only trained on beer. But he was big, and fuck, he could fight.'

Former detective-sergeant Roger Rogerson

Pop!

The screwdriver went in.

The man's stomach exploded, the flesh no match for the force of the tool-cum-weapon sharpened on the sandstone walls of Long Bay Jail.

Tear!

The next one went in, the fast-as-lightning movement ripping a second hole in his gut even before blood had had a chance to squirt from the first wound.

Whack! Whack! Whack! Whack!

Bone cracked as the prison shiv was jammed into the man's chest. The body dropped to the floor.

Neddy wiped the snarl from his face, the blood from his weapon, then turned and walked away. He didn't say a word as he left the 12 Wing yard. He didn't have to.

He was Arthur 'Neddy' Smith, convicted murderer, standover man, famed police informant, and Long Bay's most feared prisoner.

Neddy's reputation as one of Long Bay's notorious enforcers was cemented on 13 August 2002, when he attacked a man alleged to be associated with Glenn Flak, who co-partnered with Smith in a previous crime. At this point in time, Neddy was suffering from Parkinson's disease, which crippled his huge frame.

'Neddy used to work in the library,' said a former Long Bay inmate who recalled the incident. 'A bloke came in one day and told Neddy he was a good mate of Flakky's. Ned had fallen out with Flak because he was dirty he got pinched for the murder and Flak got off. Ned later attacked the bloke in the yard and this was when he claimed his Parkinson's was bad. But I tell you now, it couldn't have been that bad because I saw what he did. He just lunged at the bloke. It was brutal. That bloke did not stand a chance.'

Neddy Smith's Long Bay legacy began in 1963 when he stepped off the truck and walked straight into the belly of the Birdcage. It was the first of his four prison sentences. The handcuffed hulk, standing 6 feet 6 inches (1.98 metres), was a nobody who had just been told he'd be 'fucked up the arse' when he got to the Bay.

But soon they would all fear the blond giant, even though he was only 18. Neddy had admitted to feeling unsettled when he first got to Long Bay, but there was no doubt in his mind he'd be killed before he was fucked by anyone. He was eventually confronted.

'You'll be moving into my cell after dinner,' the man, about 30 years old, said. 'OK?'

So Neddy responded by hitting the prisoner repeatedly with a steel tub, cracking his skull. The young inmate was locked up for assault and was confined in solitary for two weeks.

He was then placed in 1 Wing, a section of the jail for offenders 25 years and younger. Trouble seemed to be Neddy's middle name, and he found any excuse to start a fight with somebody, for whatever reason. He even claimed to have stabbed an inmate during his first stint in Long Bay, after a discussion got out of control.

Roger Rogerson has no reason to doubt Smith's claims.

'Ned was a huge powerful man,' said the former detective-sergeant, a decorated then disgraced police officer who claimed Smith as his 'informer'. 'I mean, he was big and intimidating. His size commanded respect and had plenty running scared. He wasn't afraid to throw them and he often did.'

But Neddy's size would have counted for little in Long Bay if he couldn't fight. And fighting alone could not have sustained him for so long if he hadn't been smart. Neddy was a big brawler with a brain.

'Neddy was a head sweeper,' said a guard. 'I've known him for a long time. Ned never had to push his way into power; other prisoners just let him lead. He had long stints as head sweeper in both 4 Wing and 12 Wing. They would step aside whenever he walked by. I think it was more out of respect. He didn't bully anyone, he was just number one.

'But don't be mistaken. They didn't respect him for nothing. Neddy could hold his hands up. He was a great fighter, don't worry about that.'

And that's exactly what a famed Sydney heavy found out . . .

Neddy stood in the yard, the silence broken only by the sound of him slowly cracking his knuckles. He then clenched his fists, before shaking his shoulders and arms in preparation.

'Where is this cunt?' he said. 'Is he gonna show up?'

Abo Henry stood by his side. 'He'll be here, Ned,' he said. 'If he doesn't, he's dead.'

Henry was Neddy's partner in crime. On the outside, they'd bashed, biffed, robbed and run riot. Inside . . . well, things were the same.

'Tom Domican arrived out of the blue,' said Henry. 'No one had heard of him. The journos had made him into some bad-boy gangster and he believed his own shit. He'd shoved his weight around town. One day I was standing in the gym, in the CIP (Central Industrial Prison) and as I walked past he stopped me and introduced himself. "I know who the fuck you are," I said to the cunt.

'Then he started to rubbish Ned. He said that Ned gave him up over this and that, and had accused him of running him over. I told Tom that he was talking shit and if he had something to say he should go over and tell Ned or stop shooting off his mouth.

'So I went over and saw Ned. It was lunchtime, but we were out in the yard because we never used to get locked up. "Listen," I said, "that Tom bloke told me you gave him up when you got run over by Terry Ball."

'"What?" Neddy said. "That fucking Dog."

'"He's locked up over there," I said, pointing to the wing. '"Let's wait till he comes out after lunch and just run up and put one on him."'

Crack!

An electronic trigger sounded and the reinforced metal door opened. The prisoners spewed from the wing like lemmings, the cold grey yard transforming into a swirling sea of prison green.

'There's the cunt,' said Henry.

Neddy slowly pushed his head back, his neck cracking as his wispy blond hair met his rising shoulders. He snarled and then charged, the colossus blasting his way through the flooding green, towards his target.

'Did you call me a Dog?' Neddy shouted as he towered over Domican.

Domican stood his ground. 'Yes,' he said, in his thick Irish accent. 'Because that's what you are. The truth is you're a Dog.'

Swoosh!

Neddy let the lightning rip, his right knee dropping before his left shoulder sent the hook flying towards the Irishman's chin.

But Domican danced, his quick feet ensuring the fist flashed past his face, smashing nothing but air. 'Not here,' he snarled. 'Let's do this in the gym.'

Neddy turned and walked. He reached the cyclone gate, which was securely locked. They weren't getting in.

Henry recalls vividly what happens next:

'So Ned's knocking on the door, and the next thing you know he just turns around and smashes Domican right on the chin. It was a massive hit. I remember looking at Tom, and you could tell it hurt him because his hands were shaking as he tried to pull them back up. Neddy hit him with another right, and Tom rocked before shaping up again. Then Tom unleashed a roundhouse kick. It was a ripper! And had Neddy been 6 foot (1.82 metres) like me instead of 6 foot 6 inches (1.98 metres), the kick would've hit him on the chin and put his lights out, but he was able to block it with his shoulder.

'Quick as a flash, Neddy smashed Domican with a left hook and the bloke was gone. He looked like Bambi on ice. Tom had no control and his legs gave way. Neddy got on top of him and just starting laying in. Tom was fucked and couldn't even throw a punch. Neddy put in about 20 before I pulled him off and told him it was enough.

'The cunt wasn't seen for three days. It just fucking ruined him. I remember I was playing racquetball about a week later and the next minute someone pointed. I looked around and Tom was behind me.

'"You got a fucking problem?" I asked.

'"Na," he said. "I don't have a problem with you. I want to join forces with you."

'I told him to fuck off.'

The Neddy–Domican brawl has become part of Long Bay legend, facts twisted and truth embellished over time.

'We've all heard the story,' said a former inmate, recently released after serving a two-year sentence for a drug-related crime. 'They were two heavies; Domican running one wing and Neddy running another. They came together to prove who should run the jail, and Neddy smashed him. Neddy got the jail.'

The story from the new wave of guards is much the same.

'I do know Neddy went over and broke his jaw,' said an officer. 'He was in the CIP and Tom was head sweeper of the other wing. For whatever reason, Neddy walked straight into the other yard, through the circle and put a couple on his chin and broke his nose. That was the end of that; Tom didn't fight back. It was just a stand-off between two jail heavies. It wasn't over drugs, just a matter of who was tougher. These things happen.'

*

It's years later since the infamous Long Bay Jail fight, and Tom Domican is now sitting by a fire, the flames slowly eating away the bitter Irish winter that fills his home.

'How did you get this number?' he asks down the phone line. 'You know I'm living in Europe now.'

Despite being below zero in Ireland, his new home, Domican's temperature soars above the 31 degrees, which has Long Bay inmates refusing to leave their cells on this hot Australian summer's day.

'Fucking Abo Henry said what?' he remarks before taking aim and shooting straight.

'Well, the truth of the matter is I got beat,' he admits. 'It's as simple as that. I got king hit and I could not beat what Neddy had. You win some and you lose some. And that is one I lost. You just have to take it in your stride. What you should never do is brag about your wins or bullshit about your losses.'

Meanwhile, Domican laughs at the jail-yard legend that painted him and Neddy as opposing sweepers.

'A sweeper?' he asks. 'A jail heavy? I was only in there for, at most, ten days, and I had the fight with Neddy on the day I arrived. All the stories are shit.

'I was moved to Long Bay after spending three years in the Goulburn tracks because I had to come up for a court trial. It was as soon as I stepped in there that Henry came over and said: "We have a cell for you."

'I turned around and asked, "Who's we?"

'"Me and Neddy," he said.

'I told him, "No thanks."'

Domican is adamant that former detective-sergeant Roger Rogerson put Neddy on the Dog and blamed him for running him over.

'He said it live on the 6pm Ray Martin show. He said I ran him over. It was also fact that he was a Dog. Rogerson put him on the Dog and there was no fucking way I wanted anything to do with a Dog because I had 12 police inform-ants about to testify against me.'

Instead, Domican organised his own cell, refusing to be associated with the man who had accused him of a crime.

'I went off and Abo went back like a little puppy dog and told Neddy that I'd called him the Dog that he was,' Domican said.

They soon met in the yard, feet flying, hooks hitting and bones breaking.

'I called Neddy a Dog to his face,' Domican said. 'And he said, "Let's go and fight."'

'I knew I had no hope of beating him. I'd been in solitary confinement for three years at Goulburn and the only exercise I got was walking from the van to court. I was so skinny at the time, I was almost a skeleton. I'd lost three pounds and weighed no more than 9 stone (57 kilograms). And here I was, about to fight a bloke who was 19 stone (121 kilograms) and had been training every day. It was never going to be a fair fight, but I wasn't going to back down.'

Domican does not dispute the loss, but he laughs off any claims he was 'embarrassing'.

'I got knocked down six times and I got up six times,' Domican said. 'Neddy could not knock me out and I took everything he dished up. And to say I went into hiding after the fight is bullshit. Henry did not try to fight me as he says – he took me up to get stitches, and from all that I copped from Ned, I only got two.

'It was both of them who went missing, who moved up into the Grass Castle [the jail block that housed police-informers]. They both went into protection after the fight and started giving up cops. I was only in Long Bay for another week and was sent straight back to Goulburn after the trial.

'That is the truth of the matter'.

Maybe the truth lies somewhere in between. Regardless, Neddy won this clash of the Sydney street-kings and so his legend grew.

The skinny teenager sat in the corner of the yard, alone and silent. He had quickly worked out that words could kill in Long Bay. As he rested his back against the cyclone fence enclosing the 11 Wing yard, he looked at all the big blokes strutting around in prison green. A man wearing a white shirt and blue shorts emerged from the crowds. The only man in jail whom he had ever seen in anything other than green.

Fuck, he thought. *He's heading straight towards me.*

Soon Neddy Smith was towering over the boy.

'Are you John Elias?' Neddy asked.

'Yes, sir,' the boy replied.

'You know who I am, right?'

'Yes, sir. You're Neddy Smith.'

Even in 1979, Neddy was the Long Bay kingpin. John Elias – the 16-year-old who would go on to play professional rugby league – was shitting a brick.

Neddy nodded. 'I appreciate what you did,' he said with a generous smile. 'I owe you. Tell everyone that you're with me. And let me know if you need anything. I can get you whatever you want. In fact, I've already found you a good job.'

John Elias was locked up in Long Bay two months after his 16th birthday. Accused of attempted murder, he was refused bail and locked up with the 'big boys' while he awaited trial.

'I was shitting myself when I arrived,' Elias said. 'I'd heard plenty of stories about the place. I didn't look at anyone and I didn't say a word. I don't think I spoke for two months.'

Elias was rightly afraid, bunking alongside murderers and thieves. But a violent jail stabbing soon turned Long Bay into a comfortable home. A place he would never have to fear . . .

First Elias heard the scream, loud and painful. He walked behind the toilet block and came across a man splattered with blood.

'His eyes locked onto mine,' Elias said. 'And I froze. It was like he was looking straight through me. But he didn't stop. He just kept on jamming it in.'

Then he saw the body beneath him. Knees pressed against his victim's chest, the veteran inmate continued to stab.

Again and again. The sharpened toothbrush was a white-and-red blur, fast-moving and relentless.

'He was sticking it into his neck, his ribs, everywhere,' Elias recalled.

'The bloke underneath wasn't moving and I thought he was dead for sure. But then he turned his head and looked at me. That's how I knew he was still alive. The bloke doing it saw me too, but he just kept on ripping in.'

Elias turned his back, and walked across the field towards the touch football game he had just left. He held his bladder, choosing not to piss. He also decided to shut his mouth, deciding there and then that he wasn't going to say a thing.

His cell door cracked three days later. Two detectives were standing by the door.

'They told me they knew I saw it and asked me to give the bloke up,' Elias said. 'I was the only witness who could put him away. The other bloke was in bad shape and they told me he might die. They said they would get me off the charges, and if I spoke up, it would be my last day in jail. I think most 16-year-olds would have jumped at the chance, but I couldn't. I said no. They told me no one would ever know but I just couldn't be a Dog.'

His silence paid off.

'Turns out the bloke who did it was a mate of Neddy's, and after that I was sweet,' Elias said. 'I was treated like a king. Neddy took me under his wing and would invite me into his room to watch videos, eat and drink.

'Neddy's cell was a palace. It was three times the size of

a normal cell and he had lounge chairs, a television, a video player and even a fridge stacked with food and beer. I had my first beer in that room and I'd be in there all the time, watching Westerns with him.

'All the stories about Ned getting whatever he wanted? Well, they're true. He had prawns at Christmas, new-release movies and more food than he could eat.

'I did not have one drama under Neddy's care, and to be honest I was happy there and didn't care if I got out. He was one mean fucker who could knock anyone out, but he kind of became my father figure.'

Neddy Smith immediately came into power as soon as the prison gates shut behind him.

'He got it because of his reputation on the street,' former detective-sergeant Rogerson said. 'He was in the papers a lot and all the crooks and guards knew who he was.'

Neddy ran with a who's who of Sydney's underworld. A heroin dealer, armed robber, and tough man for hire, he was affiliated with infamous criminals, including George Freeman, Warren Lanfranchi and Warren Fellows. Son of a father he never knew, Neddy's street fights were legendary – and plentiful, including his claim to fame of making light work of British and Commonwealth boxing champion Bunny Johnson, and the reputation stuck.

'Neddy was always sweet,' said Henry. 'He was a sweeper and in charge of his wing. He could pretty much do what he liked and ran the place as he pleased.'

Neddy's first prison sentence, two years for a rape he has always denied, ended in 1965. He was in again from 1968 to 1975 and 1978 to 1980, and in 1989 he was given life, when he was convicted of murder in company for the brutal road-rage stabbing of tow-truck driver Ronnie Flavell. His partner-in-crime, Glenn Flak, was arrested but later acquitted.

'Flak was Robin to Neddy's Batman,' Rogerson said. 'And they had a big falling out. Ned was a bit unlucky to be convicted, to be honest. He just told too many lies. He made three statements – one in the witness box, one in the dock and one to police – and they were all different. In the end, that was enough.

'The detectives tried to get Neddy and Flak to go against each other. Ned at one stage said he would give evidence against Flak. They had separate trials, so Ned's case went first. They wanted him the most and he was found guilty. In the meantime, Ned changed his mind and refused to give evidence. They held on to Flak's case for whatever reason and would not bring him into court. But his lawyers forced the Crown into a trial. They dragged Ned from the cell to the witness box, expecting him to talk, and he told the judge that he would never ever give evidence against Flak.

'When they got pinched, Ned claimed he didn't do it. He kept on referring to the other bloke. Problem was, all the witnesses described the big bloke as responsible for doing the damage, not the little one. Ned's six-foot six, and Flak's short.

'Ned went on about the other guy when he got arrested, without actually naming him. Flak said nothing, which was within his rights. That brought Neddy undone and put him away for life.'

Despite being slowly crippled with Parkinson's disease, which he was first diagnosed with in 1981, Ned was the undisputed King of Long Bay when he walked in for his death-do-us-part stint.

'There is one moment I will never forget,' said a current guard. 'Neddy was in the MMTC and I was working on a gate near the main clinic. There's a spot where the prisoners come and get their pills. It was only a little window and the crims used to come and stand behind a locked gate when it was time to get them and it would just be utter madness when they opened it. They would push, kick and run like mad to get there first.

'Neddy came down one day to get his pills. I saw him standing at the back. We cracked the gate but no one moved. They all stood there, waiting. Ned walked slowly across the yard and to the counter, and they all stepped aside. The other inmates didn't move until he'd walked back through the gate, and then they were off like rabid dogs.'

Neddy's daughter told her boyfriend to sit down.

'Nat, you have to go and meet Dad,' she said. 'He knows we're seeing each other, and he's demanded to meet you. Sorry, but we're going to have to go in.'

Nat Wood, who would have carved out a lengthy career in the Australian Rugby League (ARL) had it not been for injury, was one tough kid. But meeting Neddy in his Long Bay prime would have scared the shit out of anyone.

'I first started going out with my missus when I was 19,' Wood said. 'I'd known her and the Smith family from when we were kids. I was playing football for the Tigers at the time and I hadn't seen Neddy since I was a child. My missus said I needed to meet him and warned me that he would try and head-fuck me big-time.

'I was a cocky cunt and I didn't really care. I thought I'd be sweet. So we went out there with my missus, her two brothers, and her mother. Neddy had his own special visit area, big and fit for only someone who was someone. We were sitting there and he grabbed his missus and sat her on his lap. He started pashing her. But while he was kissing her, he was looking over her shoulder at me the whole time. I was thinking, what the hell is going on here? I just put my head down and looked away. But he kept staring at me and I started shitting a brick.

'All of a sudden he stops and says, "Are you playing hide the sausage with my daughter or what?"

'I was already a bit nervous, because when I came in I saw him walking and people would just move out of the way. They wouldn't even look at him, all terrified. He was still fighting fit. Still I wasn't scared, but I did look to my missus for support. She was looking at the ground. Then I looked to her mum. Same thing.

'*Fuck*, I thought. I knew it was a trick question. If I said no, he would think I was a liar. If I said yes, he might want to bash me. So I looked him straight in the eye.

'"What do you reckon?"

'He looked straight back at me. "You're mad if you don't," he said, and we all laughed.

'Neddy was a big deal in Long Bay and he got more privileges than most. At Christmas we would go to the jail for a barbecue. All the families would go out on the football field, and there'd be 200 people in line waiting to get their snag. Neddy would just walk straight to the front of the line. We'd stand around, not knowing what to do.

'"What the fuck are youse doing?" he'd yell. "Hurry up. I'm not lining up. They can get fucked."

'Neddy was a hard man and he had a lot of respect. I got on very well with him. He was a real good bloke to me and he helped me out with a few things. He's a bit of a joker once you get to know him. He loves a practical joke and loves to take the piss out of people. That's probably why I got on with him so well. We would play plenty of tricks on each other.

'He was mates with boxing trainer Johnny Lewis, and one day a story came out in the paper with Johnny saying that I would make a good boxer. I got to the jail and Neddy had read the story. "Why didn't you tell me you could fight?" he asked me.

'"What difference does it make?" I said.

'"Bloody oath, son," he said and nodded.'

Neddy Smith is now a shadow of the man who once ruled Long Bay Jail, on and off, since 1963. Crippled by Parkinson's disease, he takes up to 40 pills a day.

'He has his good days and his bad,' said a guard. 'Some days, he remembers your name; others, he doesn't have a clue who anyone is. But he's still regarded as part of the Long Bay institution among the more veteran inmates. Still respected and treated well.'

Neddy now lives in a single cell, in the new state-of-the-art forensic hospital of the Long Bay complex.

'It might be called a hospital, but it's still very much a jail,' said a guard who works in the unit. 'Far newer and cleaner than the rest of the prison, but a cell all the same. The only difference is he has a hospital bed and access to medical treatment and professionals.'

Neddy's health has deteriorated to the point where he no longer has control of his own motor skills.

'He used to spend his days on a typewriter writing his memoirs and he once asked me if he could have a laptop, but the request was denied,' a hospital guard remarked. 'That really took its toll on him because the Parkinson's made it impossible for him to use a pen and the typewriter was taken away. Now he just rambles all the time. You wouldn't think he was once such a big jail heavy.'

His family still visit and the letters still come, but he's no longer feared as much as he used to be.

'Most of the new crims don't even know who he is,' said a guard. 'They're a new generation, who respect no one and nothing. Neddy means shit to them. Sure, they might know his name, but to them he's just an old man who's about to die.'

6

RAPING

Scarface

'You will shower with the gorillas in the mist down at Long Bay Jail. You'll find big ugly hairy strong men who've got faces only a mother could love, who'll pay a lot of attention to you – and your anatomy.'

Magistrate Brian Maloney, warning a 19-year-old of what would happen to him if he appeared in his court again

He was already broken when he went out into the yard. He was not yet 25, but he'd seen enough of this life. He no longer wanted to live, at least not this way. He walked with his head down like usual, but instead of sneaking his way towards the wall, the side that cast the deepest shadow, he pushed and barged his way to the middle of the yard.

He stopped and raised his head, his blue eyes surveying his surroundings – and then connecting with the ugly face.

'Hello, sweet cheeks,' the tattooed man said. 'How about a kiss?'

The blond kid did not respond. Not with words. His tender eyes suddenly became tough.

What's he going to do? thought the tattooed man, as he saw those submissive eyes turn into steel. *Hit me?*

The veteran prisoner clenched his fists as the kid pulled a razor from his pocket. He was going to hit him, oh and then do so much more, but first he wanted to let the kid take his shot.

Fffit!

The tattooed man jumped back as gushing blood splattered his face. This kid he'd been raping – the one *everyone* had been raping – had turned the weapon on himself.

The blade whistled through the air before slashing the boy's flesh, his jaw exposed from the force of the cut that went from his chin to his ear. The next sliced his nose through; straight across the bridge and into his right cheek. With the third, he almost took out his eye.

The blond boy's pretty face was now a monstrous mess. And that's exactly what he wanted.

He was cutting himself because he didn't want to be pretty anymore.

'The poor kid was just sick of getting raped,' said a former inmate. 'He was a real good-looking bloke, feminine and skinny. He was young, knew no one in there, and could not defend himself. He let it happen once and didn't say a thing because the bloke who did it said he would kill him if he did. He was scared and didn't say anything, and by not fighting and not Dogging, he made it OK for everyone else to rape him too. He was just passed around, and then all of a sudden he couldn't stand it anymore. The poor prick couldn't stand up to them; he found it easy to stick himself in the face with a knife. It was just bloody horrible. I didn't see him after that. He never came back.'

Being raped is every prisoner's worst fear. Most would rather be killed than raped. Those who commit the rape in jail call it 'prison sex' and do not consider themselves gay. There are two options for those who are raped – either fight back and it stops, or do nothing and it continues.

'It's mainly the young Aussie kids who get raped, because they don't have any links to gangs and come in as loners,' said a former inmate. 'The ones who do it? Well, they could be anyone. There are plenty of blokes in jail who root each other, but most of it's consensual. A lot of blokes basically become poofs while in jail and call it prison sex. Then they get out and go back to their sheilas, pretending like it never happened.

'But some do end up getting raped. Blokes just run into the cell of the person they want and give it to them when they're alone. Some young inmates end up being forced to share a cell with the bloke who is raping them. They end up copping it every night, and they never say anything because they're scared of being killed. You're locked up most of the day and night, so it's not hard to get at them while they're in their cell.'

Former prison guard Dave Farrell confirmed that men were raped in the prison and repeatedly forced to perform sexual acts on their attackers, leading to embarrassing, painful injuries.

'I've seen people go to the clinic and get treated for chafe because they were forced to give too many head jobs. It's absolutely appalling the things the inmates do to each other. These predators grab these young blokes and make them do 20 head jobs in a cubicle. The only reason the authorities find out on some occasions is because these young blokes go to the nurse's station with injuries like chafed lips.

'There have been other instances where someone's been raped and they haven't shitted for days. These blokes will not put a complaint in, not officially, but they do ask to be moved.

'These are vile people. I have struck tough prisoners who will stand up to this kind of thing on behalf of someone else. Some of them will hear a story from a guard or another prisoner, and they will belt the people responsible. If you don't believe that this goes on, then why would the department issue condoms? They were very popular, especially the flavoured ones. It's a harsh world in there.'

Long-time guard Roy Foxwell agreed that rape was rampant in Long Bay.

'It happened to some poor bastards,' Foxwell said. 'It's not something we like to think of as guards, and it's something we would never condone, but we knew it happened from time to time. Some blokes would get fucked and then they would fight back. That's what would stop it. But some would let it happen, and some of them would turn homosexual. I found that head jobs were far more common than rape. People were forced into giving another crim a head job. Sometimes many at a time.'

Former inmate Ian Mathie was terrified of being raped when he was sent to Long Bay Jail for the first time. He was 18 and weighed 75 kilograms.

'My first cell was four-out,' Mathie said. 'There was a big bastard in there, a massive bloke. I didn't know what his crime was, but he was a scary-looking cunt. This mother-fucker had tattoos all over him, and they were calling him Sailor Sam. I couldn't sleep. I was tossing and turning all night, thinking he'd be trying to get me at any moment. I was looking at him and I ended up catching his eye. He just looked back and said, "You're not my type."'

Mathie admitted men were raped in jail, but he said most of what he saw involved homosexual prisoners.

'There was a lot of poofterism back in those days,' he said. 'A lot of blokes were in there for a long time, and they rooted blokes, as well as bashed blokes who rooted blokes. There were a lot of poofter bashings, but I can tell you, there were a lot of poofs who could fight too, and did hit back. There were some tough poofters who knew how to get themselves a bloke. Me, I stayed well clear of the poofs. I couldn't wait to get out of the place.'

(Sexual) Abuse of Power

'We had homosexual guards too. Some of them went a step too far.'
Former Long Bay guard Roy Foxwell

The young inmate walked up to the prison guard. He had to tell him – even though it wasn't guaranteed that, in doing so, the guard wouldn't bash him, help him or, worst of all, rape him.

'Chief,' he said, 'one of your guards is a poof. He just put it on me and I'm not like that. He's rooting another prisoner and I don't know what I should do. Will he root me too or can something be done? I don't want to get anyone into trouble, and I don't want to disrespect any guard by fighting back . . . but I will if he has another go.'

The prison guard looked back at him. 'You won't have to fight back,' he said. 'Tell me everything you know.'

Soon Roy Foxwell confronted the guard in question.

'I ended up interviewing this officer and he admitted that he was gay, or, as he put it, "camp",' Foxwell explained. 'He said, "I'm not going to admit to anything but I'm gay. I didn't touch this prisoner, but the other one, he touched me. He made the advance and we had a sexual relationship, but it was brought about by his action, not mine."

'This was in the 70s and even though this was the Dark Ages, it wasn't on. I don't think behaviour like this was ever on.'

The 'camp' guard had been driving a truck around the jail; his job was to deliver supplies to different areas of the institution. Clearly, he'd been delivering more than just bread, milk and grain.

'A prisoner worked in the stores department of one of the jails. He used to help the guard get the bits and pieces off the truck and into the storeroom. He and the prisoner would then disappear and have sexual relations in the back of the room,' Foxwell said.

The officer would've been able to continue his clandestine affair with the prisoner, seeing as his sexual partner consented to his advances and didn't dare tell anyone else of his storeroom relations with the guard. But the officer wanted more than just the storeman – he also wanted the young inmate who sat beside him in the truck.

'The crim who told me about it was the one who helped him deliver supplies,' Foxwell said. 'He let it go until the officer put the word on him.

'The guard resigned when he heard the evidence. He didn't want to be embarrassed, so he left quietly.'

Another officer became extremely emotional when he was forced to admit to a similar crime.

'He was having a homosexual relationship with a prisoner,' Foxwell explained. 'This was more sinister because the crim wasn't exactly consenting. He came forward and went as far as signing a statutory declaration to stop the guard.'

The accused officer said it was bullshit. He called it 'lies' and a 'complete fabrication'.

'So I asked him: why would the prisoner lie?' Foxwell said. 'Why would he embarrass himself and put himself at risk if you hadn't done anything? Then I showed him the stat dec. He burst into tears and resigned too.'

She-Man

'While I didn't wake up as Elle Macpherson, I did wake up with a feeling of completeness that was lacking in my life, previously. I woke up as me, Maddison.'

Former Long Bay inmate Maddison Hall, a murderer named Noel Crompton Hall before sex-change surgery

According to guards, Noel Crompton Hall was a big man, muscular and strong.

'So it was weird to see him when he started getting around in a mini-skirt,' said a guard who wished to remain anonymous. 'He was homosexual and the boys used to love him. He would suck them all off and do whatever they wanted when it came to sex. He would also offer himself to anyone for drugs.'

After being locked up for the murder of a man near Mildura, New South Wales, in 1987, Hall decided he was a woman trapped in a man's body. He began dressing like a woman, and told anyone who cared to listen that he was indeed a woman. Hall said he first saw a doctor in 1985 and spoke about his gender problems. He claimed he was given 'treatment'. Hall was certainly different to the other men at Long Bay Jail. Soon authorities would agree that he wasn't a man at all.

Lyn Saunders slammed the bonnet and walked away from his car. It was stuffed. He was on the side of a dirt road somewhere in the south-west of New South Wales. Christmas was just three days away and he needed to get home. The 28-year-old had promised his mum he would be there to unwrap his share of presents that were sitting under the family Christmas tree.

Saunders had little money, so his vehicle was going to have to stay exactly where it was. The only thing that was moving was his thumb. He hoisted it high in the air every time the roar of a car engine sounded over the relentless chirping of the crickets.

Vroooooooom!

The third car blasted past, sending wind, dirt and petrol fumes into his face. This was hopeless. Maybe he'd have to walk to Adelaide?

Screecchaaa!

Finally. The screeching brakes snapped him from despair and he looked down at the rubber the fast-stopping car had left on the road.

'Where you heading, mate?' said the man, passenger window already down.

'Adelaide,' Saunders replied.

'Jump in,' said the stranger. 'I'll take you as far as I can.'

Saunders was hoping he'd be taken all the way to his family home. But he was okay with being dropped anywhere in South Australia and at worst, he was preparing to be dumped somewhere in Victoria. He never once for a moment thought he'd be stuck in New South Wales. Forever . . .

The man walking his horses suddenly stopped. His animals continued, along the road and onto the dirt, but the shock of what he was seeing stiffened the trainer to a standstill.

He had stumbled across a body. Lyn Saunders – what was left of him, anyway.

The hitchhiker was stone-cold dead, his head ripped apart by a shotgun shell. The stranger who'd picked him up, Noel Crompton Hall, had fired the kill-shot point-blank into Saunders' face. Hall's sawn-off had already blasted one into his back, but that wasn't enough to finish him off, so Hall aimed a little higher, and moved the gun a little closer. He placed the shortened barrel – much easier to conceal than the full-length shotgun – into Saunders' mouth and pulled the trigger. The pair had been arguing just before hitting the Victorian border, so Hall stopped his car, pulled out his gun and blew Saunders' head off.

Hall then returned home to Campbelltown, New South Wales, to his wife, as though nothing had happened. He thought he'd gotten away with it. But he hadn't.

Eighteen months after the cold-blooded murder, a popular primetime program showed pictures of the slain victim. The show detailed when Lyn Saunders went missing, when he was found, and how he was killed.

Hall might have forgotten about the young man he'd murdered, but the victim's mother hadn't, nor had the horse trainer, who was still having nightmares about blasted brains and blood. Hall was arrested shortly after the episode of *Australia's Most Wanted* was aired, after an anonymous tip-off led police to his front door. Hall was charged, convicted and sentenced to life in prison.

Now in Long Bay, 'wearing skirts and sucking blokes off', Hall decided he was a woman. The name 'Noel' just didn't sound right, never did, at least to him.

'He started saying his name was Maddison,' said a

guard. 'He said he wasn't a man and claimed he was a woman.'

And, eventually, the prison agreed. In a controversial and widely reported decision, the Serious Offenders Management Committee recommended Noel Crompton Hall be transferred to a female jail. Yep. That's right. Despite having a penis, it seemed that Hall was woman enough to be transferred to the all-female Mulawa Prison.

'After that happened, we all sat back and wondered how we could do it too,' said an inmate who knew Hall. 'Fuck, we would've all got around in mini-skirts if it meant being shifted to a jail you could room with a woman. Imagine how much fun you would have being locked up in a wing full of females.'

However, Hall's stay in Mulawa was short-lived. His cellmate claimed he had raped her and Hall was charged with sexual assault. Other inmates also claimed that they were assaulted by the predator, but their accusations remained just that. Furious prison officials shanghaied the she-man back into an all-male prison, this time to Junee Correctional Centre. Had they been erroneous in sending Hall to a female prison, or were they making a mistake sending the criminal back to a male prison? It was utter political madness.

Now back in a male prison, it was alleged Hall prostituted himself to other prisoners for drugs. Claiming to be a victim of the system, Hall remarkably and successfully sued the Department of Corrective Services for 'psychological trauma' in 2000, and was given $25,000 in an out-of-court settlement. The ruling made him litigious, and in 2001 he went to the Supreme Court – a behemoth of a man, his bulging chest pulling his buttons apart and his sleeves strangling his biceps – in a bid to have his sentenced overturned under the 'Truth in Sentencing Act'. His life sentence was repealed, cut to 22 years on top and 16 years and six months on the bottom.

On a roll, with his sentence cut to a minimum of 16 years, meaning he could be out in just five years, and with $25K in his pocket, Hall finally decided it was time to officially become a 'she'. With support from the Department of Community Services Gender Centre, Hall was given permission by Corrective Services to undergo full sex-change surgery. The decision outraged the media, and then the public.

'To save confusion, he should not have had "gender reassignment" surgery until he left jail,' wrote Miranda Devine, in a column published in Sydney's *Sun Herald*. 'Prisoners give up the right to such luxuries. But now there are reports the $25,000 operation was funded by the taxpayer via compensation Crompton Hall brought against who? The Department of Corrective Services. About guess what? Not being allowed to have a sex-change operation. It couldn't get any more surreal.'

A guard recalled taking Hall to the hospital for the sex-change procedure.

'I wasn't there for the operation but I did the escort,' said the guard. 'Hall went in a man, and I took him home a woman. My partner on the job, who was a female, had to go into the surgery, which was weird, because they deemed Hall a woman, even though she was a man. I was in the ward when she came back, and I had to watch Hall with her legs spread, getting cleaned before the new dressing went on. Really, it was something I didn't have to see. Hall was such a huge guy before he became a woman. He was in protection and it all started when he began taking hormones and grew tits.'

Noel Crompton Hall was now officially a woman and was up for parole. She was already free from being a man, and she would soon be free from being in prison. Soon almost became sooner than expected. In 2006, she was about to be granted parole when it was revoked at the eleventh hour.

Her barrister, Phillip Young, blamed this on the 'media bloodsport of flushing out paroles'. To be fair, the media were relentless, but also, again to be fair, maybe with good cause.

'Sex-change killer will strike again' read the headline in Sydney's *The Daily Telegraph*, nine days before the parole was revoked. Journalist David Fisher had obtained a letter from Hall's ex-wife, one that she'd sent to the Attorney-General expressing her concerns about the pending release.

'I believe Noel Crompton Hall is not of stable mind whatsoever and will repeat offend once back in society,' wrote the woman identified by the paper as Sharon.

'Noel and I have two children from our marriage. Along with believing Noel will very quickly reoffend once he is released, my biggest fear is he will try and locate his children, while both my son and daughter have expressed openly and strongly they do not want any contact with him. Obviously I knew firsthand the violent, twisted, lying nature of Noel Hall. I had been beaten by him and had the same gun (that he used in the murder of Lyn Saunders) shoved in my face. It has taken me time, encouragement, family love, a new partner and a child to rise above it all, but honestly, the scars remain.'

The family of Lyn Saunders also took aim at the HIV-positive killer in the lead-up to his parole review.

'He is a clever individual and he has not done this (the gender reassignment surgery) because he is a woman trapped in a man's body, but because he wants to screw with the system.'

The same guard who escorted Hall to the sex-change operation agreed.

'Hall was a clever crook. He worked the system well, and the payout and surgery were the result of it. He was always smart and was given good jobs. At one stage he worked in the office of one of the bosses. Regardless of his motives, he was a huge piece of the Bay. He was a big fella, a murderer and he'll go down as an all-time inmate because the government effectively paid for the operation. I never really asked him why wanted to do it, to become a woman, but I honestly believe that was just his go.'

No amount of hysteria could stop Hall from being released in 2010. After 22 years in jail, almost the maximum under the re-determined sentence, Hall was free – a man when he entered; a woman upon exit.

7

ROOTING

Lovers' Lane

'They used to ask us to put forward a recommendation for them to be moved to a cell with their lover because it would make them content and less violent.'
Current Long Bay psychologist

The guard slowly and quietly turned the key. Along with his fellow POs, he moved silently through and towards the door.

Whack!

One of the other guards kicked the door open. 'Holy shit!' he exclaimed, his foot barely back on the ground. 'What the hell do we have here?'

The prisoner's face turned the same ghostly white colour as his fully exposed bum.

'It's not what it looks life, chief,' said the prisoner as he leapt away from his cellmate, who was lying naked on the bed, knees on the mattress, hands on the wall.

'Well,' said the guard, 'if it's not what it looks like, then what the fuck is it?'

Paul Rush, a Long Bay guard who started with the NSW Corrective Services in 1989, had just begun working for the feared Malabar Emergency Unit. He was on his first overnight 'surprise' raid.

And boy was he surprised.

'I can never forget what I saw on that night, no matter how hard I try,' Rush said. 'Four of us were told to go and do the raid and we got together and snuck through the wing very quietly so nobody could hear us. We crept along so carefully that it took us a good five or six minutes just to walk up onto the landing. When we got to the targeted cell, we brought the hinge up before slowly tapping it across.'

Surprise!

'One of the inmates was absolutely chock-a-block up another bloke,' Rush said. 'We could hear the noises before we opened the cell, and we thought the guy was doing push-ups. But we were wrong. The bloke had his pants around his ankles and he was just jamming it into the guy lying face down on the bed.

'In the end they both calmly stood up, put on their trousers and assumed the search position. We didn't even have to tell them what to do, they just lay down on the floor, crossed their feet and dropped their hands on their head. It was as if nothing had happened.'

The inmate who'd been doing the rooting suddenly burst out laughing.

'And we all started laughing too,' Rush said. 'What else could you do? It was consensual sex and they were both pretty embarrassed about getting caught. They weren't homosexuals, but were two straight men doing what they call "prison sex". I wasn't surprised again after that. I knew I would see that kind of thing during raids and I did.'

The guard walked up to the prisoner. 'What's that?' he asked, pointing at his eyebrow, at least what was left of it.

'I shaved half of it off,' the skinny, harmless inmate said.

'Why?' the guard said.

'To let blokes know I'm up for it,' he replied.

Consensual sex is rife in Long Bay Jail.

'It goes on all the time,' explained a guard. 'There are homosexuals in prison who actively look for sex and straight men will take them up on their offer. The straight men claim they're not gay and say that it's "prison sex" – they won't talk of it once they get outside.'

15 Wing is known by correctional staff as 'Lovers' Lane' because several men are in open relationships with their cell-mates. They hold hands in the yard and do as they please at night when the cell doors are closed.

'We've even had requests by prisoners saying they want to move into cells to be with their partner,' said a Corrective Services employee. 'They're like married couples.'

Previously it was 9 Wing: seemingly there has always been a Lovers' Lane in Long Bay, just different people in different wings at different times.

'It was just a place were there was a lot of sex,' a guard explained. 'To be more accurate, it was almost like a swingers club. There were predators, homosexuals, normal blokes who got into it and everything in between.'

PO Roy Foxwell said homosexuals have always been segregated for their own protection. 'We'd put them in segregation when they came in if we knew they were homosexual,' he said. 'You could tell by their mannerisms, by the way they reacted, the plucked eyebrows – stuff like that. If we didn't identify them at first, we eventually would. Word would quickly get around that they were gay. You'd see them hanging around with a predator or another young boy. We'd separate them in their own cell and they'd be in a yard with others like them.

'You'd think it'd be for a free-for-all, but the homosexual men tended to want the more manly blokes who weren't locked up with them. It was like putting a bunch of women together. They weren't into each other.

'It was harsher for them in the old days. Homosexuality in the prison was tolerated in the late 70s and 80s but not before. They would've been flogged back then, not protected. Some partnered up with a heavy who liked a head job, and who'd mother and stop them from being bashed.'

But not all homosexual inmates were protected. Sometimes they were belted. On one occasion, a guard punched, kicked and left a gay inmate alone and lying in his own blood.

'The officer went into a cell where a cat lived,' said another guard. 'We used to call the homosexuals cats. When he opened the door, this thing came out and clawed off his face. The cat drew blood, so we belted the shit out of him. We took him down to what was called the pound, which was solitary confinement. The superintendent could put a prisoner in the pound for three days for misbehaviour, and then you could bring in the visiting justice, who could give them another 14. The first three days the prisoner got bread and water and nothing else. The three days after that they got given normal meals and then they would go back to the bread and water. This cat got flogged before he went in. When the doctor entered the pound, he almost fell over because the inmate was lying in a pool of blood. He was almost dead. But the doctors back then didn't say anything.'

Equally as bad as the bashing was the room the 'cat' had been locked in.

'Solitary was horrible,' the guard continued. 'It was just a mattress on the ground. There was a light but no window and you'd switch it off and leave them in the dark if you didn't like them. They'd have a can of water that would sit in the corner and a night-tub to shit in. There was nobody to talk to and they'd only be let out for an hour a day.'

Wanking
'They were all beating off. It was the closest thing they could get to a root.'
Long Bay inmate

Sexual acts in prison are not always violent, forceful and foul. Sometimes they can be outrageously and crudely funny . . .

'Fuck!' The prisoner's head rose from the form guide on his table. 'They're gonna kill me.'

After a while he swore again. 'Fuck!' he screamed, even louder. 'Who won that race?'

The shouting from the prisoners was more than a match for the battery-operated wireless radio that sat on the table next to the form guide, scribbled and marked.

'Put it back on!' a fellow inmate screamed.

'What are you fucking doing?' followed another.

Soon all the prisoners began to chant: 'We want more! We want more! We want more!'

The swearing inmate, distracted by the din, forgot about the trotter that came racing home and won him some cash – and laughed. He thought about all the poor bastards now pulling up their pants, job not even half done.

The guard came shouting into his room.

'How dare you show porn,' said the governor as his lackey ejected the tape. 'You'll be in the shit for this.'

Tape in hand, the governor and the guard stormed from the wing. On their way out they passed the frustrated prisoners, who were hissing, booing and pleading for them to give the tape to the man with the form.

'I had a job playing videos,' said the inmate, who didn't fear for his safety after he heard his fellow inmates begging for the tape to be returned. 'We used to get two new releases a week, and I'd play them on the machine in my cell, which would be fed to the entire jail. The guys could watch the normal free-to-air channels if they had a TV; we had channels two, seven, nine, and ten. But they could get the video I was showing if they tuned into channel one. I was given the job of controlling the feed, and I had the only video machine in the jail linked into the feed.

'The guards would give me movies like *Streetfighter*, *Point Break* – stuff like that. Some screws were okay and would also record Anthony Mundine fights for us from their Foxtel and bring it in the day after for me to put on.

'When we were locked up at night I would put the video on. It could really be a pain in the arse at times, because I'd be asleep at midnight, long after the movie was over, and people would start yelling out for me to put another film on. They'd also come at me in the yard with special requests, like a movie their mate had told them about, or they'd asked me to replay a Mundine fight. I just couldn't win because everyone always wanted different.

'My mate also had a player and he would always tape stuff off the TV. He was a horny bastard and he sat up for months taping any tits, arse or sex scenes that came on. He got a bunch of the late-night SBS stuff, as well as that scene from *Basic Instinct* with Sharon Stone. He made a compilation and he would put it on and flog himself. Some guys found out he had it, and all of a sudden everyone was begging me to put it on. So one Friday night I grabbed the tape from my mate and whacked it in just to shut them up. They cheered when it came on, but I wasn't even watching because I had a few bets I was keeping track of. I was actually pissed off because they were yelling so loud I couldn't hear my radio that had the trots on. They were all beating off. It was the closest thing they could get to a root.

Then all of a sudden a screw stormed into the room and turned it off.'

The prisoners, all blue-balled and frustrated, forgave the video-playing inmate. But the governor didn't.

'He put me up on charges of showing porn,' said the inmate. 'Of course it wasn't porn and I got off, but boy did I have to go through some shit. It still wasn't over when the charges were dropped. I had blokes coming up to me for weeks telling me to put it back on because I cost them a wank. And my mate wasn't too impressed with me for losing his tape.'

Conjugal Visit
'They still get sucked off now.'
Current Long Bay guard

The prisoner looked over to the guard. So did his wife. 'Okay,' he said, needing no question to provide the answer.

The guard turned away as the inmate let go of his wife's hand. He pushed his chair back, the metal legs squealing as they scraped against the concrete floor. His wife walked around the table, past the guard and towards her incarcerated man.

Squeeeek!

Metal scratched the floor again; this time the chair was being pushed back in. The guard knew it was safe to turn around. He'd seen nothing and would see nothing. The woman was no longer within his peripheral vision –

she was under the table and sucking the inmate's cock. He looked at the prisoner and nodded, all straight face, arms folded. No one would know a thing, except for the prisoner and the guard he was now indebted to.

'They're supervised at all times, but guys still turn a blind eye during visits,' said a guard. 'They still get sucked off now. It happens more in the private jails, especially Junee, but it goes on everywhere. You'd get blokes who'd only let prisoners have hand jobs, but there'd be others who'd let them go all the way. A lot weren't comfortable with it, especially new blokes, so I'd tell them to stop. I had no dramas with the inmates doing it, especially if it was discreet; but other people were in the room, in a big common room, and they could see it.'

An older guard, now retired, said it was less likely to be allowed in the 1980s. 'It was only possible in one Long Bay visiting section,' he said. 'It was more common at Parramatta because they were all contact visits, which meant you could hold hands and touch each other. Back when I was at Long Bay, contact visits only ever took place in the Malabar Training Centre (MTC). I looked after visits in the non-contact section, where there was a plank and wire between the prisoner and their visitor – they couldn't touch.'

But over in minimum security, the old huts and hills were home to plenty of humping.

'All sorts of shit went on there,' the guard continued. 'In some of the camps, they used to sit around on the grass in summer with blankets over them during visits. When you saw that, you knew what was going on. It wasn't permitted, but you had to catch them in the act. Sometimes you just turned a blind eye.'

Boom Gates and Babies

'They found pornos, viagra, blankets and sex toys.'
Former Long Bay parole officer

The prisoner told the parole officer he was doing 'real good' and had been well behaved of late.

'That's because I am really happy,' he said. 'I have a girl-friend now and she comes to visit me after she sees her brother. It gives me something to look forward to, and I find it gets me through the days and also helps me to avoid trouble.'

The parole officer was impressed. But he needed some further details for the report he was about to write. He contacted the jail's 'visits' section for some information on the woman who had inspired the prisoner's improved behavior.

'No one's been in to see him,' said the administration officer. 'He hasn't had a visit all year.'

When the parole officer met with the prisoner again, he asked who his female visitor was, who her brother was. So the prisoner gave him names.

'I think you're making this up,' the parole officer said. 'I checked your visits and you haven't seen anyone.'

The prisoner became silent. Beads of sweat formed on his forehead and his hands began to tremble. 'Oh,' he said.

'Yeah, no, I mean the bloke told me that his sister wants to be my girlfriend. She sent a letter saying she was going to visit me.'

Alarm bells went ringing and the officer decided to dig into this case a little more. Once again he rang up the visits section. 'Let me know when this sister comes in to see her brother,' said the parole officer. 'We'll check it out then.'

Sure enough, the officer received a call the day the sister came to visit the brother. As expected, she didn't meet up with the newly happy prisoner. Well, not officially . . .

A guard, at the request of the parole officer, followed the woman. He watched as she walked out of the visiting area, past the cafeteria and towards the gate. Nothing strange so far. But just before she reached the boom gate, she looked to the left and then to the right. Coast clear, or so she thought, she darted into the open door of a nearby building.

The guard followed her into the prison art gallery, a place where some inmates worked and low-classification crims were allowed to do craft. When he entered the building, only about 30 seconds after the girl had gone in, she was already half naked, the 'improving' prisoner in the nude.

Busted.

He had been receiving visits indeed. The inmate had his very own Aladdin's sex cave, with the officers finding a stash of pornography, sex toys and viagra.

The sex was stopped and his parole was denied.

The prison was left highly embarrassed by the 'boom gate sex' incident, but it was all kept hush-hush and the public was none the wiser. Aside from what the guard had witnessed, there was no evidence – well, none that couldn't be discreetly thrown out.

But not all sexual conduct in jail is so easily stopped this way. There has also been one incident that saw a woman impregnated by a heavily guarded prisoner . . .

The medical courier came in with a refrigerated box. He was one of the first 'un-uniformed' people who had ever been allowed in the highly secretive Special Purpose Unit – home to the most protected prisoners in Australia. He was here to see a notorious gangland criminal, and after his visit he left with . . . the criminal's sperm. The specimen was then sped to the prisoner's girlfriend. This 'special delivery service' happened not once but twice, and on the second time the couple conceived; the inmate fathered a baby from jail.

Remarkable but true. A high-level investigation was launched when the media broke the story ten months after the baby was born. It was reported that three of the state's highest-ranking officers were involved in the embarrassing scandal that became known as 'Spermgate'.

'It was an extremely famous incident,' said a Long Bay guard. 'We all knew about it but couldn't say anything. It was all kept very secret, and I think the prisoner was allowed to do it because of his importance to the police.'

8

DRINKING AND GAMING

Long Bay Brew

'The screws went down to the pharmacy and bought a bunch of laxatives from the chemist. They loaded up the brew with all these pills that would give you instant diarrhoea. And four prisoners ended up spending half the day on the shithouse.'
Former Long Bay PO Roy Foxwell

Michael Vita watched as the inmate, head bowed, first stumbled left and then right. Vita didn't stop his wobbly march as he attempted to cross the yard.

'You,' the veteran Long Bay governor yelled. 'Come here.'

The man in prison green ignored the order.

'Stop now!' Vita shouted.

This prisoner looked up slowly. 'Whatzz thhhhat?' he slurred. 'Stooooooop?'

The prisoner's eyes were glazed over.

'I asked him to walk in a straight line,' Vita said. 'And he fell flat to the floor. It was pretty obvious he was drunk, so we searched him. We didn't expect to find anything, because they usually drink in their cell.'

What happened next was a first for Vita and, most likely, the prison too.

'He pulled his pants down and there was a bladder strapped to his leg,' Vita said. 'It was full of prison brew. Attached to the bladder was a tube, which ran up his leg, through his shirt and up his neck. He'd been sucking on the bloody tube as he walked through the yard. Can you believe that?'

Alcohol is freely available in Long Bay. As one prisoner puts it: 'If you want it, you can get it. Especially if you have the money or the pull.'

But it is also a huge issue.

'So many problems in jail are fuelled by alcohol,' Vita continued. 'You'll find that a lot of the bashings and most of the fights are perpetrated or caused by people who've consumed the stuff.'

Prison brew is lethal and quite easy to make. Grab some orange peels, yeast, a packet of lollies, a garbage bag and you're on your way.

'They'll use just about anything,' Vita continued. 'If you work in the kitchen or have access to it, and many prisoners do, all you need are some fruit peels and yeast from the bakery. Anything with sugar in it will start the fermenting process.'

Hard-boiled lollies were a favourite of the past; the red-and-white kind were given out at Christmas. Glucose tablets, given to diabetics, are a more recent ingredient.

'We had to keep our eye on the ball,' Vita said. 'If you had a good nose you could smell it because the stuff really stank. They'd sometimes make the brew in common areas or in their rooms. The wings were 18 cells long with two levels.

'We knew then never to go walking on our own when we went out looking for the brew. We certainly wouldn't go up the stairs and down the landing – you'd get bashed otherwise. The inmates used to take advantage of that, and wait for periods of time when there were only two of us in with 72 of them. We'd usually find the brew in green garbage bags, and this is what's referred to as a "bladder". They'd be hanging in the stairwells, buried in the ground, or stashed inside the toilet.

'It was a deadly brew and many a riot can be blamed on it. The inmates were off their heads on it in a minute. If we didn't find it, well, it was too late – you were in trouble. We couldn't reason with a prisoner who was drunk on the stuff. You just had to close the wing, get out there, put your gear on and do your best. Something bad was coming and you had to prepare for the worst.'

Former Long Bay guard Grant Turner, a hard-nosed screw who worked with the much-feared emergency unit, found a mother lode of brew in a sweeper's cell.

'We spotted it under his bed,' Turner said. 'It was a huge plastic drum full of the stuff.'

Turner asked the prisoner what it was. The guard already knew, of course, but wanted to see how the inmate would try to get out of this one.

'It's my special brew, chief,' the prisoner said matter-of-factly. 'The best in the jail. It's about two days from being perfect but you can try some if you want.' Grabbing the drum with two hands, he heaved it from under the bed and screwed the cap off, sending alcohol vapour into the air. 'Here, have a smell.'

Turner decided to amuse him. 'What makes it so good?' he asked. 'Why is it the best?'

'Check out my feet,' the inmate replied. 'They're grape-crushing machines. I used to make wine on the outside.'

Turner looked down and laughed. The prisoner did indeed have massive feet. But rules were rules. 'Sorry, mate, we can't let you have that brew. We're going to have to take it off you,' he said.

The prisoner was shocked. After all, he was a sweeper and thought he was entitled to a bit of the 'blind eye'. 'Well, at least give me a sip,' he said.

The guard reluctantly nodded.

'So he grabbed this gigantic container and started to skoll the entire thing. He jammed as much as he could down his throat. We had to wrestle it out of his hands,' Turner recalled.

It wasn't unusual to find large quantities of prison brew here and there. Back in the early 70s, the guards discovered a mother lode bubbling away in a 20-litre container.

'It was in the Metropolitan Remand Prison (MRP), where they knew a brew was being made,' said former guard Roy Foxwell. 'The guards found it and wanted to find out who'd made it and who was going to drink it, so they left it where it was. The screws went down to the pharmacy and bought a bunch of laxatives from the chemist. They loaded up the brew with all these pills that would give you instant diarrhoea. And four prisoners ended up spending half the day on the shit-house.'

The guards couldn't work out why the prisoners cared so much for their hair.

'There's a list of things prisoners can buy,' said a current guard who asked not to be named. 'Aside from their rationed items, they can purchase things like toothpaste, better-quality clothes – still green, of course – shoes and soap. You could also get a couple of different types of shampoo, and we noticed that Pert 2in1 was selling out. The inmates were all buying it and we couldn't work out why. Blokes without hair on their head were stocking up on the stuff.'

The prisoners were not longing for a healthier scalp or shinier hair – they'd come up with another ingenious way to get drunk.

'We found a couple of bottles hidden in freezers,' said the guard. 'And then it twigged. We looked through the ingredients list. Pert was the only shampoo that contained alcohol.'

But this didn't mean the inmates were eating shampoo slushies.

'The inmates worked out that alcohol doesn't freeze,' explained the guard, 'so they'd put the shampoo in the freezer and freeze everything except the grog.'

Needless to say, Pert is no longer on the Long Bay prison shopping list.

A popular cleaning product also got its fair share of Long Bay prisoners drunk. It also put a few in the hospital.

'Brasso was very popular back in the day,' the guard continued. 'It also contained alcohol, but the prisoners were clued up to the freezing process and would drain it with a sieve. Sometimes they would make alcohol, sometimes poison. It was a fine line and pretty dangerous, but a risk they were willing to take.'

Of course, you could always just get hold of the real stuff if high school chemistry wasn't your thing. After all, Jim Beam, Jack Daniel's, Johnny Walker Blue . . . they all taste better than Pert.

'The screws would bring in whatever you wanted, provided you were a somebody,' said infamous Sydney gangster Graham 'Abo' Henry. 'They brought me beer, scotch, bourbon – whatever grog I wanted. Sometimes they'd even smuggle it in a hot water bottle.'

Meanwhile, in minimum security, they prefer drinking out of glass.

'Some blokes used to climb up that pipe and go straight over the wall,' said former two-time Long Bay inmate Ian Mathie, referring to the prison's 3-metre high fence.

'The guy who showed us how to get out was a little

Aboriginal bloke. He used to work on the masts in the Navy and knew a thing or two about climbing.

'He made easy work of all the pipes, brick walls and barbwire cyclone fences to get to the shop for grog. When we had money, we'd send him off to get a bottle of scotch. They were never the big ones, just the hip flasks, but that was plenty enough to get you drunk. So we'd sit around playing cards at night, drinking scotch. I don't think the screws cared too much unless you pissed them off.

'Every Thursday, our climber mate would escape just to get pizza. He'd come back over the fence and sit there eating his pizza in the yard. The screws didn't give a shit because they knew he was coming back.'

The Game One

'I just love games, chief.'
Long Bay inmate

Booze isn't the only thing on the Long Bay banned list. Sometimes guards would go looking for the sinister and end up finding something completely unexpected . . .

Once again, they weren't there.

'Where the fuck is everyone?' the wing boss shouted at morning muster.

The fellow screw shrugged. 'Still asleep, I guess?' he replied.

'Again?' the boss shouted. 'Is narcolepsy contagious?'

That was the obvious diagnosis, given several inmates had made a habit of missing muster.

The guard found them in bed, nicely tucked in and oblivious to his shouting. He woke them up by rolling them onto the floor.

'I'm just tired, chief,' they'd say.

And no one knew why . . . not until the overnight raid.

'We went in looking for drugs,' said former Malabar Emergency Unit (MEU) guard Paul Rush, 'and didn't find any. But we did come across contraband – a PlayStation 2. We found it hidden in a toaster box, wrapped up in foam. You would've never known it was there. The only reason we found it was because we tipped the room over, suspecting something else. Now, a PlayStation isn't the smallest thing in the world. We had no idea how he got it in because this was a medium security jail.'

When the inmate was confronted about his console stash, he simply replied: 'I just love games, chief.'

Rush rated it as one of his strangest finds. 'It was always hard to get him out of bed in the morning,' Rush said about the video-game-playing prisoner. 'And we couldn't work out why until we found his PlayStation. He used to get out of bed as soon as the door was shut and stay up until 5am playing it. And it wasn't just him. He used to rent the thing out to other blokes, too. I dare say he was making a bit of money doing it. We actually got some intel from another inmate tipping us off to search his cell. We later found out he had the shits because this bloke wouldn't rent the PlayStation to him.'

And whatever did happen to the PlayStation 2?

'It may have ended up in one of our lunchrooms,' said a guard. 'A lot of things like that didn't get destroyed and made their way to the officers' annexes.'

9

INJECTING

Sharpen and Share

'They didn't give a shit about the prospect of getting AIDS.
Not one bit.'
Long Bay sweeper

'The new bloke has HIV,' the wing sweeper told the junkies. 'Whatever you do, don't go sharing needles. Use your own if he gives you some gear.'

The sweeper, an old-school tough guy in for armed robbery, hated junkies. They made everyone sick. Still, no matter how much he despised them, they didn't deserve to die. None of them deserved to be sentenced to death.

He walked into the shower block two days after delivering the life-saving advice.

'They were all sitting there, smacked out with the new bloke,' said the sweeper.

'What's going on?' he shouted, looking at the used syringe on the ground.

The junkies hadn't listened to his warning; a hit on offer, they'd jammed the infected syringe into their bruised and belted veins.

'They didn't give a shit about the prospect of getting AIDS,' the sweeper continued. 'Not one bit.'

A day later, he approached one of the men he saw share the needle with the HIV-positive prisoner.

'What were you thinking?' he asked. 'I told you the new bloke has AIDS.'

The prisoner was adamant. 'Na, we told you he's sweet,' he replied. 'He said he didn't have it. And anyway, we bleached the needle.'

The sweeper shook his head and walked off.

Later, he found out that all five men who'd shared the syringe contracted HIV.

'They're probably dead now because they weren't the type who would bother to get help,' the sweeper said. 'The prison junkies don't care about anything except getting a hit. I used to ask them if they were worried about AIDS. They'd say, "No, what you do is put it in bleach, pull it and clean it out. Then it's sweet."'

'Bleach is everywhere in jail. They reckon it kills everything, including AIDS. They were so desperate that if their syringe went blunt, they would rub it on the sandstone wall to make it sharp. The scary thing is more than 50 percent of the inmates are on the gear [heroin]. It's fucking everywhere and it's just horrible. The things you see these blokes doing for a hit . . . It's disgusting.'

Don't believe him? Well, there aren't too many things more disgusting than sticking your arm up your mate's arse. Unless you're the mate, and he's performing the action.

'The worst thing I saw in Long Bay was definitely the gear,' said former inmate Abo Henry.

'The crims would put it up their arses. I saw blokes being chased by the screws because they knew they had it, and they would shit in their own hands as they were running to get it out.

'I even saw one bloke bent over in his cell with another bloke's arm up his arse. He had his wrist and everything up there, looking for his mate's gear. The guy couldn't get it out himself, so he promised the other bloke half if he could get it for him.'

AIDS was a possibility. Hepatitis C was a certainty. An eight-year study commissioned by the Australian Government revealed that one in three male prisoners in Australia had the incurable disease in 2001. The epidemic had been predicted in 1999, and the NSW Drug Summit recommended the introduction of a prisoner needle exchange program. Using clean needles would make the risk of contracting the disease in prison six times less likely.

The prison union opposed the move.

'You're giving an inmate a loaded gun,' Tony Howden of the NSW Prison Officers' Union told ABC reporter Sean Murphy in 2001. 'He could just use it to stab anyone. It's a death sentence if it has HIV in it. And long term . . . Hepatitis C is a death sentence.'

Prisoner Shaun Cook told Murphy he'd taken a hit with a dirty needle.

'That's happened to me before, you know, like there's no bleach, so you think about it,' he said on the ABC program *Lateline*. 'And you take that risk. Then after, you think, oh, maybe I've got something.'

Educational programs were introduced in Long Bay to warn prisoners of the dangers associated with sharing needles. They were also shown how to clean a needle with bleach and cold water.

Suzi Morris, a spokeswoman for NSW Corrective Services in 2001, spoke to the *7.30 Report* about the program.

'All our educational programs teach the inmates how to use safely,' Morris said. 'I know that might sound strange in an environment like this where it's a legal issue, but we understand and realise that drug use happens and that for some people it's not going to be abstinence.'

Drugs were bought and sold inside the jail. Just like in the outside world, it was lucrative for the sellers and dangerous for the buyers.

'There was an internal network; a smaller version of what happens outside,' said former PO Turner. 'There would be a dealer who'd secure the money from people on the outside or who'd do it for favours on the inside. It was a lot more expensive inside than out. In terms of the gangs, like the Lebos and Bikies, some of these blokes were massive, so their mates on the outside would bring it into the jail for them, for free.

The Smelly Safe

'We watch you until you shit them out, or until the bags burst and you die.'
Former PO Roy Foxwell to a suspected drug smuggler

Prison guard Roy Foxwell answered the call.

'Mate, we have one here that's jammed full of gear,' said the federal police officer on the phone. 'She was going to bring it into the country and take it straight to jail. She won't submit to an X-ray or an internal search. Can you come help?'

Foxwell agreed and hung up the phone. He was getting the drugs – if he didn't get it in the hospital, he would get it in the cell.

'Look, lady,' he said beside the woman's hospital bed after having left Long Bay to make the visit. 'You have two choices. You give us the drugs now and we'll charge you with importing. Or we take you into a glass cell and we watch you until you shit them out, or until the bags burst and you die. If you don't die, you won't just be charged with importing, but also for bringing them into jail. It's your call.'

Foxwell knew it was an offer too good to resist.

Half an hour later, when Foxwell was called back into the woman's room, she had her answer ready for him: she would submit to an enema.

And out came the drugs.

Dropping Pants

'You wouldn't think someone could get a syringe up there, but that was commonplace.'
Long Bay guard

The officer on patrol rested his elbow out the open window, eyes firmly on the field.

'Hey, slow down,' he said to the guard driving, as he saw an inmate jump at the sight of the car. 'We could have something here.'

An inmate ducked down behind the other two prisoners who stood with him, as though he was trying to hide. Then, strangely, he dropped his pants.

As the official Long Bay seizure report said of the incident: 'He was seen inserting something into his anal region and appeared very nervous.'

The guard floored it and soon both officers were out of the car and standing in front of the inmate, who seemed even stiffer now, thanks to the object stuck up his arse.

'Stop!' yelled the guard. 'We have reason to believe you are carrying contraband.'

The inmate stood still. He didn't say a word.

The two officers took the inmate back to the Area 7 interview room.

'We began to strip search prisoner [name removed],' said the report. 'During the strip search [name removed] was told to take off his underwear. As this occurred, a packet fell from his buttock area. Officer [name removed] secured the item and the search continued. Nothing else was found. Officer [name removed] then gave [name removed] the official caution and asked [name removed] a number of questions. During the questioning [name removed] admitted to ownership of the packet and said he had found the syringe on the oval. The packet was unwrapped and a cap was found with a syringe. The syringe was placed into a sharps container and put into an evidence bag in plain view of [name removed].'

The guard expanded on the report: 'He had the drugs and a syringe shoved up his blurter. You wouldn't think someone could get a syringe up there, but that was commonplace.'

So how do the drugs get in? Well, in the safe, of course.

'There are only a couple of places you can hide something on a human body,' said former guard Grant Turner. 'Up the blurter is one of them, and for a woman the other is in their vagina. They call both of them "the safe" or sometimes "the cupboard".

'They usually wrap the drugs in a couple of balloons or condoms, and they insert it when they go into visits or when they take it from one side of the jail to the other. Some keep the drugs in their safe for storage so that it isn't found or stolen by anyone else. They will leave it up their blurter until they're ready to use it.

'But, sometimes, the safe is used for things other than drugs. I once found a bloke who had an eight-inch blade up his arse. He was keeping it there until he had an opportunity to stab the bloke he wanted to knock.'

Often, the contraband is taken from one safe and stored in another during visits. They can also be removed from a safe, only to be swallowed.

'The women would bring it in their safe and they would get frisky with the husband,' said Turner. 'The bloke would eat it and then shit it out or vomit it up later when they got back to their cell. They could eat eight condoms in one go. It was just disgusting. Some blokes would even put syringes up their arse during a visit.'

Veteran Long Bay guard (and later governor) Michael Vita confirmed drugs were passed in visits. Despite being supervised, there were too many inmates for any guard to watch and keep a full eye on.

'They used to bring drugs in and we couldn't stop it, no matter how hard we tried,' Vita said. 'We would've needed one guard per prisoner to prevent it from happening, and we were watching tens at a time. As much as we supervised visits, you couldn't stop someone from kissing their husband, and most of the time you wouldn't see it anyway. They would just pass it from mouth to mouth and it was in. There were times when we were able to catch them in the act, and then we'd put the bloke in solitary and wait until he passed it. But for each crim you caught, there were ten who got through. They brought everything in. Everything. Heroin was the biggest problem during my time.'

It comes as no surprise, then, that drug use was widespread in Long Bay.

'When I was in 10 Wing the laundry was at the back,' said an inmate. 'They'd be able to lock it up and sit there, shooting up all day. The guards didn't care because they weren't hurting anyone but themselves. The blokes would get their family or friends to smuggle the drugs in or they could just buy them. The girls would get the balloons and pass it over through a kiss. The crim would swallow the things so that they could get them back through the check. Straight after the visit, you'd see them run to the toilet for a shit. Then they'd be elbow-deep in crap, going through their shit to get the balloon holding their hit. It was so disgusting, and a sight that will never leave me, no matter how hard I try to forget.

'But sometimes bringing it in was way easier. The blokes on work release would be given it while they were sweeping a road and just bring it back. They would organise a drop and bury it for someone else to pick up.'

Serve and Seize

'They would split the thing open, whack the drugs inside and just throw it over.'
Former Long Bay inmate Ian Mathie

The tennis ball hit the grass, bouncing once, then twice, before rolling onto the asphalt that marked the end of the freshly cut yard.

'It's mine,' said the inmate, hands swiping at the Slazenger ball rolling away.

'Bullshit,' said another inmate, who was trying to stop the rushing ball with his feet. 'It's fucking mine.'

The ball was eventually caught by the first inmate. Frustrated, the second prisoner pulled back his fist in preparation for a punch.

Boooop!

Then another ball bounced into the yard.

'Sorry, mate,' he said, bringing the loaded weapon down from his chin.

'This one must be mine.'

Former inmate Ian Mathie witnessed the men fighting over the ball. He was in the minimum-security section of the jail during his second stint in Long Bay.

'It was a great spot to get drugs in,' Mathie said. 'Tennis balls were always coming over that fence. They would split the thing open, whack the drugs inside and just throw it over. From there, they would either use the drugs themselves, or if they were doing it for someone else, they'd take it into another part of the jail.

'For the blokes who were taking it themselves in the minimum-security section, it was pretty much just marijuana. They were almost out of prison and couldn't risk being caught with anything heavier or they would've ended up going back into maximum with more time added on to their sentence. But heavy stuff did come in and they'd take it into the other jail, either because they were being paid or threatened.'

So how do you know exactly which tennis ball is yours? And what stopped those clenched fists from punching face?

'Well, if you weren't expecting something, it wasn't yours,' Mathie said. 'And you'd be game to pinch someone else's because you had no idea who ultimately owned it. The junkie picking it up was probably just a courier who was going to take it in to a heavy inside. You could take your chances, but you might end up with a shiv in the neck.

'The person who was getting it would know when it was coming in because they'd get a visit and would be told to look out for a ball on a particular day at a particular time. But still, there were days when four or five balls would come over the fence at the same time. That was a fucking good laugh unless it was you who was expecting a ball.'

PO Turner confirmed that the tennis ball was a popular and successful way of smuggling drugs into jail.

'They would just hit them over the wall with their racquets,' he said.

'They'd pretend they were taking the dog for a walk and hit a few tennis balls to their dog, and then all of a sudden they'd shank one and whack it over the fence. That went on a lot behind 12 Wing and also in minimum security. The guys in minimum security would then take it into the other jails. If they didn't have a job in another jail, they'd make someone who did take it in. The most common way was to smuggle it in the meals.

'Food in prison was delivered into the wings on carts and they'd give the stash to the bloke on whatever wing it needed to go to. The bloke would then walk to the food base and pass it to whichever inmate was given the job of making the collect.'

Seek and Destroy

'If you feel anything abnormal, you tip them up onto their head, strip them and find out what it is. Don't even give them

*a second, because if they get the opportunity they'll throw the
gear out the window or eat it.'*
Former Metropolitan Security Unit (MSU) Long Bay guard

SUBJECT: Operation visitor search at Long Bay. On Saturday
[date removed] officer from the Metropolitan Security Unit
and Drug Detector Dog Unit conducted a visitor search at
the Long Bay Correctional Complex boom gate with the
following results.

Searches:
109 × visitors' property searched
203 × visitors PAD (passive alert dog) searched
5 × vehicles denied entry
109 × vehicles searched
1 × field can issued

Contraband:
4 × knives
1 × tablet
1 × syringe
4.2 grams of white powder
Quantity of GVM (green vegetable matter aka 'pot')

This is what you'd normally find in an average bust during
a visitor search: drugs, syringes and knives. Unfortunately,
searches are few and far between. And even with sniffer
dogs, guards and police, not everything is seized.

'There wouldn't be a day you conducted a search that you wouldn't turn something up,' said a former MSU guard. 'We used to get the police to come down and we would search everyone who came through the front gate of the jail. We'd line them up and the dogs would go over them. When the dogs sat down, that's when we knew to run in.

'We would also get the dogs to go over the visitor cars as they were entering the parking lot. Because the car park is on Corrective Services property, as soon as they drove in, if they had a needle, a weapon or drugs, anything deemed inappropriate, they'd be charged as though they'd taken it into the jail. We would stop them, knowing they'd have a bag of whatever, and get the sniffer dogs in. Then we'd get the police in to make the charges.

'We normally had a lot of fights before the police came in, especially with the Bikies and the Lebanese. They thought we had no power at all and they acted like we were just some member of the public, walking over and asking them to submit to a search. They did not like being disrespected.

'Once the cops came round, they'd change their tune. We had powers of arrest but not of search, and this applied only to prisoners – not civilians. So we would hold them if the dogs pulled them up, or if we suspected or found anything, and we'd wait for the cops to come.

'We used to conduct these types of searches every weekend, but now the unit in charge of it has been axed because of cuts. We stopped a lot of the gear from coming through, and now it's all getting back in.'

One bust uncovered a jaw-dropping amount of cash,

which is banned inside jail. You can only guess the amount of drugs that had got in as a result.

'We did a bust one weekend and found thousands and thousands of dollars in a can,' said the MSU guard. 'They had their own kitchens in some of the jails, and one day we went in and found a tin can. The can looked perfectly normal; it had been modified so it had a screw-off lid, which meant you could open and close it in a second and it would look completely sealed. When we worked it out and opened it, they had a little bag of baked beans in a false compart-ment under the stash as a decoy. We wouldn't have found this out if not for the tip-off, and it was just genius. That's how inventive and cunning these blokes are. We discovered they'd made the drug trade a cash business inside prison and they were all handing over money during visits. The money would come in and then back out into accounts. It was an unbelievable find, because cash isn't allowed in jail.'

Guards searched every inmate and every visitor when they came into Long Bay. Most of the drugs that weren't hidden in a safe were found.

'When you do a search on somebody, it's like doing a karate chop with your hand,' said a former MSU guard. 'You start from the neck and run that karate chop all the way down to their groin. You then rub it from the tip of the spine to their arse and around to their balls. If you feel anything abnormal, you tip them up onto their head, strip them and find out what it is. Don't even give them a second because if they get the opportunity, they'll throw the gear out the window or eat it.'

*

Now that the cell doors were firmly shut and the wing completely dark, the inmates no longer had to hide their drugs.

Or so they thought.

'The midnight raids were when we knew we would get the drugs,' said former Malabar Emergency Unit (MEU) guard Paul Rush. 'We'd target them overnight for illicit drugs because we knew we'd get them every time. We would bust open their cells at 2am, and find them passed out in a corner with a fit [a prison-made instrument that can be used to smoke or inject drugs] or bong in their hands or on the ground next to them.

'The inmates weren't worried one bit because these raids were very random and they thought they'd have their hit and hide it before their cell was opened for morning muster.

'We had an interesting way of waking them up. We'd get a cup of warm water and place it on their stomach or chest before tapping them. They'd wake up, spilling the water all over themselves, mistaking it for piss. Then we would give them the good news about what we'd found in their possession.'

SIM Cards and Steroids

'And it just wasn't the prison officers. Nurses, psychologists – they were all caught. A lot of the women workers were caught out having affairs with the men and they would be manipulated into bringing it in.'
Former Long Bay PO and governor Michael Vita

The officer walked towards the prison guard, a piece of paper in his hand.

'This here is a search warrant that gives us the legal right to inspect your car,' said the officer. 'Please open your boot.'

Karaha Pene Te-Hira, a prison officer for 22 years, knew he was done. He did as he was told, aware that he'd be wearing green if he ever walked into a prison again.

The officer fumbled through the contents of the prison guard's boot. Te-Hira's bank records had been seized and he'd been taking less than $100 out of his account each month. Authorities suspected he had a stash of cash. They were right.

'He had almost ten grand in his boot,' said a current guard who wished to remain unnamed. 'He was smuggling shit in for the prisoners and making a fortune.'

In fact, the inspecting officer found exactly $9500 in the boot of the Long Bay Metropolitan Special Programs Centre (MSPC) Special Activities Officer's car. Te-Hira soon admitted to selling prisoners contraband, which ranged from shoes and SIM cards to steroids.

The easy way to get contraband into a prison is not by using your 'safe', swapping spit or catching sailing Slaz-engers. No, it's much easier and less riskier to pay a guard to bring it straight through the front door.

'If it wasn't the inmates bringing it in, then it was the staff,' Vita said. 'Our internal criminal investigation unit nailed a few during my time. We would be told something or suspect something and we'd pass the information on to them. And it just wasn't the prison officers. Nurses, psychologists – they were all caught. A lot of the women workers were caught out having affairs with the men and they'd be manipulated into bringing it in.'

In 2012 the prison did not do the nailing. Te-Hira was hauled before the Independent Commission Against Corruption (ICAC) after Corrective Services NSW sent a report to the watchdog, alleging the guard had been trafficking telephones and illegal drugs into the MSPC.

Te-Hira had been a guard since 1990. He began working at the MSPC in 2006 and was suspended in 2009, following the execution of the search warrant. It was alleged and then proved that Te-Hira smuggled in contraband for his sweeper in exchange for car radios, favours and cash. Te-Hira told the commission that his trafficking activities started not long after his employment in the MSPC.

'I just got too close to them,' Te-Hira said. 'And it just went from there.'

One of the inmates he became friendly with included prisoner Omar Zahed, a sweeper in the MSPC. Te-Hira smuggled shoes and steroids into the jail in a prison officer 'standard-issue clear plastic bag'. He placed papers on either side of the contraband to hide it from the other guards.

Te-Hira would receive the objects to pass on to Zahed and the payment from his sister when the pair would meet at a car park in Summer Hill.

Sweeper Zahed also allegedly paid for a stereo and DVD system to be installed in Te Hira's car at Xtreme Car Audio Blacktown in exchange for steroids.

Following a lengthy and thorough investigation by ICAC, Te-Hira was found to have engaged in corrupt behaviour by:

1. Trafficking contraband, including food, clothing, shoes, mail, mobile telephones, chargers, SIM cards, steroids

and a plunger for steroid injection, into the MSPC for inmates Zahed and Prisoner X over a six-month period in 2012.

2. Trafficking a pair of shoes, which he delivered to Zahed on or around 14 June 2012, into the MSPC, in return for cash and a pair of shoes.

3. Trafficking a pair of shoes, which he delivered to Zahed on or around 28 June 2012, into the MSPC, in return for a pair of shoes.

4. Accepting a benefit of at least $500 towards the cost of having a car stereo and DVD installed into his car.

Corrective Services sacked Te-Hira after the ICAC recommended he be dismissed. The disgraced guard was only spared jail time because the Director of Public Prosecutions could not prosecute as more than six months had passed since the offences.

Te-Hira's colleagues were furious. His former mates turned their backs on the 'dirty' guard.

'That type of thing is just not on,' said one guard. 'Ninety-nine percent of the guards find corruption disgusting. Prisoners taking drugs and getting things like phones to commit more crimes sicken us. Pene betrayed us all and there were blokes in here who wanted to flog him. But Pene was very embarrassed and sorry for what he did. To his credit, he asked if he could come in and front all the guards. He wanted to apologise. He never got to do it, because the guards refused to go near him. They could never look at him again after what he did.'

Care Bears

'It was also known (regardless of its official name) as the "AIDS unit" or "Death Row". Prisoners' mail was routinely labelled AIDS and visitors were informed the prisoner they wanted to see was in the "AIDS Unit". This was the way some family members and friends learned that the person they were going to visit was HIV-positive.'

NSW Department of Corrective Services Research Publication: Lifestyles Unit – Evaluation Study

Future Long Bay governor Michael Vita walked from one prison to the next. He saw a guard come out of the hospital.

'You fucking Care Bear,' he shouted at the man walking from the new 'therapeutic' wing.

The fellow guard stopped.

'Mate, have you gone soft?' Vita asked. 'What's the go with working in there and calling the crims by their first names and letting them call you by yours? It's just not right.'

Little did Vita know that he would soon become a Care Bear too.

'Long Bay was the place that really kicked off the Special Units,' Vita said. 'Ron Woodham (former boss of Corrective Services NSW) was really the innovator, and even though he was as hard as nails, he recognised the only way he would get ahead would be to start looking at all the special needs of the prisoners. Ron had already started up the emergency units, and after that he began opening up more therapeutic units like Special Care Unit, the Crisis Support Unit and so on.

'Ron wanted to make a run for the top job and he had brains enough to know that he had to cater for everybody. He had to try to rehabilitate them and he surrounded himself with people who could help.'

Vita established the Lifestyles Unit in Long Bay in 1992, working closely with drug-addicted and HIV-positive prisoners.

'The Lifestyle Unit was a voluntary program for people with AIDS/HIV, but we kind of ushered them into it. There was a lot of hysteria over AIDS and the prisons couldn't segregate HIV-infected prisoners or do mandatory tests anymore. I think this was a way of keeping them all together. The conditions were really good in the Lifestyles Unit and prisoners were encouraged to enter with the provision of better food and privileges. While in there, inmates had proper, first-class medical treatment and counselling. They were never in cages and a lot of their sessions were group sessions.'

AIDS was a controversial issue in Long Bay. The prison's first response to the epidemic was to throw all the HIV-positive prisoners into the same room and forget about them. In 1985 the first compulsory segregation unit was established. Prisoners known or suspected of being HIV-positive were locked away in a special unit called the Malabar Assessment Unit. A corrective services report slammed the facility.

'The unit was grossly inadequate in resources, and was the subject of a number of complaints under the *Anti-Discrimination Act*,' the report said. 'It severely restricted the inmates' access to facilities normally available to inmates in the correctional system. It was also known (regardless of its official name) as the "AIDS unit" or "Death Row." Prisoners' mail was routinely labelled AIDS and visitors were informed that the prisoner they wanted to see was in the "AIDS Unit". This was the way some family members and friends learned the person they were going to visit was HIV-positive.

'In 1989, the Prisons AIDS Project assessed the purpose and activities of the MAU and found that, while the physical accommodation and layout of the unit was adequate, both the staff and the inmates were dissatisfied and unhappy. Those involved felt that little was being achieved by placing HIV antibody-positive inmates in a segregated unit. Furthermore, there was increasing pressure from many sectors on the discriminatory nature and legality of a segregation unit and its violation of human rights.'

All rhetoric aside, the threat of legal action forced the jail to rethink its position. But the institution, and all the inmates who did not have the virus, were more than happy to keep the rot contained.

'The hysteria started hitting in the mid-80s,' Vita said. 'People were concerned prisons would become the epicentre for the disease because of all the drug use. They thought everyone would get it and they thought segregation was the only way to contain it.'

Despite the fears, HIV/AIDS affected only a small number of Long Bay prisoners. On 5 November 1990, compulsory HIV testing was introduced to all admissions into the NSW correctional system. From 1993 to 1994, a total of

12,032 admissions were tested, with 55 prisoners recording a positive result. Only 0.46 percent had the 'prison disease'.

At the end of 1994, again due to outside pressure, mandatory testing was scrapped in favour of voluntary screening. Between the years 1994 and 1995, it was estimated that an average of 22 inmates in the NSW Corrections System were HIV/AIDS positive.

Long Bay's Lifestyle Unit was the softest solution the prison could find.

'We had an average of about five inmates in there at any one time,' Vita said. 'At most it had seven or eight. Eventually it was turned into a hepatitis unit but it was shut down in 1992, and we went back to a policy of integration rather than separation. Whether inmates had AIDS or not became very confidential and the only person who could know you had HIV was the superintendent or the governor.'

10

PROTECTING

The Special Protection Unit
'I only made her suck me off.'
Long Bay prisoner Gary Murphy

Michael Vita cracked the cell.

'You know I didn't do shit,' said the inmate who was about to be locked away. 'I only got a fucking head job. I shouldn't be in here at all.'

Vita, the governor of the new Special Protection Unit (SPU), glared at Gary Murphy. He wanted to punch him in the face. Instead, he pretended he didn't hear what the vile creature, who was given a life sentence for his role in raping and killing Anita Cobby, said. Vita was responsible for running a Long Bay wing that housed New South Wales' most horrid criminals; the first of its kind in Australia.

'I only made her suck me off,' Murphy continued as he entered his cell. 'I swear.'

Vita slammed the cell door and twisted the key so hard it almost snapped. He then drew a gulp of air, rolled his shoulders and walked away. He had already forgotten what the man said about the 26-year-old beauty queen who'd almost been decapitated after being gang-raped by five men.

'I would have gone insane if I'd listened to what they all said,' Vita reflected. 'They were the worst of the worst.'

Gary Murphy was just one of a group of 'sickos' locked up in isolation at 11 Wing in Long Bay Jail, in an experiment that would begin the epidemic of 'protection'.

Next to Murphy, in an equally boring and sterile cell, was Neville Towner, a man who smashed a rock over a four-year-old girl's head as he was raping her because she 'wouldn't shut up', before throwing her lifeless body into the Nepean River. Across from them, past the dining table and 51-centimetre TV that all six 'protections' huddled around to watch *Midday with Ray Martin*, was where Gary Murphy's brother, Michael, was kept. He was also sentenced to life for the brutal murder of Cobby.

In all, there were six loathsome, violent and disgusting criminals in Long Bay's Special Protection Unit (SPU), who were separated from the rest of the prisoners for their absolutely heinous crimes.

Opened in 1988, Long Bay's SPU was another attempt at solving one of the prison's age-old problems:

How do we stop the killers from being killed?

The simple answer was to put them all together.

'Rapists, child abusers, murderers and, more often than not, all three of the above,' Vita said. 'These were the most-hated prisoners in the jail, men who'd committed crimes that made them prime targets in jail.'

There are some crimes even the most violent of criminals can't tolerate, even killers. If you are convicted or suspected of being one of these three things, consider yourself an immediate target: a paedophile, a rapist or a Dog.

'They are the worst,' said Abo Henry. 'Disgusting fucks who you should kill on sight. In jail, anybody who has touched a kid is the walking dead. Rapists aren't far behind and, as for Dogs, it's just a matter of time.'

'Prisoners have their own code,' said Vita, further expanding on the matter. 'They always have. There are some crimes that rate above others, and people you or me would consider sick rate others sicker than them.

'Historically, the prisoners who've been most at risk are those who have raped or killed children and, back in the day, women. Nowadays, for whatever reason, maybe values have changed, raping a woman is not something that will get you killed. But abusing children – that's something even the worst prisoners won't condone.

'When you put a group of people in a room, a pecking order is developed. But before judging you on your personality, your toughness or your intellect, you are judged on your crime. In 1978, when I was in the Metropolitan Remand Centre, you were bashed for a rape on a woman but, as I said, that has changed. And you were killed for raping a child – and that will never change.'

What did change was the 'let them get what's coming to them' attitude that prevailed in prison society until the late 1970s. Most were happy to see these men suffer in prison. To be honest, most still are. But minority groups, such as the Prisoners Action Group and other bleeding hearts, forced institutions to ensure the safety of all inmates.

'We'd like to bash most of them ourselves,' said a current prison guard. 'But we have an obligation to protect those who cannot protect themselves. Seriously, they are treated better than us. If it comes down to it, the department will take their word over ours. You'll be sacked in an instant for even looking at one of these scumbags the wrong way.'

The rapist looked at the killer.

'Uno,' the rapist said.

The killer threw his cards on the table and shook his head.

'Let me see,' said the infamous Queensland paedophile, also locked away in the SPU. The most despicable prisoners played cards to pass the time and had no choice in the company they shared.

'The 1988 SPU was the first of the very strict protections,' explained Vita. 'We already had protections prior to this, but these blokes were so hated that they couldn't even survive alongside other protections.

'The SPU was at the end of 11 Wing, opposite the Special Purpose Centre (SPC). There were seven cells on each side, and a wall separated them from the other prisoners in the wing. Despite having 14 cells in SPU, there were only six inmates vile enough to end up in there.'

Vita remembers each and every one of their crimes vividly.

'Frederick Many raped a woman on the Central Coast, and was sentenced to 14 years,' Vita said. 'He bashed her and put her in the boot of his car. The victim was smart enough to chew off her fingernails and spit them out in the back. The police found the guy and then discovered her fingernails. It was this evidence that ended up getting Many convicted.

'Then there were Michael and Gary Murphy, two of the pricks who killed Anita Cobby. They were slimy bastards and I had to work with them face-to-face. I found it difficult talking to them, knowing who they were and what they'd done. And I would've never picked them out to be killers. The old story that you need to have horns and look evil to be evil is just wrong. These guys were polite and looked respectable. Gary was the overt one of the two and he developed mental problems as the years went on.

'We also had a grub called Towner who'd killed a kid. And then there was the sicko who killed a woman and buried her. He then went back and dug her up and raped her corpse. Lawrence was another one, a despised criminal who killed two Aboriginal kids in a toilet at a rugby league knockout competition. And lastly there was Dennis Ferguson, who was sentenced to 14 years after raping three young girls in a motel in 1987. He was a beady-eyed little . . .'

*

A key cut by an inmate just weeks after the introduction of the state-of-the-art Saf-lok key, which was brought in to stop prisoners from picking handcuffs. (Picture supplied by Roy Foxwell)

The block of wood and metal used to create the key-cutting template, stolen from prison workshops. (Picture supplied by Roy Foxwell)

The first cut key was found in a shaving brush hidden in the inmate's cell. (Picture supplied by Roy Foxwell)

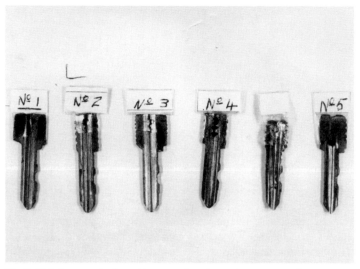

Six Saf-lok keys cut in Long Bay were found in prisons across the state. They were to be used in a mass escape attempt. (Picture supplied by Roy Foxwell)

Drugs seized after an 'internal' body exam. (Picture supplied by Roy Foxwell)

Drugs medically removed from an inmate's stomach after he tried to smuggle them into Long Bay. (Picture supplied by Roy Foxwell)

Drugs removed from an inmate's rectum. (Picture supplied by Roy Foxwell)

Tunnels built at Parramatta Jail by convicted murderer Anthony Lanigan after he convinced Long Bay guards he needed to be moved from Long Bay to Parramatta. Lanigan returned to Long Bay after the failed freedom bid and escaped from the prison in 1995. He remains at large. (Pictures supplied by Roy Foxwell)

Smoke pours from a Long Bay wing during the 1975 Christmas riot.
(Picture supplied by Grant Turner)

Automatic weapons used by Long Bay guards. (Picture supplied by Grant Turner)

Guards conducting a riot drill in the infamous Long Bay supermax, Katingal. (Picture supplied by Grant Turner)

A cell in Katingal. Inmates were deprived of all natural light, and oxygen was delivered through an air-conditioning system. (Picture supplied by Grant Turner)

Katingal was a mirror image from the outside. Here is one side of the building that was knocked down after the Nagle Royal Commission branded the facility inhumane and recommended its closure. (Picture supplied by Grant Turner)

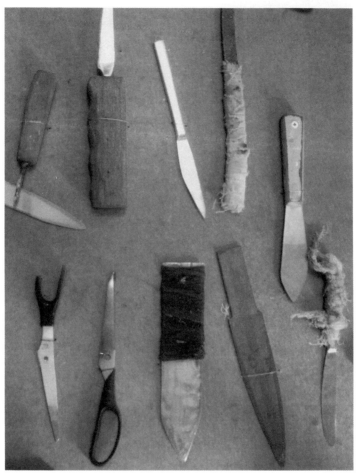

A collection of prison shivs seized by Long Bay guards during a raid. (Picture supplied by Dave Farrell)

The shower blocks in Long Bay are considered to be death traps, where many bashings and murders take place. (Photo: News Ltd/Newspix)

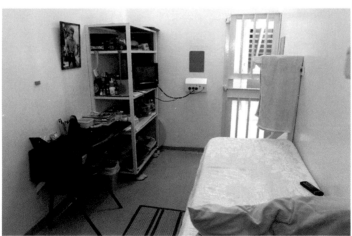

A 'sweeper' cell in Long Bay. Sweepers are allowed privileges above other regular inmates. (Photo: News Ltd/Newspix)

An aerial view of Long Bay Jail in the early 90s, with each building identified by post-it notes. (Picture supplied by Dave Farrell)

Aerial shot of the prison in the early 2000s. (Picture supplied by Grant Turner)

Arthur 'Neddy' Smith, Long Bay's most feared prisoner, was a convicted murderer, standover man and a famed police informant. (Photo: News Ltd/ Newspix)

Graham 'Abo' Henry was one of the jail's most infamous 'sweepers', and was Neddy Smith's right-hand man. (Photo: Steve Moorhouse/Newspix)

John Elias first entered Long Bay at the tender age of 16, only to become a professional footballer later in life. (Photo: News Ltd/Newspix)

Ian Hall Saxon: the Long Bay enigma. The rock 'n' roll promoter escaped the jail in 1993 and was recaptured two years later. (Photo: News Ltd/Newspix)

According to a guard, shamed entrepreneur Rene Rivkin first arrived in Long Bay in a soft-top Bentley, gold worry beads in hand. (Photo: Chris Hyde/ Newspix)

Company director Rodney Adler spent time in Long Bay, and was placed in protection, alongside sex offenders and other inmates who were vulnerable targets. (Photo: Gary Ramage/Newspix)

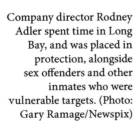

However, such extensive protection came at a price. Those who were imprisoned in SPU were safe but completely bored.

'They were confined to a small wing,' said Vita. 'Their only common room was the corridor in between the cells. It was only about 20 metres wide and as long as the seven cells. This was where they had their meals and visits.

'These inmates were at such a risk of being killed that they couldn't be taken anywhere. They had a 20 metre by 10 metre yard, but they rarely went out there because it looked into another yard, and the other prisoners there would abuse them. We would open their rooms up at 8.10 and we would lock them back up at 11.40am. They would go out again at 1.15pm before being shut in for the night. There was a TV in the hall, and they watched it whenever they weren't locked in their own individual cells. This was just a scumbag unit – it wasn't designed for them to be entertained or to facilitate interaction with others.'

Despite these limitations, it was clear none of these despised criminals would complain, or even consider the thought of it.

'They would have been killed if anyone got hold of them, so they liked being locked in,' Vita explained. 'They never gave us a drama because they knew they couldn't survive on the outside. When they did act out, we would threaten to throw them out with the angry men in gen pop. That would shut them up quick.

'These men knew they were disgusting. And they knew their place.'

Occasionally the guards overheard horrid conversations regarding details of the prisoners' crimes.

'The Cobby killers would sometimes start discussions about what they'd done,' Vita said.

'I didn't want to hear any of it. They often talked to the other inmates because they wanted to be accepted. They didn't have many visitors, as you would expect. I can remember being quite disturbed by Gary, because he would tell everyone he was innocent. The prick told me that all he got out of it was a head job. In his mind, he'd done nothing wrong. He would tell everyone because he wanted to be absolved of it.'

Former prison officer David Farrell, described by former prison governor John Heffernan as the toughest guard who worked in Long Bay, said the Murphy brothers who'd killed Anita Cobby were 'nobodies' when it came to this hard-nut jail.

'They were insignificant to look at,' Farrell said. 'They weren't hard men at all. That poor woman might have stood a chance against them if the rest of their mates weren't there. Gary and Michael wouldn't have lasted a second, had they been in gen pop. They acted tough because they were in segregation and would egg each other on. But in the end, they're really just wimps who only preyed on the weak.

'I knew Anita Cobby's father well. I met him on several occasions because he sat on the Serious Offenders Review Board. He was a thorough gentleman, and I could never understand how he was so calm about things. He was obviously a religious man because he never once asked me to get at them. I was absolutely gobsmacked by the way he dealt with things; he was so forgiving and understanding. He was heartbroken to lose his daughter but he was strong enough to deal with these horrible criminals in a sympathetic way.'

Protection has always been around in one form or another. Different prisoners need different levels of protection, ranging from not sharing a cell, or being locked up in a specialised wing like the SPU, or even in a secret prison where you don't have a name. Not all protection inmates have committed horrible crimes. Many ask to be placed in protection because they were simply afraid.

'Protection requests became an epidemic and that's the reason we had to open the SPU,' said Vita. 'Prisoners would come in and say, "I can't look after myself," and we'd put them in 1 Yard, which was the first level of protection. Some started off in general discipline, got a smack in the mouth and asked for protection.

'And then you had strict protections, which were the sex criminals and the Dogs. The Dogs were the informers and most of them had hits taken out on them.

'After that you had the strict-strict protections, like the ones in the SPU.'

A former inmate said several prisoners might have been killed had he not stopped them from going into protection for no other reason than being scared.

'Nearly the whole jail is in protection now,' said the inmate. 'There's protection, and then there's strict protection.

The whole thing is a joke. Some blokes who didn't even need protection would claim that they had to have it.

'I was a sweeper in reception and I'd have to speak to them about why they wanted protection before they were officially sent to the boneyard. Some of their answers were just shit. One bloke said it was because he owed a guy some money and he thought that guy was an inmate in Long Bay. I said, "Don't go in protection over that. No one's going to kill you for a little bit of cash. But you'll certainly be killed for going into protection. Instead of one bloke going after you, the whole criminal world will want you dead."

'I pulled plenty of blokes out of protection before anyone else knew they'd been in there. Like this real tough cunt called Stevie – a serious man on the outside. I couldn't believe he'd asked for protection. He ended up being all right, but he would've been killed. The thing is you might only be inside for a couple of years, but you'll be knocked down as soon as you get out because you'll be known as a Dog. Down at the remand centre you could see them through the cage at the end of 13 Wing. The inmates would throw shit at them over the fence and threaten to kill them. And none of us would forget a protection's face. Word spreads and these blokes would try to get on with their business once they got out but would quickly wind up dead.'

Dogs were once considered as bad as paedophiles.

'Dogs were fucked,' said two-time Long Bay inmate John Elias. 'You were done for if someone could prove you were a

Dog. Before my time you were killed if someone called you a Dog. It was such a severe and serious thing, that no one would ever call another prisoner a Dog unless they knew for certain that they were.

'The term eventually got overused to the point where you'd have to produce paperwork to prove someone was a Dog. That paperwork would be a statement of brief or a court document proving that the inmate had given someone up. This paperwork could be sold because there was always someone who was ready to take out a contract on them. I remember there were some staunch cunts who got exposed as Dogs and nobody was spared. When the paperwork was out you'd be fucked.

'One bloke was a bit of a leader within his Lebanese gang but after some paperwork was produced about him being a Dog, his mates fucked him up. They took him out to the boneyard and flogged him.'

You could also be killed for 'crying wolf'.

'In the old days it was just as bad to call someone they knew wasn't a Dog,' said a former inmate. 'You'd be knocked for sure.'

Raymond John Denning is remembered as Long Bay's most famous Dog. He was a respected figure in the criminal world, both in and out of jail, before he became a police informer later in life. He died of a 'drug overdose' shortly after he was released from prison. Denning was not known as a heavy drug user, and it was rumoured that he was killed by a 'hot-shot' – where someone injects you with a lethal amount of drug, like heroin, to make it look like a murder – for being a Dog. According to former detective-sergeant Roger Rogerson, Denning was the man who led police to infamous Long Bay escapee Russell 'Mad Dog' Cox.

'We used him to get to Cox,' Rogerson said. 'Denning just got him a message and they met up. Denning knew where he was going to be and he told us. We were there and that's how we got him.'

Paedophiles in Prison

'We're always searching their cells and confiscating things like Target and Kmart catalogues, which they'll sell and pass around because of the kids in their underwear. We've got to a stage where we'll go through the newspaper and pull anything out that has a picture of a kid in it.'
Current Long Bay prison officer

PO Grant Turner cracked open the cell.

'This is a random search,' he said. 'Please stand still while we inspect your cell.'

The convicted paedophile smiled. 'Of course, sir,' he said. 'You're more than welcome to look at anything.'

'They are all so sickeningly polite,' Turner explained, reflecting on his past experiences with these despicable crims. 'They are so nice it is utterly creepy. They are "Yes, sir" and "No, sir" to everything.'

Contrary to what Turner had said, this search was not random at all. The intelligence unit had been given information that this sex offender was distributing child

142

pornography to other inmates, and so it was Turner's job to search the compound.

Turner tipped, pulled and ripped apart the cell.

Nothing.

Maybe the intelligence was wrong.

'See? I have nothing to hide,' said the inmate. 'Can I help you with anything else?'

Turner turned towards the inmate and noticed a folder behind his feet. 'Pass me that, please,' he instructed, pointing at the pile of papers the inmate was trying to conceal.

The prisoner was no longer nice.

'He told me I couldn't have it,' Turner said. 'He told me that they were his legal documents and he was allowed to have it.'

'Give it to me now,' the officer shouted. 'I don't care if you're allowed to have it or not. I've been instructed to check everything in your cell. *Everything.*'

The prisoner begrudgingly handed over the folder.

'It was his brief, all right,' Turner said, remembering the incident. 'And it had police photos of all the children the man had abused. It was full of pictures of little kids, some of them showing the injuries they had sustained.'

Turner soon found out this inmate had been distributing the pictures to other convicted child sex offenders in the wing.

'He was loaning the pictures in return for favours,' Turner said. 'You can imagine what the other inmates were doing with them.'

The inmate was not charged because he was indeed allowed to be in possession of the photos, for legal reasons. But Turner informed the authorities of the discovery.

'They banned them from having photos in their brief after that,' Turner said.

Paedophiles are the lowest form of jail citizen. The criminal code demands that you squash a 'rock spider' on sight and never give these 'creepy fucks' a chance to spin another child-catching web. But they're not so easy to get, locked away in private and heavily guarded wings.

The thought repulses most – especially those who have to protect them.

'They're given the most privileges of any prisoner,' said a guard who asked to remain anonymous. 'All the older paedophiles are held in a special unit in the hospital. They range from ages 50 to 80. And it makes me sick because of the treatment and care they receive. They have nurses looking after them around the clock, they get all their medication for free, they have their arses wiped and they get better and more frequent meals than the rest of the prisoners.

'It's fucking disgusting. It costs a shitload to keep these vile humans in here and we're paying for it. These are putrid people who deserve nothing.'

Most imprisoned paedophiles are known as extremely manipulative inmates who are rated as 'high risk' when it comes to the prospect of re-offending once their sentences expire.

'They can't be trusted for a moment,' said a former parole officer. 'They will say all the right things to us and do all the programs, but often they slip up and reveal their true intentions. Some will blatantly admit that they'll do it again but honestly believe they haven't committed a crime. They think we can't do anything to stop them after their sentence expires. But we can.'

The *Crimes (Serious Sex Offenders) Act* was passed in 2006 because of the high rate of re-offenders among this sickening class of criminal. The Act's main provision is to keep a sex offender in jail indefinitely.

'And it often needs to be used,' said the former parole officer. 'There's no point rehabilitating some of these men. Most of them think they've done nothing unlawful and claim that their relationships with children are a beautiful thing.'

The family man, a guard at Long Bay who was enjoying his day off work, opened his letterbox. He jumped back as the angry posse of catalogues leapt at him like a junk mail Jack in the Box. Bending over to pick up the rubbish, he found an envelope between the unwanted advertising: white, inkless and without a stamp. He was immediately suspicious. He ripped apart the seal and was soon holding a fistful of polaroids.

They were pictures of his kids.

'Paedophiles are vicious things,' said one of the guard's colleagues. 'Everyone thinks they're gutless old men who only harm children. But they're as cunning and as dangerous as they are sick.

'A guard in our unit was sent pictures of his kids one day as a threat after he uncovered and busted a Long Bay paedophile ring. We screened the inmates' mail, and found all this gibberish was going in and out. We thought it was nothing at first, but this guard studied the letters for weeks, thinking there was something to it. And he was right. The gibberish was a code and the paedophiles inside were sending other paedophiles outside information on children. They were telling them where they could get them and who could be got. The guard passed on the information to the police and the ring was shut down. But the paedophile inmates eventually found out that it was this guard who fucked them over and the paedophiles on the outside began stalking his kids.'

Of course the guard wanted to retaliate. And so did each and every one of his colleagues.

'But we had a duty of care, we couldn't even leave the floor open for a second to let the other animals at them, let alone touch them ourselves,' said the guard, outlining the frustrations of the prison inmates and staff.

'A split hair would result in an inquiry. And the first person there would be the ombudsman and he just wanted a scalp. He's normally not on the uniform's side and would go after our jobs.

'As guards, it was our responsibility to protect the scum and give them top-class protection. It was the worst job in the jail, seeing to these paedophiles. Most of the officers who work in this unit have young kids, and as dads we couldn't help but think about what these filthy bastards would do to our children if they were given half a chance. Of course we wanted to bash them, but we couldn't. You could back in the 60s, but certainly not after the Royal Commission, where routine bashings of prisoners by the guards were exposed.'

Guards fear Big Brother is watching their every move.

'There are cameras everywhere,' said a current Long Bay PO. 'There's no way in the world you could do a thing to one of these pricks. You'd be sacked for pushing them over, even if they provoked you by spitting on you or telling you they were going to fuck your kid.'

Despite the rampant security, these convicted 'kiddy-fiddlers' will always find filth.

'We're always searching their cells and confiscating things like Target and Kmart catalogues, which they sell and pass around because of the kids in their underwear,' said one guard. 'We've got to a stage where we'll go through the news-papers and pull out anything that's got a picture of a kid in it.

'I despise these pricks, and I'm really blunt with them. I don't even see them as people, let alone crooks. They are a different breed. And they're always putridly nice, responding with things like "Yes, mister", "No, mister", and it's sicken-ing because you know the levels of evil they've stooped to in their lives.'

Paedophiles have enjoyed protection without scrutiny since the Nagle Royal Commission. But the conviction of Brett Peter Cowan in 2014 for the murder of 13-year-old Daniel Morcombe may prompt a review of the special and expensive care given to these horrid criminals, following a social media tsunami demanding this killer receive the most brutal of penal punishments.

And it seems that the negative sentiment about paedophiles in Long Bay is shared among prisoners, too, although the degree of concern has shifted over the years. Would they attempt to kill Cowan if they were given access to him?

'He would've been in serious danger,' explained a former inmate who was in for murder. 'If a paedophile walked into the wrong place years ago, they'd be fucking stomped on. But now the criminals don't seem to care so much. A lot of the old-school crims are out now, and there's no real criminal code in jail anymore. Most of the blokes there are just drug-fucked junkies who would sell their mothers for a hit. It's not like the guards will let them near anyone anyway. There'll be seven of them escorting the scumbag to see a nurse. But the funny thing is, I don't think they even need the protection because most of the new-age inmates don't care. They'll only kill someone if there's something in it for them.'

And Justice for All
'If they got hold of them, they'd kill them.'
Long Bay inmate

The notorious paedophile walked in. He was a man who needed no introduction; his heinous crimes had been splashed in print and had headlined the 6pm news. He winked at the guard who awaited his arrival.

Knowing full well of the crimes this new inmate, Dennis Ferguson, had committed, the guard fumed. 'You are a fucking scumbag,' he shouted straight into the criminal's face. 'And you will be treated as one.'

Ferguson smiled. 'Do you know what it's like?' he said. 'What it's like to have sex with a six-year-old? It's just love. Do you understand love? This is what I love and they love it too.'

This was the invitation the guard was waiting for.

Whack!

'I smashed him,' said the guard, now retired. 'The heap of shit fell to the floor telling me that I didn't understand "this beautiful love". Ferguson was a fucking monster and I do not regret doing what I did. Not one bit. But I was lucky to get away with it because it happened a long time ago. There's no way a guard today could do it.'

Or could they?

The guard stormed down the landing and snarled at the gang rapist through the locked cell.

'Clean that fucking shit off now,' he screamed.

Bilal Skaf puffed out his chest, grinning. 'Fuck off,' he said. 'Or I'll rape your wife too.'

The guard pulled the key from his belt, opened the door and calmly walked towards the inmate. He looked at the wall he had been called to inspect before locking eyes with the skinny smartarse.

'I rape prison officers' wives,' read Skaf's graffiti, which was scrawled in black texta across the wall.

'Piece of shit,' the guard said, standing over the smiling criminal's face.

'What are you going to do?' Skaf shouted back. 'Nothing. That's what!'

The guard smiled. Then –

Whack!

First came the heavy right.

Crack!

And then the left.

Splat!

The guard picked up the 22-year-old and threw him into the concrete wall.

'Then I grabbed his head,' recounted the guard. 'And I used his face to clean off the texta.'

Bilal Skaf did not enjoy his Long Bay stay. First he was bashed.

'I gave him a real good touch up when he came in,' said the guard. 'Skaf was nothing and he had only just arrived. Someone asked me to give him a hand with this rapist bloke who was playing up. I went in there and saw this really little bloke with a big mouth. It was Skaf, and he was standing there, all pumped up, looking at me, with the graffiti on the wall behind him. I towelled him up and wiped the wall down with his face. He had no remorse whatsoever for the crime he'd committed. He never said sorry for anything he did in jail either. He was quite happy to cop a hiding, and that's exactly what he got.'

Next, Skaf learned his Lebanese brothers would not protect him. He was now alone.

'He thought he was going to be some sort of Lebanese

hero,' said another guard. 'That he'd become part of their gang and be sweet. But Michael Kanaan [a Lebanese Australian triple murderer currently serving three sentences of life imprisonment, plus 50 years and 4 months with no possibility of parole] had put the word out for him to be bashed. The Lebanese hated Skaf as much as anyone because he'd tarnished their whole race and made innocent Lebanese people targets because of his disgusting crimes.'

Skaf was jailed for 55 years after being convicted on 21 counts of aggravated rape, assault and kidnapping. In 2000, he'd led 14 Lebanese Australian Muslims on a series of gang rape attacks on Australian women. One of their victims was raped 25 times at Bankstown, in an attack that lasted six hours. It's alleged she was called an 'Aussie pig' and told she'd be raped 'Lebanese style'.

'What this trial showed was that he was the leader of the pack, a liar, a bully, a coward, callous and mean,' said Judge Michael Finnane in his sentencing remarks of Bilal Skaf. 'The worst of all offenders who conducted himself as if the proceeding were a joke.'

Skaf began his sentence, which was later reduced to a maximum of 28 years on appeal, in Long Bay. He was placed in protection in 2 Wing after receiving death threats from fellow inmates.

'He would be in his cell, crying every night,' said an inmate. 'My mate did the plumbing in that wing, because the shitters were blocked up all the time. He'd go in there and unblock them, and I would carry his tools for him. I would walk past Skaf's cell and he'd be crying. He thought he was a tough cunt when he went in – he believed all the Lebos were under the impression he was a legend because of what he'd done to the Aussie girls, but they hated the cunt. They wanted to kill him as much as anyone else, maybe more. He drove me mad with his crying, and I'd scream at him, calling him a little girl. He was just a little punk. A nothing.'

Skaf's only ally in Long Bay was his brother Mahmoud, a member of his rapist gang.

'I probably had more dealings with Mahmoud,' said a guard who currently works at Long Bay. 'He was a vicious little shit. I worked in the hospital before it became the Medical Training Centre. Any maximum-security prisoner who needed medical treatment was moved in there. That's where I had plenty of dealings with Mahmoud. He had a mouth like his brother, but he was nothing too. They both ended up in protection because everyone wanted them dead.'

Skaf did not back down despite the bashings and the death threats. He claimed that he started a gang while in jail called W2K – Willing To Kill – and threatened to shoot court officers and prison guards. He drew pictures depicting rape and sent white powder that looked like anthrax to prison boss Ron Woodham.

But Skaf also sobbed in his cell and attempted to commit suicide. His Long Bay horror ended when he was transferred to Goulburn supermax after prison authorities said three prisoners were plotting to inject him with a needle containing HIV/AIDS drawn from an infected prisoner.

'That might have been bullshit,' said a guard, disputing

the claim. 'I think the politicians just made it up because they wanted an excuse to send him to Supermax. I worked in his wing and didn't hear of any such plot, neither did the other guards. Regardless, he was a piece of shit and we were happy to see him leave.'

Another guard revealed a few protections have had near misses while being locked away in Long Bay Jail.

'There have been some very close calls,' he said. 'I've seen several that have been stopped at the last moment. I jumped on a bloke just after he slashed a Dog's eye. He would've been killed if we hadn't got to him in time.'

The same guard witnessed three men murder an alleged Dog while working at Silverwater Jail.

'I was in the MRRC (Metropolitan Remand and Reception Centre) when they killed Johnny Tram. He was a Dog and they killed him over the John Newman assassination. They stabbed him 27 times, with industrial scissors, in front of everybody. He was in there, doing his work, and these three Asian guys just walked up to him and started stabbing. The officer grabbed him, but the attackers didn't stop. It was brutal. He died on the spot. As soon as I heard about it, I rushed in to help. I saw the last one go through and watched Tram die. I believe he had some information on the Newman murder and that's what got him killed. They'd put a hit out on him and got him. He was sewing linen sheets at the time. It was the worst thing I have ever seen in all my years working in jails.'

Former prisoner Abo Henry said a paedophile was brutally bashed while in Long Bay.

'There was a bloke who did 16 years for raping and killing a kid,' Henry said. 'He had a couple of weeks to go. He said he wanted to get out from the main jail and finish his time in protection. He was warned against it, but he thought he'd be sweet after 16 years. He thought that no one would know him. Anyway, they found him in the weights room with his head caved in. A mate of Neddy Smith's was the main suspect, but he beat the charge.'

Four sex offenders and one Dog were murdered in Australian prisons between 1980 and 1998.

'The general prison population fucking hated the protections,' said an inmate. 'If they got hold of them, they'd kill them. Now and then there would be a little bit of a slip-up and they would grab one. Say, one of them had been on protection for a while and they thought the circumstances had sorted themselves out.'

In that period, Long Bay recorded the second-highest number of prison homicides in Australia with five men killed whilst in custody.

11

MURDERING

The Knock-Up

'He indicated to me that if he were placed two-out or were made to mix with other inmates in the yard, it would be highly likely that he'd hurt someone.'
NSW Corrective Services forensic psychologist

Craig Behr looked into the cells as he walked down the wing. He passed by a tattooed giant, an old man with a beard, and then a skinny kid, who looked like he should still be in school. Behr, 24, who was in Long Bay for aggravated break and enter, and sexual assault, hoped the guard behind him would yell out 'stop' right at that moment. The skinny one seemed like a good cellmate, better than the old man and less intimidating than the giant.

Behr knew he was about to go 'two-out' because he was never allowed to be left alone. He was being moved because his old cellmate – the one he liked – had gone out on a visit. Behr had not cut, bruised or tried to kill himself since being transferred from Goulburn to the Long Bay Hospital 33 days ago. Maybe it was because his cellmate had stopped him. Maybe it was because the counselling and treatment he'd been receiving discouraged him from any acts of self-harm. Either way, Behr was being relocated, and he didn't like it.

'Hurry up,' said the guard as Behr slowed down, hovering in front of Skinny's cell.

But Behr was out of luck. The guard continued to walk before stopping in front of cell No. 20. He looked at the card in his hand, nodded and then stuck a thick key into the door.

The metal swung inwards, and Behr studied his new cellmate. He was relieved.

The man did not have tattoos, he wasn't old, and best of all, he was no giant. Behr was not scared, but he should have been.

The 23-year-old did not know his new cellmate had to be 'locked in' at all times. He did not know that when the harmless-looking guy wanted a shower, he had to be escorted by three guards. And he did not know that this man standing just a metre away from him had told a prison psychologist that he intended to hurt his cellmate if he was put two-out. And apparently the guard now walking away knew none of this either. If he had, Behr might not have been kicked to death.

*

Michael Alan Heatley had made his point clear. Three days before the guard opened his cell door and sent the new inmate into his room, he had sat down with a Department of Corrective Services psychologist, and said that he would kill should they make him share a cell.

'Mr Heatley's risk of harm to others is currently assessed as high,' the psychologist wrote in a report. 'He indicated to me that if he were placed two-out or were made to mix with other inmates in the yard, that it was highly likely he'd hurt someone and stated that he had been experiencing homicidal urges for the past 18 months.'

So why was he now two-out? Why was this scrawny prisoner standing in *his* room?

This must have been a dare. He'd already told the prison authorities what he would do.

'I didn't want to kill the man,' Heatley later said. 'I didn't even know him. I'm not schizo, but I do have a mental problem. I'm homicidal; I've told them that for days. Then they tell me this morning that they're putting this guy in with me, even though I begged them not to. I told them I'd kill him, but they just said, "You're full of shit."'

Heatley suffered from chronic psychosis. He was twice acquitted of armed robbery on the grounds of mental illness. He claimed that he smoked, sniffed and drank his dead father's ashes, and believed he was the racehorse Phar Lap.

He was not Phar Lap, of course, and his father wasn't dead. No . . . he was also in jail; like father like son. Tony 'Grub' Healey, was a notorious bank robber and had been a fellow Long Bay inmate. Known as the 'Tellers' Terror', he had committed 25 armed robberies. He was also a two-time escapee.

'Give me 20 years,' Grub had screamed at the judge after being recaptured at his second escape attempt. 'I don't give a fuck, I don't care. I'll find a way out.'

Grub Heatley might as well have been dead, as far as his son was concerned. Michael hardly knew his dad, the old man having been incarcerated for 23 years of his life. It's fair to say that Grub wasn't much of a role model, nor was Michael's uncle, who was also in jail for murder. Michael was already a convicted armed robber like his dad, but not a killer like his uncle.

Not just yet . . .

'HELP!' came the desperate plea.

The inmate in No. 21, right next to the cell where the scream had come from, sprang from his bed and ran to the door. He looked out the small window and into the corridor. He couldn't see anything, but he could hear banging followed by what sounded like a body hitting the ground.

At 12.15pm, Long Bay Jail inmate Johannes Schmidt hit the button on the Emergency Cell Call System. He wanted to help the man who seemed to be in obvious pain, but he was locked in his cell. Thankfully, the guards were coming. Well, they should have been coming.

Maybe they didn't hear it?

Schmidt tried hitting the button again. It was 12.21pm.

Was it broken?

More noise came from the cell about five minutes later. Schmidt heard shuffling, a noise that sounded like a body being dragged across the floor. Finally, at 12.35pm, a guard walked past his window and towards the cell next door. It was completely silent.

The guard opened the door and was welcomed by the sight of Heatley standing tall. Then he saw the body on the floor.

'I think he's had a heart attack,' said the inmate. 'He isn't moving.'

Behr was lying in a pool of vomit. Heatley was right about one thing: he wasn't moving. But it wasn't because of a heart attack.

Behr had been kicked to death.

Deputy governor Nigel Lloyd was informed of the death at 1pm, when he was told a prisoner had suffered a heart attack in 13 Wing. He went to the cell and stood silent as he looked at the body. He did not know the man who was lying dead on the floor.

'I don't think it was a heart attack,' said the guard, standing by his side. 'I think he's been murdered.'

The guard was right.

The postmortem report stated Behr's cause of death was 'consistent with head injury and that he died at approximately 12.15 hours on 27 March 2004.' The forensic pathologist who conducted the autopsy concluded he had suffered head injuries that led to impaired consciousness, vomiting, inhalation of debris, brain hypoxia and then death. In other words, Heatley kicked the crap out of him and Behr choked on his own vomit.

So the prisoner was murdered. Killed by an inmate who was supposed to be kept in isolation. Found 23 minutes after guards failed to respond to the first emergency call.

Needless to say, some serious questions were about to be asked.

Michael Heatley was soon in police custody. He told them that he was the one who'd activated the emergency alarm so that he 'could get out of the cell'. And that he'd repeatedly warned prison staff that he should not be placed in a cell with anyone else. Heatley pleaded guilty to the lesser charge of manslaughter after he was charged with murder.

Seven months later, Heatley sat in a court dock, watching on as Behr's mother, Janet, broke down.

'To have to hear the offender coldly and callously state he would take my son's life and that he meant to do it,' she said. 'It was a devastating experience.'

Heatley jumped from his chair. 'Your son was trying to sex me up, lady,' he screamed. 'You try to make me out as a cold-blooded killer when your son was trying to sex me up. I am not going to sit here and listen to this anymore.'

He was sentenced to eight years for manslaughter. Again Heatley was locked away – this time, and for the rest of his time – by himself.

The murderer had been arrested, charged, sentenced and jailed. But this was still a 'shit-fight'.

'They put Behr in a cell that he should never have been in,' said a guard who worked in the hospital at the time of the attack. 'Heatley stomped his head in and it was a bloody mess. It became a big shit-fight because they tried to sink a lot of officers over it. The boss had a psych report saying Heatley should never have had anyone in his cell, but it was never passed on to the officers. They should have been warned, but they weren't.'

That was one of the reasons the Coroners Court of New South Wales launched an inquiry into the 'Death in Custody'. The other reason was because it took the guard on duty 23 minutes to respond to the call.

'It happened when it was our lunchtime,' said the guard. 'And during that time you just lock the prisoners up and leave a couple of guys to guard the wing. One of the crims heard something and tried to use the 'knock-up', which is an emergency system that goes back to the gate. He tried to warn us what was going on, but we had this other crim who was continually using the knock-up. The guy trying to warn us couldn't get through because the other guy had blocked it again. We probably would've been able to get to Behr and save him had the call not been blocked. The officers never got the message that this guy was being beaten to death. Behr was in for raping a very old woman, about 80, so he probably got what he deserved. But that isn't the point because it never should have happened to begin with.'

The coroner was scathing in his report. In his official finding he said, 'There was a near total lack of appropriate action by various Correctional Officers after the prison psychologist submitted a report which labelled the prisoner "high risk" and directed he not be placed in a cell with another inmate.'

The coroner also slammed the guards' failure to answer the emergency intercom.

'I find that he should have answered the knock-up from cell 21 much earlier. It was ultimately answered when she opened the call at 12.39 pm. This delay bears some significance because that 23-minute delay after inmate Schmidt first made the call must be judged against the background of the evidence of Dr Botterill, who says that the death appears to have occurred in a progressive manner. Therefore it cannot be ruled out that had there been a more timely response, some resuscitation efforts could have been implemented, which could have been successful.'

Despite the controversy of official inaction, in the end this was just another murder in Long Bay Jail . . .

It's Raining Death

'This was payback. They mutilated him because he mutilated one of them.'
Current Long Bay PO

The man walked to the end of the wing, into the wide-open entrance and turned left. Steam smacked him in the face as he smelt the stink of the sweat-stained tiles.

'This is for our brother,' came the faint voice, drowned out by the rushing water.

Pop!

It felt like a balloon had burst under his ribs.

'Ow!' the man shouted in pain, his shoulder instinctively turning away.

Pop! Pop!

Two more explosions this time, both in the centre of his back. He now knew he was being stabbed.

'Arrrghhhh!' He launched his right fist towards the direction of the voice. The punch was powerful, but he bruised nothing but air.

'Fuck!' he screamed.

Not because he missed, but because he was now facing his attackers. All five of them.

He knew he was going to die.

Whack! Whack! Whack!

Three different shivs – a wooden stake, a sharpened toothbrush, a shard of glass wrapped in plastic – were jammed into his body.

Whack! Whack!

Two of them twice.

Crack! Bang!

Then one assailant used his foot, and the other his hand to brutally beat him up.

Lights out.

He couldn't have felt the next blow; he was already lying on the floor.

Crack!

A shiv smashed though his skull and stabbed his brain.

Long Bay veteran Raymond Carrion, a convicted armed robber and suspected murderer, was found dead in the 12 Wing shower: fully clothed but his body almost emptied of blood.

Long Bay's showers are a death trap – full of soapsuds, shivs and silent attacks. This is the best place to kill, or to be killed, in Long Bay. There are no guards, no warning, and no hope for those marked men who enter alone.

'The shower was the place to knock them off,' said Abo Henry. 'There were no doors to lock. You could just walk up behind anyone and give it to them. Each wing had a shower block up the very end. They would just follow you in and give it to you.

'Sometimes they just wanted to hurt you. They might have boiling water, and they would wait round the corner, make sure the screw wasn't there and just whack you. I've seen cunts hit that way. It's horrible. I'll never forget the smell of burning skin.'

So frequently were these unfortunate bodies found, bashed, bloodied, maimed and murdered, that the jail once lobbied for funding for individual showers to be placed in cells.

'We did our best at putting in plumbing and toilets in each cell,' said former governor Michael Vita. 'But the inmates never had their own showers, and that was always a very big problem. You had to go to the bottom landing and right past all the 18 cells to shower. There was a chamber and all prisoners in that wing would have to shower in the same place. We would try to stage the showering times so that they didn't go when they felt like it or all at once, but it wasn't as easy as it sounds. It wouldn't be unusual for you to be at the front of the wing in your office and hear commotion coming from the shower block. A lot of crims would be hanging around that back area where the showers were. There were eight open cubicles in each wing, so you could never really police it. It was what was known as the 'get square area'. A lot of the time the area would just be left open and the prisoners could shower as they pleased. I can't even begin to remember how many came out of the shower who were either shivved or hit with an iron bar. It was just bang, bang, bang – the victims wouldn't even see it coming, and with the shivs, they wouldn't even know what had happened until they saw the blood.

'It happened a lot during the time I worked there. I would say someone was stabbed or bashed in the showers at least a couple of times a month. I saw at least 20 of those instances, personally.'

Neither Vita, Henry, nor anyone else saw the attack that left Raymond Carrion dead. Well, that's what they all told the police anyway. Officially, nobody knew why Carrion had been killed, his lifeless body found on the shower block floor of the Metropolitan Medical Transient Centre at 2.10pm on 5 July 1998.

Unofficially, and truthfully, it was a racially motivated act of revenge.

Raymond Carrion was stabbed in the shower as payback for stabbing someone else in the shower. Carrion, 36, was originally due in court two days after his death, for the murder of Maurice Joseph Marsland, an Aboriginal man dubbed the 'Eastern Suburbs rapist'. Carrion was one of three people charged after the convicted rapist was brutally beaten and stabbed on 13 February 1996 in Goulburn Jail.

'I can remember speaking to the Goulburn superintendent straight after that murder,' said Vita. 'And it wasn't just another death in the "Killing Fields", as the jail was known at the time because of the murders that took place there every week. No, this one was something else. The super had thought he'd seen it all, but he hadn't. Despite all the bodies, he said it was the most sickening thing he'd ever seen during all his years working in a jail.

'Alan Chisholm was the man who responded to this incident and the body was just cut to ribbons. Marsland was a predator of the jail system and a thug. He raped people to get into jail and he also raped people in jail. He was a big, vile and violent man. Nobody liked him, especially the guards. Chisholm was a tough nut and didn't like this creature one bit, but he said to me after finding Marsland's body that nobody – even a rapist – deserved to be killed like that.'

And, it seemed, a group of inmates at Long Bay agreed.

Raymond Carrion was shifted to Long Bay ahead of his trial and placed into protection. It was unlikely he would be killed for murdering a rapist. But the government wasn't about to take a chance with their first Killing Fields killer.

Along with accused co-killers Jason Richards and Mark

Morris, Carrion was due in court for the murder of Marsland on 7 July 1998.

'I don't need protection,' Carrion protested as he was being locked up with men more repulsive than the one he'd just stabbed to death. 'I don't want to be with these fucking disgusting creatures and Dogs.'

Carrion had been in and out of Long Bay for much of his life. He and his brother, Roy, befriended future professional rugby league player John Elias during a stint in 1980.

'I had an unbreakable bond with a group of blokes, including Ray and his brother Roy,' Elias said. 'They were big time when I went in and I was a nobody. They were from Punchbowl like me, and I used to see them walking around with their old man when I was a kid. They came into Long Bay after me and I asked them if their dad used to go to the local TAB, and we became friends. They were a bit older than me, about 19 and 20, but they were tough bastards in for a big armed robbery at Maroubra. They had respect in jail, even though they were young, and they were great touch players too. Ray and Roy both made my time in Long Bay more bearable.'

Given Carrion's long-standing reputation in Long Bay, surely he didn't need to be in protection?

'Ray was in segregation,' explained a current guard who asked not to be named. 'Even though he was in protection, they wouldn't call it that because of his name. He was in 12 Wing, at the back in segregation. He was an old school crim and he didn't want to be known as a Dog. Anyway, the sweeper convinced the executive that Ray was okay. He said he wouldn't have issues with anyone in his wing and that Ray didn't need protection. The sweeper said he could guarantee his safety.'

But the sweeper did not know that a hit had been put out on the man he'd just vouched for. Carrion had killed a rapist: a despicable predator and thug. But in doing so, he'd also murdered an Indigenous prisoner during an unprecedented time of death that saw people band together for protection, giving rise to the deadly race gang.

'The Aboriginal guys had heard a bunch of white guys had killed one of their own,' the guard continued. 'They didn't care what the dead bloke had done – they just saw it as a hit on their own. The Aboriginal guys had vowed to kill all the blokes who had murdered him.'

Carrion walked through the wing, proud he'd told security to shove their protection. Most celebrated his return, slapping skin and patting his back. But some – five to be exact – waited by the shower, ready to cut him up.

'He went into the shower block and he was stabbed viciously. It was very bad. I know the officer who was the first to respond and he said it was horrible. Carrion was beaten, cut and stabbed. They didn't just kill him – they sent a message. He could've been done with one to the heart, but they mutilated him in the same way he mutilated one of theirs.'

The Aboriginal group also tried to get one of the others accused of Marsland's murder.

'Alan Richards got stabbed 27 times at about the same time,' said the guard. 'But he lived. If any of them should've died, it should've been him. He was a sick fuck and a double murderer. Ray was just an armed robber who got someone who deserved everything he got.'

Stabbed in the Eye and Nobody Knows Why

'Something very evil is taking place.'
Long Bay inmate solicitor Doug Humphreys

Henry John Blunden put down the brass lock he had just finished polishing.

'That's me, boss, I'm done,' he said to the prison guard. It was 9am. 'I'm going back to my cell.'

Blunden walked out of the workshop and back to 12 Wing.

Two hours later he was found dead, alone in his cell.

At first the guard thought he was having a nap.

'He looked like he was sleeping,' said a guard who was working in the remand centre at the time. 'The door was open, and he was just lying on his bed. There was no blood.'

The prison guard told Blunden to wake up, but the inmate did not move. He yelled a little louder, yet the prisoner did not budge. Then he rolled him over.

'That's when he saw the empty eye socket,' the guard continued.

'Blunden had been stabbed in the eye and it had been plucked out. But this wasn't what had killed him.'

No one saw or heard a thing.

'They'd shocked his heart and killed him that way,' said the guard. 'It was strange because there was little blood and no signs of struggle.'

The crime remains a mystery.

'It's an unsolved jail murder. People have their suspicions but no one was ever charged.'

Jailhouse detectives claim Blunden was killed for either being a Dog, or because he was innocent of the crime he had been charged with, but not convicted of.

Blunden's alleged crime was horrible. He was due to appear in court a week after his mysterious death for the murder of an elderly Eastwood couple and their adult son. It was believed that he'd killed the son, a contract plumber, three months before shooting Oliver Dresler, 61, and his wife Thelma, 63, in the chest and dumping their bodies in a metal trunk at a tip near Wellington in central western New South Wales in 1993. The decomposed body of their son, John, was also found in a green trunk on a property owned by his brother.

Despite being seen moving furniture at the Dreslers' house following the murder, and allegedly telling a neighbour they'd moved out, Blunden pleaded not guilty and always maintained his innocence. Another man was charged with the murder – 35-year-old builder George Mrish.

Blunden was being held in the remand centre at Long Bay while he awaited his trial. He'd been an 'anonymous' and 'quiet' guest for nine months before he was found dead.

'He was well-behaved and went about his own business,'

commented a guard. 'You wouldn't even have heard of him if he didn't turn up dead.'

Some say he became an informer and had given police information about other crimes in exchange for favourable treatment in the matter set for trial; but he did not go into protection, which would have kept him alive if he had, in fact, been a Dog.

'During this period he was never in protection,' said a prison spokesperson shortly after Blunden was found murdered in his jail cell. 'He'd never requested it and was never thought to be at risk at all.'

Meanwhile, Blunden's lawyer, Doug Humphreys, hinted at a far more sinister reason for his death.

'We now have four murders in relation to this,' Humphreys said. 'Something very evil is taking place.'

The lawyer said his client had told him he'd been scared for his life a week before his murder. He claimed authorities were well aware of those fears despite the public denial.

'Nobody really knows why he was murdered and we knew nothing of his fears,' said a guard. 'Maybe he was a Dog and we didn't know about it, or maybe he was suspected of being one. But maybe he was just killed so nobody else went down for the murder. Either way, he's dead – another killed in the jail.'

Another guard was almost certain Blunden was taken down for being a Dog.

'I believe the person who got him had been paid by somebody else,' the guard explained. 'It was a professional hit on behalf of another criminal. Whoever killed him probably didn't know him and just did it for the money.'

Squashing a Spider

'The one that me and Freddy got accused of . . . that rock spider. Yes, we fucking knocked that.'
Long Bay inmate Troy Layton, testifying against James Murray in Sydney's Central Court

They waited and watched, desperate to get at this vile creature. Men like this one were to be killed on sight . . . especially this one.

'You'll most likely get killed if you're a rapist,' said former guard Grant Turner. 'And you'll definitely get killed if you're a police informer. And they will not only kill you, but hunt you and torture you if you've raped or murdered a child.'

Noel Edward Holden had done both. He was a despicable creature who'd kidnapped his neighbour's daughter, raped her, killed her and then buried her in a shallow grave near Guildford in Sydney's West.

'It hurts when I think about it and I sort of get a mental block,' he told police after being arrested for the terrible crime. 'She was asleep and I put her to bed where you found her.'

During his trial, Holden claimed he had not seen Svetlana Maria Zetovic on 7 November 1973, the day she went missing from her family home.

But on 9 November, when the six-year-old was found

dead and covered in grass clippings in his yard, the 45-year-old told police that he'd stabbed her after she'd nursed his cat and said she wanted to go home. Svetlana had been struck through the heart, strangled and sexually assaulted.

Former Senior Constable Wayne Brooks detailed the grisly discovery to reporter Lindsay Simpson in 1986.

'We walked around the whole area,' he said. 'Going from house to house. We went through swamp and down the maze of underground drains. I was walking down the side fence (of Holden's yard), and the bloke in the middle kicked a pile of grass cuttings with his foot. That's when he found her. She was just like a china doll. I remember her face. She had a sort of ivory colour skin and she was looking up at us.'

Holden told the police he did not want to hurt Svetlana after she came to ask him if she could see a horse being fed.

'I only wanted to look at her, but she cried,' Holden said. 'I cannot remember what I did.'

There were fears for Holden's safety even before he was brought to trial. More than a hundred people greeted him with threats and hysterics as he fronted the Fairfield Court of Petty Sessions a week after Svetlana's body was found.

'A number of people have very emotional feelings about this matter,' said the police prosecutor when objecting to bail. 'Holden might come to harm if he were to be released.'

The labourer, who lived next door to the victim in Linthorne Street, Guildford, would indeed come to harm.

He was given a death sentence when he was sent to Long Bay Jail.

*

Noel Holden was found dead in his cell on 17 August 1986, 12 years after he'd sexually assaulted and murdered the six-year-old girl. Just like little Svetlana, he was strangled and stabbed, but he was also kicked and punched. The walls of his cell were splattered with blood, the floor littered with shards of his shattered skull and pieces of his brain.

Most in the prison felt that this 'rock spider', as he was described by PO Alan Braithwaite in Sydney's Central Criminal Court, got what he deserved.

'That was common knowledge in the jail,' said Braithwaite.

Other guards who knew Holden did not disagree.

'He was a foul creature,' said a guard. 'A child rapist and killer. He was a classic example of a rock spider, and there weren't too many tears shed when he died.'

According to the chairman of the NSW Prison Officers' Association, Pat Armstrong, Holden had been in protection for 'two or three years' at the time of his death. Holden had survived but asked to be taken out of protection to secure better visits and more yard time.

'Over the years he took himself off,' Armstrong said. 'He hoped that he'd blend in with the rest of the population. The trouble was, someone recognised him.'

But Holden was always going to be identified. Protections walk around in a yard separated from the jail's general population only by a cyclone fence. They are watched, noted and sometimes marked for death.

'We wanted to kill all of them,' said Abo Henry. 'But they were hard to get. The screws would follow them wherever they went. You could see them through the fence. Down at remand, you could look them straight in the eye at the bottom of 13 Wing. People from gen pop would give them a spray and tell them they were dead. We were in one yard and they were in another, and some blokes would just stand there threatening them the whole time. They'll go up to the Metropolitan Remand Prison (MRP) to see the doctors. I remember one cunt spat at me. I promised to kill him, and I will, if I ever see him again.'

Holden was a man well and truly marked for death. His murder was described as particularly brutal.

'The crims jumped on his head from the top of the bunk,' said former guard David Farrell. 'They absolutely belted the shit out of him. Police managed to get the people who did it because of the tread marks on the bloke's face and head.

'Holden was a child molester and people were always after him. He was a very small guy and a vile piece of gear. Everybody knew who he was and what he had done.'

Leaving protection was not a wise move for Holden. But even being locked up with offenders guilty of crimes like his would not have guaranteed his life.

'We can't protect these guys 24/7,' said Farrell. 'We knew he was a target, but the blokes who got him had all the time in the world to watch, wait and come up with a plan or a time that they could get him alone.

'All the men in protection have done terrible things that make them a target, but that doesn't mean they won't target each other. These men are far from model citizens and are not always well-behaved. They'll come up with their own little hierarchy, and end up standing over the weak. People think the old poofters and paedophiles are harmless, but some of these old men are the grumpiest and most violent things in prison. I've seen them arm up with walking sticks and frames. Just because they're old sex predators or informers does not mean they're not dangerous. It certainly does not mean they won't go after a fellow inmate who needs protection just like them.'

Prisoner Troy Layton fronted the Sydney Central Criminal Court and testified that James Francis Murray and Frederick Owens told him that they'd 'knocked' a rock spider while they were smoking Indian hemp in a cell. Murray and Owens were the two men charged with Holden's murder after several inmates gave evidence that implicated the two in the jailhouse killing. Layton said he smoked four cones with the pair after Murray told him: 'The one that me and Freddy got accused of . . . that rock spider – yes, we fucking knocked that.'

12

CUTTING

Scary Eyes

'I couldn't be with her for another moment . . . I just knew I would be hurt.'
Female employee from the Department of Corrections

The prison officer wiped the sweat from her brow, straightened her shoulders and clenched her jaw. Body now firmly jammed into the seat, her brain ordered her mouth to stop being a scared little girl and speak.

Stuff this. Who is she? And what the hell is she going to do? Have a look at her. How can you be scared? she thought to herself.

She slowly lifted her gaze: past the papers, through the pens and towards the woman who sat on the other side of her government-issued MDF desk. As the prison officer's gaze rose, the white desk gave way to the inmate's green jumper, then she caught sight of her stomach, her breasts, followed by her chin.

But she couldn't see her hands, which were cuffed and strapped to the bottom of the desk.

The woman jerked back in her chair and stamped her feet into the ground, the chains strapped around her ankles singing as they rattled against the floor.

The officer snapped her chin from her chest, deciding it was now or never, and looked the prisoner in the face.

'I looked into eyes, expecting to see the end of the world,' she recalled of the experience. 'But they were just eyes. Normal. Actually they were quite bright and alert. They were almost kind.'

The official exhaled, the rushing air relaxing those tight shoulders and cooling her face.

But maybe you should be scared? the voice in her head asked. *Why else would she be sitting in front of you like this?*

The veteran employee looked away from her eyes and to the hefty leather straps holding down the prisoner's hands.

They're there for a reason, the voice continued.

She glanced at the two prison guards. Both were giants, strong and fit. The first was standing behind the prisoner's left shoulder, eyes firmly planted on the back of her head, arms tightly folded and a heavy frown on his face. The other guard, slightly smaller but equally imposing, stood no more than a foot from her right shoulder. His knuckles went from red to white as he pumped his fist into a ball.

'I've been in that room with serial killers, murderers and rapists,' said the Corrections employee. 'And I've been with all of them alone. Up until that point, I'd never sat with someone who was cuffed. And I'd never had to have guards in the room to make sure I was safe. So it was strangely scary.

'I mean, I've talked to triple murderers and felt safe. But here was a woman, cuffed and guarded, and I was more scared of her than the serial killer.'

Though the restraints and security provided some sort of barrier between her and the female prisoner, the official still felt afraid. She thought of Hannibal Lecter and his leather mask as she finally shot off a sound.

'Hi,' she rattled. 'Nice to meet you. I hope all is well.' She glanced at the guards, then at the cuffs.

Of course she isn't bloody well, the voice in her head said.

The official felt as though she was in a scene from *Silence of the Lambs*. 'I was shitting myself,' she would later say of that moment.

And then Sydney's very own Hannibal spoke.

'I'm great,' she said brightly, her voice genuine and kind. 'I've been moving through my program, and I'm really excited about the prospect of learning how to become the good person I know I can be.'

The officer smiled.

See? the voice said again. *Told ya not to be scared.*

The officer slumped her shoulders, unclenched her jaw and went to work. As she conversed with the female prisoner, she was impressed to find that she was the opposite of what she'd expected her to be – the inmate was nice, smart, attentive and chatty.

Crack!

The officer was smiling and nodding when the prisoner stopped mid-sentence. Her head snapped to the left and then to the right, quick as a flash. She proceeded to speak, rescuing the sentence and pretending the thunder hadn't cracked. But her eyes were now full of dark clouds.

'Sorry,' the officer said shakily, jumping from her chair. 'I need to go to the toilet. This is over.'

She wanted to run from the room. Only the cuffs and the guards stopped her from sprinting. But whatever the case, she just couldn't look back.

'She kept on talking but there was this evil in her eyes,' said the officer. 'It sounds stupid, I know. They kind of just glazed over, widened and froze. They were the scariest eyes I'd ever seen. I couldn't be in the room with her for another moment. I just knew I would be hurt.'

The most feared prisoner in Long Bay Jail is not Neddy Smith. Nor is it a Rebel, a Bandido, or a Brother for Life gang member. The one who needs chains, leather straps, and a military-style guard is not a kickboxing king or a Kings Cross thug. No, the most dangerous inmate in Australia is Rebecca Butterfield: a softly spoken woman whose last victim was stabbed 60 times.

*

PO Grant Turner walked into the Long Bay Hospital.

'You're on A Watch,' he was told. 'You'll be monitoring Butterfield. Be very careful.'

Big deal, Turner thought to himself. He'd never heard of Rebecca Butterfield before and was more concerned by the boredom of sitting outside a room for eight hours, watching a restrained woman.

'What's to be careful about?' Turner asked.

The fellow guard pulled out a report; Turner scanned the list.

2003 – Ms Butterfield requires stitches after cutting her own throat

2004 – Ms Butterfield requires more stitches, again cutting her throat

2005 – Ms Butterfield tries to hang herself, then cuts her throat

2006 – Ms Butterfield cuts her throat and almost bleeds out

2008 – Ms Butterfield is severely burnt after setting fire to her cell

2008 – Ms Butterfield severely bangs her head and inserts items under her scalp

2009 – Ms Butterfield headbutts a wall 105 times and splits her skull open

'Oh,' Turner said. 'I see.' He grabbed a chair and sat down in front of the cell. He was advised that there was to be no contact with her.

Butterfield was contained in an observation cell of her own within the concrete grounds of the hospital – they would never put her in with anyone else. There were five cells in total, and all had perspex windows. On her door was a hatch that allowed for food to be passed inside.

Turner looked curiously at the woman lying down in the see-through cell. Twenty-seven years of age at the time, she was unremarkable – except for the scars.

'Fuck you,' she screamed. 'What are you looking at?'

Butterfield ignored Turner for an hour or so. And then she asked for a pencil.

'She told me she wanted to draw,' Turner said, recalling his encounter. 'And she made a good argument for getting it. But we were on strict instructions not to give her a thing.

'Butterfield was as manipulative as she was dangerous. She would make up lucid stories about why she needed something like a pencil, saying she'd been having nightmares and part of her therapy was to draw what she'd seen.'

Turner refused her request. But at other times POs were not so resolute. Butterfield would use whatever she could get her hands on in order to inflict self-violence.

'I was told that she always cut herself,' Turner said. 'She would attack anyone who tried to treat her.

'On that day, I was to sit in the corner and just make sure she didn't cut herself. I also had to ensure there wasn't anything in her cell she could cut herself with. She had constant wounds, which were open all the time. If she got hold of a pencil, a paperclip, or a toothpick, she would use it to open up an old wound. She would stick whatever she could find under her skin, hoping it would get infected.'

Turner would later see Butterfield cut herself to ribbons with a broken light, confiscate a sharpened toothbrush she'd intended to stab into a nurse's stomach and witness her kick a pregnant healthcare worker in the stomach before almost strangling a doctor to death.

Rebecca Butterfield seemed like a normal young woman. On the surface she was a happy teenager, polite and intelligent. She had been brought up in a good home. But her smile hid a dark secret, one that would eventually make her angry enough to kill.

She kept that secret for most of her life but that rage, which was just a whisper in her head at first, soon became a roar. Butterfield finally went to police and revealed her shocking history of sexual abuse. A man she alleged had been abusing her was charged and taken to court. Had things gone differently, Butterfield might never have ended up in jail, but her accused perpetrator was found not guilty and the charges were dismissed on 3 April 1996.

The humiliation of first disclosing the confronting details of the alleged crimes, and then watching the man she claimed had committed them walk away, enraged the teenager. For years she'd lived with the traumatic secret on her own, and when she finally had the courage to expose her demons, she was called a liar.

Butterfield's official criminal history began 25 days later, when she was charged with malicious damage. The failure of the police and the court to convict her abuser left her with a hatred of authority and a growing anger. Butterfield began with small crimes, hurling bottles at police cars and screaming abuse. She also assaulted police and resisted arrest.

Her acts of violence escalated when she assaulted a taxi driver who'd taken her to the police station at her request. She was seemingly making a statement against the law. Soon she would go too far. Not long after her first assault, she committed her second. Her rage had now turned bloody.

Butterfield was charged with maliciously wounding a person with intent to inflict grievous bodily harm in 2000. She'd stabbed a neighbour who accused her of fabricating her allegations of sexual assault. Butterfield was sentenced to six years with a non-parole period of three.

But Butterfield's history of violence had only just begun . . .

Now incarcerated in Emu Plains prison, Butterfield picked up the scissors. She held them tightly in her hand and calmly walked towards the other inmate.

Whack! Whack! Whack!

The sharp steel went in and out, bursting skin and organs, spraying the walls, the floor, and her face with blood.

But Butterfield couldn't stop.

Whack! Whack! Whack!

Bluce Lim-Ward, aged 31, was found with 34 stab wounds on 7 May 2003. Serving a six-year sentence for fraud, she'd approached guards just two hours before the attack, saying she feared her cellmate was about to attack her.

Lim-Ward died on the way to the hospital. Butterfield, now 28, was no longer that angry teenager throwing bottles at cars.

She was a killer.

'A disturbing feature of the case is there was absolutely nothing to suggest that the victim had done anything to provoke the prisoner,' said the sentencing judge. 'Her past history indicates that unprovoked and violent attacks upon others have been part of her criminal history.'

Butterfield banged her head against the wall.

Tap.

She did it again and again, soft and slow.

Tap. Tap.

She continued, but this time a little harder and a little faster.

Tap, tap, tap.

Then harder and faster again.

Thud, thud, thud.

Her forehead was red, the speed with which her head was hitting the wall approaching a heavy-metal beat.

Whack, whack, whack.

Blood began to spurt from her head.

Smash. Smash. Smash.

Butterfield was again raging, but locked in a room all alone, the only person to attack was herself.

The guard rushed in as she smashed her own skull, the force of the blows now breaking bone. Everything within close proximity was covered in red. The guard launched from behind, locking her arms before driving her to the floor.

'She had head butted the wall 105 times before she was stopped,' said the guard who was there that day. 'Her skull was ripped apart and you could see brain. It was absolutely horrible.'

Rebecca Butterfield is among a rare group of prisoners known as 'self-harmers'.

'She does it for the attention,' the guard said. 'After her head was stitched up, she ripped apart the stitches and jammed things into her head. For whatever reason, she doesn't feel pain and she will hurt herself in any way she can for a thrill. She once tried to cut off her head using a toilet seat. She put her head into the toilet and smashed her neck with the seat. Some of the things she's done are just unbelievable.'

None more so than on the day she found her match.

'She set herself on fire in 2008,' said a guard. 'Lit herself up and watched her skin burn. No one knows how she got the match, but she was saved in the nick of time. She suffered severe burns but she was kept alive.'

Former PO Grant Turner said he was once forced to knock her out. He feared she was going to kill again.

'We had to take her to Westmead Hospital because she'd hurt herself that bad,' Turner said. 'The doctors thought that they'd need to amputate her arm, because her cuts were so bad. We took her in, put her on the bed and strapped her down. We cuffed her hands and legs, and belted her to the bed.

'When we were done the nurse walked in. She was heavily pregnant. When she was close to the bed, Butterfield kicked her right in the guts. The chains of her leg cuffs were quite long and she had enough freedom to move. And she was able to generate a lot of force. The nurse rushed out and the doctor stormed in, running to the bed and shouting at her.'

Turner warned the doctor away. He was too close. But it was too late.

'She ripped her fingernails right into his jugular,' Turner said. 'And then she started to strangle him. She hooked in and was trying to kill him. I jumped in and dropped my elbow straight into her head. I had to knock her out, otherwise the doctor was going to die. He just about passed out. He's lucky to be alive.'

Turner said that, apart from seeking attention, Butterfield hurts herself so she can get close enough to kill.

'She had constant wounds,' Turner said, 'and more often than not, we had to take her to the doctors or to the hospital to have whatever she stuck into her wound removed. And when you were within distance, she would attack.

'Everybody knows Rebecca Butterfield. She is absolutely off her chops. You could never go one-out with her. Apart from the violence, she would make accusations against you. We almost got sacked for giving her a radio. In the end, she could not have access to anyone. She was just too bloody dangerous.'

So dangerous that Butterfield might be the first non-sex-offending prisoner to be kept in jail 'indefinitely' when her sentence expires. Butterfield is due to be released from prison in 2015 and authorities are already considering making an application to the NSW Supreme Court to prevent her from being released under the controversial Crimes (Serious Sex Offenders) Amendment Bill 2013. Several high-risk sex offenders have been kept in jail past their maximum sentence following the passing of the act in 2006. But Butterfield is likely to become the first non-sex-offender to be detained in jail, following her sentence under an amendment bill that 'provides for the supervision and detention of high-risk violent offenders'. The controversial bill was amended on 19 March 2013, after the public bill, originating in the Legislative Assembly, was passed by the both the Legislative Council and the Legislative Assembly of New South Wales.

'I've examined this bill and find it to correspond in all respects to the bill as finally passed by both Houses,' wrote the Assistant Speaker of the Legislative Assembly in the 23-page amendment.

Prison authorities will make an application to the Supreme Court six months prior to November 2015, when Butterfield's sentence expires. Considered to be the most violent and destructive criminal in the system, Butterfield cannot be kept in jail past this date if the application is not made, or not accepted, as she is neither a sex offender nor a mental patient. Despite being kept in the hospital, Butterfield does not officially qualify as a mental patient. Officially she has a personality disorder, not a mental-health issue.

A current guard who has worked closely with Butterfield called her a ticking time-bomb who would almost immediately re-offend if released.

'There are many horror stories about her and they are all true,' said the guard. 'With some criminals they can be great one day and terrible the next. They just act out when they have a bad day. With Butterfield, she was an hour-to-hour prospect. She is such a rollercoaster and the look in her eyes is just terrifying. You know the potential is there. She isn't a scary-looking person, but she is very scary when she gets that look in her eye. She has an evil glint.

'The headbutting episode was terrifying and recently she pulled out a colostomy bag and threw piss everywhere. She is an amazing self-harmer and the scar tissue on her body is unbelievable. She has a dent in her forehead and scars everywhere. Butterfield freaks people out, and I think that's why she harms herself. And it is almost impossible to stop. You could put her naked in a concrete room and she would still find a way to hurt herself. She can't help herself and no one can help her either.'

It's My Balls

'He was probably the most difficult prisoner I've ever had to deal with. You had to keep your eye on him every second.'
Long Bay guard

Slowly and, most importantly, secretly, he let the nail grow. It was the perfect plan. The jail guards would never suspect a thing.

Michael Rodda studied his nail, which towered from the end of his big toe. It was thick, milky and, after four months, finally ready to become a weapon.

Using his right thumbnail, also cunningly grown and gone unnoticed by prison surveillance – from the guards staring at him through his custom-made perspex cell to the lenses of the video camera mounted on his cell wall – he picked and pulled at his toenail. With his hand under the bed cover (he wasn't strapped down this time) he picked at the corner of his toe. Rodda carefully sliced and sawed, making sure the much stronger nail on his toe did not crack the one on his thumb. Suddenly the corner of the nail gave way; a slight break in the layer allowed him to grab and gently rip it off his foot. Moments later, he was holding a two-inch piece of toenail, as milky white as it was strong and thick. But the job wasn't done.

Rodda spent the next two days grinding the nail against his cell wall, filing away the side to make a pointy end. A sharp end.

It was showtime.

He ripped off the blanket and sprang from the bed. Nail in hand while the guard leapt from his post on the chair and towards the cell door, Rodda pulled down his pants. Before the camera on the wall could even focus, the inmate pushed Long Bay's first prison shiv made from a body part into the base of his scrotum.

And then he let rip.

Blood poured as the nail tore the skin, the flesh split from his anus to the base of his penis. By now the guard had cracked open the door and was rushing towards Rodda when the inmate sent his hand into the open wound.

'He ripped out his nuts and dropped them,' said the guard. 'They were still attached but they were dangling, with no skin to hold them in.'

The nurse entered Rodda's cell after the guard had noticed the blood on his bedsheet. It had been a month since the self-harming inmate had severed his genitals. The bleeding was stopped, the torn flesh first sterilised and then sutured after he was rushed to hospital. But as the nurse walked towards his bed, the prisoner was screaming.

'It's my balls!'

The nurse ripped off the blood-soaked sheet. She was in no danger of being attacked, with the prisoner already cuffed, both his hands and feet bound tightly by leather against the bed's steel frame. She almost fainted when she saw the open wound. Not because of the blood or the balls, no . . .

Because of the creatures wriggling out of his skin.

'He had maggots in his nuts,' the officer continued. 'Dead set, there were maggots in his balls.'

Rodda had taken his stitches apart soon after the operation to fix his genitals.

'He got hold of a fly that had made its way into his cell,' the guard said. 'It could have flown in under the door or through the window. He must've picked his wound and put the fly or the fly's eggs inside. And that's how the maggots grew.'

*

Another infamous Long Bay self-harmer, Michael Rodda was sentenced to six years jail for starting a bushfire on the Central Coast. The troubled man embarked on a series of sick stunts that would have been unprecedented had it not been for Rebecca Butterfield's track record for violence. His history of self-mutilation makes for difficult reading. A prison report documented some of his more horrific incidents, which included inserting objects into his body, either through cutting himself, opening a previous wound, or putting them into his anus or mouth. Plastic bags, razor blades, pens, clothing, blankets and bedding are just some of the objects that had to be surgically removed from Rodda's body. A former guard who wishes to remain unnamed watched on in horror as the inmate ate a piece of material, which subsequently forced the prisoner to have a lobotomy.

'He was standing there in the nude wearing a prison safety jacket,' the guard said. 'It's kind of like a straitjacket and meant to keep him from hurting others and himself, but it didn't work. Unable to get hold of anything to harm himself with, Rodda went about eating the blanket. We stopped him, but he had ingested enough to make him very sick.

'Rodda was a real piece of work. After he cut his balls, we had to go in and hold him down as the nurses dressed his testicles. They would do the patching and cleaning up, and we'd be forced to watch. It was horrible. He was strapped down, but he was that dangerous we had to be there just in case.'

Rodda was housed in the MSPC inside the Long Bay hospital – he was obviously an inmate who could never be kept in general population. Like Butterfield, he was always in his own cell. And he was never left alone.

'He was under 24-hour guard in the end,' the prison officer continued. 'There was absolutely nothing in his cell. He would be in a straitjacket most of the time, and whenever he had to be taken out he would be stripped nude and completely searched.'

Considering the intense surveillance Rodda was kept under, the guards thought they had him under control. It would be impossible for him to rip apart a wound, eat a pen, or stick a razor blade into his belly. But they were wrong. There was one weakness in this stringent security. And Rodda found it.

'The only time he wasn't restrained was when he had to shower,' the guard said. 'We would remove his cuffs and jacket so he could wash himself. The shower in his cell was completely open and we had to watch him. That room was all glassed up and we could see everything he did from the officers' station. Plus, the place was equipped with cameras from multiple angles.

'When Rodda showered, it was the only time he could use his hands. There was a time when he had an open wound because the doctors refused to seal it. To be honest, I didn't think they could even if they tried, because there was so much damage to his internal tissue and muscle. The cut began from his navel and went up to his chest.

'One day I was watching him shower and he put his hand inside the wound, ripped the skin open and pulled his intestine out. There was blood and guts everywhere.

He was looking at me and holding his insides like it was a present. It was dead-set disgusting. After that moment, we'd have to run in and grab him every time he put his hand near his stomach. It was just unbelievable. The only thing in the shower was soap, so we thought there was little he could do. But we were wrong.'

On top of this, Rodda thought to perform surgery on himself while locked up in jail.

'Rodda had marbles,' the guard said. 'And I probably should explain what they are. In prison, some people split their penis from the base up and insert marbles along the shaft. They will tape it up and let it self-heal, consequently ending up with a penis bulging with marbles. Apparently they did this to sexually please their partner.

'Rodda already had the marbles inside him, even before I started working around there. Blokes like him didn't feel pain, so cutting apart his own dick was nothing. He would rip anything open on his body and stick whatever he could find inside – a piece of thread, a bit of dirt – so he could infect the wound. Nothing fazed or hurt this guy.

'He was cut up so bad the hospital eventually said there was nothing they could do for him. They would stitch him up, only to have him rip it back apart. The open wounds were too much and he was eventually denied treatment. Rodda was moved out of Long Bay and into Silverwater. Then he had to go to Westmead Hospital for treatment.'

Rodda was due to be released in 2009, but he did not make it out. After years of flirting with death, he finally went too far.

'He ate a coaxial cable and choked to death,' said a current prison guard. 'He ripped the cord from a TV and stuck it down his throat.'

Four years dead, Rodda is still one of Long Bay's most talked-about prisoners. But for the guard who had to keep a close eye on him, he was just a pain in the arse.

'Rodda was probably the most difficult prisoner I ever had to deal with,' the guard said. 'If he wasn't the worst, he was certainly on the podium. Working with him required 100 percent concentration for your entire shift.

'It was strange because, despite all he did, he seemed quite normal. You could have a conversation with the bloke, no problems. He loved to talk and he just wanted the attention.

'There's only one time I can remember losing it and giving it to him. He got so frustrating that I just couldn't help myself. I called him a murderer. He looked at me and said, "I'm not a murderer, I've never killed anyone." I told him, "You're a murderer because you're taking up precious surgery time that other people in need could use. You are taking a bed for no good reason. Someone could be rushed in and then denied because all the medical attention is focused on you. You are a fucking murderer."'

Another guard also found Rodda to be pleasant – at least when he wasn't harming himself.

'He was a nice, quiet character, but he would be talking you through it as he did it. It was bizarre. One of my mates was on an escort with him. When the doctor discharged Rodda, my mate said, "Oh well, I have to take you home.

There goes my overtime." Next thing Rodda said, "You'll be right" and then he pulled the stitches out of his penis and they had to take him back to the hospital. Needless to say, my mate ended up getting his overtime.'

13

SHOOTING

The Long Bay Shootout 1975

'It was just another day in jail and all of a sudden you have crims running around with guns.'
Long Bay hostage PO Paul Cafe

Prison officer Paul Cafe can finally speak about the two scars on his leg. After 29 years, he can talk terror, smashed windscreens, and bullets whizzing past his head and into his legs at point-blank range while a rabid inmate stood over him.

'He just said, "Cop this",' recalled Cafe, who is now happily retired and living in Queensland. 'Then he shoved the gun in between my legs and fired twice.'

Much has been written and reported about the Long Bay shootout of 1975, but never the truth.

'I've seen some shows, read some things, but none of it has been right,' Cafe said. 'Some people who were there didn't even get it right. They weren't in the truck. I'm the only one who can tell you what happened.'

This is Paul Cafe's candid account of the notorious and bloody escape attempt at Long Bay Jail on 8 August 1975 – a date Cafe will never forget.

Cafe saw them running: three prisoners and each with a gun.

The young guard was manning eight-post, where it was his job to assist the 'gatekeeper', letting the steady stream of trucks, as they delivered food, clothing and, of course, prisoners, in and out.

Bang!

The first shot rang out across the baking asphalt, shattering the summer silence in the entry yard. The gatekeeper, Sam Pavich, jumped as the bullet zinged past his head.

'It was Marko Motric,' Cafe said of the convicted robber armed with a gun in his hand. 'I saw him running to the left of the truck, pointing a gun and discharging it in Sam's direction.'

There were two trucks in the caged area of the Metropolitan Remand Centre; a white International stores truck and a red Bedford stores truck. The first, driven by Ray Clarke, was waiting inside the cage. The second was stopped inside the open gate. Cafe had just waved the red truck through, but it stopped dead when the first bullet was fired, screaming past Pavich's face.

'Give me the fucking keys!' A bulky forearm wrapped around Cafe's throat.

Russell 'Mad Dog' Cox, an infamous robber, was pressing a gun into the guard's face. Cafe went still. He would later find out the weapon shoved against his head was made of wood. But right there and then, it felt like the actual thing.

'A shot had just been fired,' Cafe said. 'So I had no reason to doubt it was real.'

Cafe was pushed into the gatehouse; Cox, the fitness fanatic who held the prison chin-up record, was a boa constrictor and Cafe the mouse.

'You're not going to get away with this,' Cafe muttered bravely.

Cafe was floored and another gun was aimed at his face. But this time it was real: a .22 Beretta. Motric pushed the cold, hard barrel against the guard's burning, flushed face.

'We gonna take this one?' Motric said. 'Is he a Dog?'

Cafe was hauled from the ground and towards the red truck, gun now jammed into his back. He was flung like a rag doll onto the seat. The two frenzied gunmen were taking him for a ride.

'I then saw Allan McDougall,' Cafe said of the third prisoner making a blazing bid for freedom. 'He was standing on the step by the window of the visitors' counter with a .38 obtained from the gun safe.'

Crack!

A bullet from McDougall's gun ricocheted off the ancient Long Bay oak, spitting splinters towards the truck.

Smash!

The windscreen shattered, glass flying everywhere, as the .38 finally found a home in the soft upholstery of the car seat – McDougall had made it into the vehicle. Cafe was trapped in the truck with three dangerous bandits, sandwiched in between Cox and Motric, while McDougall stared into his face.

Cox found first gear. He slowly edged the truck towards the gate, which swung open. Gatekeeper Pavich had thought about throwing away the keys, but with his mate Cafe in the truck, he opened the gate.

Cafe felt Cox's shoulder move. Soon his .38 Beretta was pointed at another guard.

'As the gates swung open, Cox began to exit,' Cafe said. 'He aimed the gun at Jeff Jones.'

But this was when Cafe reacted. He grabbed the Beretta from Cox but then –

Bang! Bang! Bang!

The firestorm had begun. The guards, perched high up in the towers, opened fire, the bullets hitting the truck sounding like a tin roof being belted by hail. The armed prisoners panicked.

'Get him up so they can see him,' one said.

Cafe was shoved out the window and onto the truck's bonnet. He clung to the window frame, smashed glass stuck in the seals ripping through his hand. And the bullets continued to pelt the truck. One after another.

Crack! Crack! Crack!

'I didn't know if anyone in the towers knew there was a hostage on board,' Cafe said. 'I saw a guard called Mal Lewis in the tower firing at us. I could hear the bullets hitting the truck as we went past the office.'

The rain of bullets continued as Cafe held on for dear life. His legs swung through the air, left and then right, with every jerk of the truck's steering wheel. But the unrelenting sound of metal pelting metal became the least of Cafe's concerns when he saw the abandoned vehicle that was about to smash into his legs.

'I saw a parked ute on the driveway and we were about to hit it head on,' Cafe said. 'I would've been crushed, so I pulled myself back into the cabin.'

Boom!

The truck spewed up into the air as the bread truck smashed into its side. The guard, Sandy Storie, had floored the grey delivery vehicle out of the Central Industrial Prison and jammed it into the belly of the prison runaway.

Thud!

Just as the Bedford's wheels had bounced back to the ground, an earth-moving truck had speared into the rear. Stan Stewart had floored the beast, jamming it straight into the Bedford's tail. The truck came screeching to a halt.

That same strong arm was again round Cafe's throat, the gun pressed into his cheek. He was pushed from the vehicle and the three prisoners huddled around him, turning Cafe into a human shield. He was shuffled towards the main gate, gun now jammed into his throat.

'We'll kill him,' the cry came.

The escaped inmates were desperate; the guards' barrel ends tracing their every move. The prisoners were outmatched, outgunned, and the only hope they had left was the hostage at the end of the .38 pistol.

An armed guard peered over the raised wall at the entrance to 2 Tower. 'He's dead,' he screamed, assuming Cafe was already gone.

The terse exchange was followed by fireworks. The guns seemed even louder following the brief pause, barking as they spat the metal missiles into the air.

Cafe was sent rolling down an embankment, McDougall's arms and legs knotted with his.

'And that's when he looked at me,' Cafe said. 'Jammed the gun in my groin and let me have it.'

Bang! Bang!

Cafe screamed in pain.

'Next thing I know [fellow guard] Alex Cook was standing over me,' Cafe said. 'He was saying I had two in me.'

The shootout was over, Cafe was rushed to Prince Henry Hospital and the wannabe escapees back behind bars.

Detective-sergeant Roger Rogerson was the first officer on the scene.

'I had locked all three of them up,' he said of the prison inmates Cox, Motric and McDougall. 'So I suppose I was seen as the right man for the job. I was sent down to investigate the matter and build the prosecution's case.'

The sun was setting as Rogerson arrived, and the trio had been locked away. With bullet holes in the ground, on the walls and, of course, the escape vehicle, Rogerson could have been forgiven for thinking he'd walked into a city razed by war.

Notebook in hand, he was ready to start. But he could only interrogate McDougall; both Cox and Motric had been shot. They were left to bleed on the Observation (OBS) floor and denied medical treatment for 26 hours.

'You might say McDougall was dishevelled when I got to him,' Rogerson said. 'The screws were big tough blokes back then and they didn't take any shit. He'd been beaten up as he should've been. McDougall was a tough old-school crim from Melbourne. He'd come up and done a few TAB jobs and robbed half a dozen banks with a bloke called Gibbs. I locked the pair up together.

'McDougall didn't deny anything. He admitted it and copped it sweet. They were caught at the boom gates, guns in hand, so there was little defence.'

Rogerson was not surprised by the trio's cunning plan, or the brutality with which they'd executed it.

'They were real hard men,' Rogerson said. 'Tough cunts. I locked Cox up for a big robbery at PYE industries. Back in the day, they were a big company that made televisions. He did them for about $50,000, which was a huge amount back then. I had some inside information through an informant and got him at a block of flats in Randwick.

'I locked Motric up for robbery too and he was mad. They were never going to try and get out of jail quietly.'

Rogerson left MacDougall and took statements from the guards.

'I am a First Class Prison Officer, attached to the officers' cafeteria,' said James Coulduck in a statement he'd given to Rogerson. 'I have been with the Department of Corrective Services for approximately ten years. About 2.45pm on Friday, 8 August 1975, I was in the cafeteria on duty. I heard the sounds of shots being fired. I ran out of the cafeteria towards the CIP gate and I noticed a prisoner with a revolver in his hand and he had hold of a prison officer and he had the gun pointed at the prison officer's head and he said, "He's dead." This prisoner was armed with a long barrel .38 calibre revolver and he was wearing brown trousers and a blue pullover. Just then another prison officer, Jeff Robertson, came running past me and I shouted to him, "Look out, Jeff, they're armed." There was an old lady, a young boy and two girls on my right-hand side and I then pushed them into the gents toilet. I went into the toilet then I looked out and I saw these three prisoners with the prison officer jammed between them. The prisoner still had the gun pointed at the officer's head and was still saying, "He is dead, he is dead."

'I then walked towards them and said, "Let him go." They continued to walk and we walked with them and I saw that Senior Officer Cook had a revolver and then the hostage prison officer fell on the ground with the two prisoners leaving the prisoner in the brown trousers with the revolver standing up.

'I then shouted to Mr Cook, "Shoot him." Mr Cook fired two shots and the prisoner fell and rolled down a short embankment. Another prisoner also fell down the embankment.

'I then jumped down the embankment and fell on top of the prisoner McDougall. Just before I fell on McDougall, I had seen a .38 revolver lying in the grass close to where McDougall had fallen. I believe that this revolver had been in the possession of prisoner Cox, as I had seen the revolver he had been carrying, thrown by Cox, as he fell back, to this position. Just as I went over the bank, there were shots being fired, but I do not know by whom. After falling on McDougall I pushed his arm up his back and with the assistance of Mr Nordstrom, I then escorted McDougall to the OBS at the CIP and placed him in Cell 6. I then strip-searched McDougall and saw that he had the sum of $32, consisting of three $10 notes and one $2 note hidden in his underpants.'

Rogerson concluded the trio had used a replica gun, made from wood, to obtain weapons from a gun 'tank' before taking Cafe hostage.

'They'd come up with a plan to hijack a truck,' Rogerson said. 'They forced Sam Pavich to open the "tank", which is a metal box that detectives leave their guns in when going to interview inmates. It could have six guns in it at times and this trio ended up with a couple of .38s and a .22. They ran out into the cage and overpowered Cafe before putting him into the truck.

'By this time the alarm had sounded and the screws ran out with their big carbines, old guns used in World War II that used to hold 15 bullets. They laid into this truck and, from memory, they put about 60 bullets into it. They were hit by a couple of trucks and were eventually overpowered at the boom gate.'

*

Paul Cafe returned to work shortly after the traumatic hostage incident.

'I had two weeks off and was sent straight back to night shift,' he said. 'There was no counselling, nothing like that. I was just told to get on with it.

'One [bullet] went through the left thigh and the other into the right thigh. They both went straight through, and I was lucky in a way because it was only a small calibre gun that I was shot with. The doctor said I would have been in some trouble if it had been a bigger calibre.

'People had me standing on the bonnet, but I was in the truck. Glass was going every which way, and then they threw me out the window. It was Cox's idea. He was driving and I was sitting next to him. As soon as the shots came, Cox told them to push me out.

'When it was all finished they gave me out and Cox was around my head with the .38. They wanted to keep me close so that they wouldn't get shot at. It all happened so fast. Nobody was to know I was there and I could see them firing. They weren't to know that I was on board. It was just another day in jail and all of a sudden you have crims running around with guns. They were firing them.

'Worst of all, a large truck was at the gate and there was no way they could close it. Once they got in they had the upper hand because we were unarmed.'

Cafe is still haunted by the memory of that day.

'It's been nearly 40 years now, but I have to carry it – it's defined my life. Some people call me a hero and others say that I should've done this and that. Everyone was putting up their hands, asking for medals. I'm very disappointed about what some people have said.'

And that shootout wasn't the last time Cafe encountered his assailants.

'I've seen Motric. They brought him back from Maitland one day. The superintendent asked me if I had any problems with him coming back to Long Bay, and I didn't really.

'Another time was when Cox was in Katingal and they thought he might have swallowed a handcuff key. It was during lunch time when three officers brought him into the jail. They walked over and gave me their guns. It was very unusual. Here I was, now holding the gun, and there was this bloke who'd caused me so much grief.'

14

RIOTING

Burn, Baby, Burn

23 August 1978, Central Industrial Prison

'They'd torn off their numbers and said to the other inmates, "Let's do it now!"'

Secretary of the Prison Officers' Association, Tim Hickie, 1978

The scream was faint by the time it bounced through the concrete yard and reached his ear. But while distance dulled the volume, the 100 metres between him and the prison did nothing for the pain emanating from the building. Soon there were two people screaming, then three and then four. And in a matter of moments, the faint noise had become a deafening roar.

Toowheeeeeeeeeat!

The whistle blasted, leaving the rookie guard with no doubts – a riot had broken out. The animals were no longer caged.

Oh, shit, Michael Vita thought. *What do I do now?*

Vita would go on to become Long Bay governor, but on this day he was just a teenage prison guard, three months into the job.

And he was scared.

'I was shitting my pants,' Vita recalled. 'The noise, the confusion, the stuff we could see flying into the yard. It was bloody terrifying.'

The Central Industrial Prison (CIP) was in flames. Smoke poured through the bars and into the yard, bottles burst through the windows and smashed into thousands of shards.

At 11.04 it had begun, heralded by four prisoners yelling, 'It's on.'

The senior guard looked at Vita. 'Come on,' he said, before turning his back and sprinting.

'I followed him,' said Vita. 'And next thing I knew I was standing in front of the armoury, lined up with another 50 or 60 guards.'

Vita's fists were not going to be enough to stop these 70 inmates from taking over the prison or rescue the guard who was trapped inside.

'They'd taken the wing officer,' Vita said. 'He'd been bashed and we needed to get him out.'

The gatekeeper opened the impenetrable steel door of the armoury and waved the guards inside. A collection of rifles and shotguns hung on the wall.

'But I didn't get one of them,' Vita said. 'Instead, I was handed a shield, helmet and baton. The baton had a little leather thong on the end; I twisted it around my thumb so if someone grabbed me they couldn't take it.'

What he wasn't given was a gas mask.

'They were in short supply,' Vita said. 'I didn't think much of it.'

It was a rookie error he would soon regret.

'As we were kitting up, we were told the emergency unit were on the way,' Vita continued. 'They'd go in first and we would follow.'

Then the guards were split into four groups. They hastily lined up and made their way towards the chaos – towards the rabid prisoners who were now threatening to kill the guard held hostage.

'They'd already flogged him,' Vita said. 'And we feared they'd do worse.'

The Malabar Emergency Unit (MEU) finally arrived – a recently formed group, more tough than trained for situations like this – looking fearsome in their bulletproof vests and black helmets. There were 20 of them, drooling as they waited at the door. The Long Bay attack dogs were ready to be unleashed.

'They cracked the cell,' Vita said. 'And fired the gas in.'

Pop!

The first canister flew through the air before landing near a cell. The second one went further in, landing smack in the centre of the jail. And soon the little metal capsules exploded, spewing noxious white clouds into the air.

'Then they went in with the pepper fogger,' Vita said. 'It was like a big blower vac full of gas.'

The MEU charged, their gas masks protecting them from the gaseous tear-duct destroyer.

'Timber was still flying everywhere as they went in,' Vita said. 'They yelled at the inmates to return to their cells.'

Vita and the rest of the guards followed. Baton ready, he was to belt anyone who wasn't locked in a cell.

'I don't remember whacking anyone with the baton,' Vita said. 'Once the gas went in, most of them gave way.'

The MEU were able to find the guard, and though he was a bloodied mess, he was still thankfully alive. They also quickly found the prisoners responsible for starting the riot, and those responsible for taking their mate. Soon they were bloodied and messed too.

With the culprits caught and the rest locked in their cells, the guards retreated. The wing was a war zone. Chairs, beds and desks had been turned into barricades. Smashed glass and burnt clothes littered the concrete floor. Broken pieces of timber and makeshift shivs were scattered all over the ground. But young Vita could see none of it as he rushed out for fresh air.

'Some of the gas got me,' Vita said. 'We trained with gas, and did exercises where we ran through the shit. We were told never to rub our eyes in a riot when gas was used. But that's easier said than done. The wind, maybe the blower, had thrown it towards my direction. I had it all over my clothes, some in my face. It bloody hurt and I rubbed and rubbed. My nose and my eyes burned.'

Apart from this, Vita had walked out of his first riot with no severe bruises or breaks. He would be in plenty more over the years as they became a normal part of his job.

'There were many riots,' Vita said. 'Especially back in the day. They were bloody scary things and there was a big potential to get caught. They were usually caused by a group of prisoners, and the rest would go along. And those responsible copped it. But most would surrender as soon as the gas went in. If you put up resistance, you would pay. We would lock them up, check their muster card and move on to the next.'

Gas was the only real weapon in a riot, since guards were not permitted to carry guns.

'The guys in the tower were the only ones armed with guns in normal circumstances,' Vita said. 'And once the crims were locked up at night, the guards would have a handgun.

'There was a fear that if you walked around with a weapon, inmates would jump on you and take it. In the tower, they used Ruger rifles. They were .337 calibres and had a magazine with ten bullets. And at night they used a .38 police special with six rounds. All we had were our shields, helmets and bats, and most of the time that was enough.'

Seventeen prisoners and one prison guard were injured in the 1978 riot. A workshop and a library were completely destroyed, with three of the six wings set on fire. Seven of the prisoners were seriously injured and taken to hospital. Guards were also harmed during the chaos.

'To make it worse, some of the gas masks issued to officers were not fitted with filters,' said secretary of the

Prison Officers' Association Tim Hickie at a press conference following the riot. 'The gas went straight into their lungs. There was almost hand-to-hand fighting in there. We know punches were thrown at prison officers because two of them had split lips.'

Bruised prisoners, battered guards, burning buildings and poisoned lungs, you'd think this was a particularly bad riot. Unfortunately, it was not.

'Run of the mill,' said Vita. 'I suppose you could say there's no such thing as a peaceful riot. That would be a protest, though, wouldn't it?'

As the smoke cleared and the rubble was removed, it emerged that this riot was sparked because prisoners wanted mail delivered in a timely manner. Apparently it was taking them too long to get their letters. They also wanted better visiting rooms.

'All they're asking for, really, is that they be treated like human beings,' said Kevin Story, a spokesman for the Prisoners' Action Group, at the time.

Ready to Riot

'When you're walking into a dark cell you don't know if they're waiting with a shiv.'
Senior assistant superintendent of the Malabar Emergency Unit (1978–1979), Dave Farrell

'Chief, can I give you my TV?' the prisoner asked. 'I'd like you to lock it up for me, if that's OK. I don't need it right now.'

Dave Farrell has been asked this question more times than he cares to remember.

'As soon as we hear that one,' Farrell says, 'we're off to get suited up. We know what's coming.'

Experienced guards like Farrell know when the jail is about to go up in flames. There are several warning signs that cannot be ignored. Long Bay Jail has seen some of the bloodiest and longest riots in the NSW prison system. And Farrell has been in most of them.

Now retired, Farrell is reminded of the Long Bay riots daily. He has lost 15 percent of the use of his hands, thanks to a rampaging inmate. But Farrell says they always knew when a riot was on the way.

'A lot of the times we'll pick up signals,' Farrell said. 'What happens is a decent screw, an old screw, will pick up on a vibe that something's not quite right. If you have a stable prisoner, and all of a sudden he wants to get out of the jail, you know something's up. When a riot is coming, you can see the behaviour of prisoners change. A sure sign was when they'd ask for their TVs to be put away. They wouldn't say any more than that, but we knew the only reason they'd want to give up their TVs was because they were scared of having them smashed.'

Another indication is when prisoners would ask to be locked in their cells.

'They'd say, "Boss, can you lock me in today?"' Farrell said. 'One request is unusual, but sometimes you'd get four or five ask on the same day. They don't want to be involved in the drama.

'Often you'd also pick up on people who'd dob them in. Some inmates might say something as simple as, "You should have a day off tomorrow."

'There are plenty of signs and you need an old head to pick up on them. That's why a good old screw is so valuable.'

Farrell was a founding member of the Malabar Emergency Unit. He received extensive siege and hostage rescue training during his career.

'There have been moments where we'd be on standby for days,' Farrell said. 'Kitted up and just waiting outside a jail. You'd be broken into four different squads depending on what your role is, and everybody knew what your objectives were.'

Farrell did not take a backward step during a riot, and throughout his time in Long Bay, he was feared by prisoners and was the guards' go-to man.

'We would go in with a baton, a shield and a gas mask,' Farrell said. 'That was enough. You don't need any more than ten in a squad, and at each riot we'd have four squads plus a back-up unit. You would set up a medical point. It's actually dangerous to have too many officers in a squad, believe it or not, because numbers just get in your way.

'During a riot, the first step is to hit the jail area hard with chemical agents. You fire the stuff in and get the rampaging inmates as confused as you can. In a hostage situation, and most of the riots involved a guard being taken hostage, one group would be sent in with the job to get the guard out. The rest of the squads would be there to stop the riot and lock the prisoners up.'

Easier said than done, of course, considering the rioting mob would spend hours setting obstacles to trip up the charging guards.

'Nine times out of ten the doors will be barricaded,' Farrell said. 'They'd use anything they had: beds, chairs and office furniture. They'd also smear butter all over the floor so we would slip. They would make it as difficult as possible for us to get to them.'

And even after all of this, there were the bottles, pieces of wood and furniture that were pelted at the guards.

'As you're going through, crap gets thrown at you,' Farrell said. 'Anything that wasn't strapped down would become a missile.'

Guards would shout and scream while entering pitch-black cells, unaware if a prisoner was cowering in a corner or about to hit them with a lump of wood.

'Normally, all the light bulbs would be smashed, so the prison was as dark as possible, which made it hard to see,' Farrell said. 'When you walk into a dark cell, you don't know if they're waiting with a shiv. You could be stabbed and not see it coming. Most times you were going blind and you were running a huge risk. That's why you needed a good group of people in the squads who could back each other up.'

Every guard who went into a flaming cell was prepared to come out bloodied and bruised.

'You get hurt sometimes,' Farrell said. 'It was part of the job. You only had a bat, and the crims would arm themselves with whatever they could find. I've had plenty of injuries over the years, as have all my mates.'

And Farrell, known to his fellow guards as 'Emu', didn't think twice about his life as he charged in to save theirs . . .

Hostage
23 October 1986, Metropolitan Remand Centre
'We all thought we were going to die.'
Current Long Bay PO Domenic 'Mick' Pezzano

Mick Pezzano sat behind his desk, looking straight at the two rookies standing by the door.

'Something isn't quite right, boys,' he said, the C-shift now in full swing. 'Nothing's going to happen today, but something will next week if we're not on our toes. Keep your ears to the ground.'

Pezzano was right. He was also wrong. Something was going to happen, but not next week . . .

Bang!

The door exploded, smacking the rookie guard standing closest to the entrance in the back. The force sent him rushing towards Pezzano's desk.

Whoosh!

He was once again upright, dragged back by a vice-like grip that crushed the back of his neck. The guard couldn't see the man who'd moved his powerful fingers to his throat. But it was hard not to miss the iron bar threatening his face.

'Give me your fucking keys or I'll kill him!' the prisoner screamed at Pezzano, the force of the demand firing hot spit into the young officer's ear.

'Yeah, and we'll also let him have it,' said the other inmate, holding a piece of timber like Babe Ruth facing the Red Sox, but instead of a pitcher, he was sizing up the other guard's face.

Mind strangled by fear, Pezzano searched deeply, and desperately, for a way out.

'The crims grabbed the two young guards,' Pezzano said. 'One had an iron bar ripped from a bedpost and the other a piece of timber stolen from a woodshop class. They had their weapons cocked and demanded I hand over the keys. I immediately recognised who they were. One was Lee Owen Henderson, a former boxer in for murder, and the other was Warren Perry, also a hardened crim. They were both thugs, gangsters – guys who shouldn't be messed with. I looked to the boys and they were just terrified. I could see it in their eyes. I myself had only been in the job for two years, but these poor blokes had only been guards for a few months. I looked back to Henderson and Perry. I was sure they were going to smash their heads in.'

Pezzano stared at the prisoners steely-eyed; the shock of their ambush had frozen him, even though he wanted to boil.

'Well?' said Henderson as he strode towards Pezzano. 'What's it going to be?'

Pezzano searched his head, but again fear denied him an answer.

'They started getting aggressive,' Pezzano recounted. 'They walked over to me and started pushing and shoving. I thought they were going to smash me and then I reacted – a scuffle broke out. And all of a sudden they backed off.'

And not because Henderson and Perry had had enough. No, the fight was over – because the inmates had the keys.

'I didn't want to give them the keys because that would've meant they'd have control of the jail,' Pezzano said. 'But they ripped them from me as we wrestled.'

Whack!

The bat hit Pezzano square in the back, the lightning of the strike frying his hamstrings, the thunder rocking his neck.

'Go!' the crim ringleader screamed.

'We were marched across the landing and into a cell,' Pezzano remembered. 'They pushed us in and slammed the door.'

The inmates were now off the leash, and they were rabid, drooling and ready to bite.

'On that night there were three of us on the top landing, guarding 70 inmates,' Pezzano said. 'We didn't carry any weapons and all we were armed with was a duress alarm. We were on the C-watch, the afternoon shift, and we'd pulled all the inmates out of the yard and into the wing at 4pm. The C-shift was always a bit of a threat because we couldn't lock them in their cells until 9.30pm. That meant there was 70 of them roaming around on the landing, free to do whatever they pleased.

'Keep in mind, it was only us three guards to keep them in line. And we're talking maximum security here, not a white-collar prison farm. We were in the office having a chat when Henderson and Perry came in. It was about 8.30pm, only half an hour before we were going to lock them in.'

But at 9pm, Pezzano, PO Ken Newberry and PO Bob Menzies were the only ones behind bars. The 70 prisoners, well, they were ripping the place apart.

'It was on,' Pezzano said. 'They took control of the whole landing and smashed everything that wasn't bolted down. The noise was just unbelievable. It was like a football stadium going off. It was horrendous, banging and glass breaking everywhere. Every window was shattered. All we could hear was iron bar on iron bar, metal on metal. It was a bloody jungle.'

Through a small glass slit in the cell door, the guards watched the pointless violence and the desperation unfold.

'The prisoners started barricading the top landing,' Pezzano said. 'They just ripped everything apart, broke everything they could and just threw it at the stairs. Seriously, there was shit flying everywhere, and in a second they created a mountain from whatever junk they could find.'

The guards were locked in the cell and safe from the rioting madness. But for how long? Let's not forget that a convicted killer was clutching the cell door key.

Pezzano launched on the intercom; a duress button could be found on the wall in each cell.

Ring. Ring.

'What?' answered the guard at the main gate.

'It's Mick Pezzano,' he screamed. 'We're being held hostage in a cell.'

'Fuck! How many of you and where?'

'Top landing, 13 Wing. There are three of us. Get us out. This fucking place is being destroyed.'

Click.

The intercom went silent.

Pezzano turned to check the reinforced steel door, which was fortunately still locked, keeping the rabid thugs – murderers, rapists and standover men – at bay. His and his men's safety assured, at least for now, Pezzano found the courage to look out the window.

It was absolute catastrophe.

The young guard regarded Pezzano. He was shaking. 'What if they come back in?' he asked. 'What are we going to do?'

Pezzano grabbed the end of the bed and hurled it at the cell door. 'We barricade ourselves in,' he replied. 'That's what we do.'

Officers Newberry and Menzies jumped off the floor, yanked the kettle and the blankets, and ripped shelves from the wall.

'Grab everything in the cell and throw it against the door,' Pezzano ordered. 'We're going to make it as difficult as we can for the bastards to get in.'

Once they had gathered everything they could and positioned it by the door, the trio stood in a huddle, vowing to punch, push, kick, scratch and slap anyone that tried to come in.

'I can only speak for myself, but I was terrified. We really felt that this was the end. It wasn't just about being bashed or killed by the crims, there was the possibility of worse. In most riots the inmates start fires, and if that happened we wouldn't have had a chance. There's no way we could've got out because we were locked in a cell. We would've been burnt alive.'

Pezzano smashed his fist into the intercom again. 'Help,' he cried desperately.

The officer on the other end of the line was calm. 'They're coming,' he said. 'Sit tight. They will get you out.'

Pezzano slumped against the wall. The door had been barricaded, and the rescue mission had been launched. Pezzano had done everything he could, and now he was utterly helpless. His life could either be saved by his colleagues or taken out by whatever dangers the riot held in its wake. Now all he and his fellow officers could do was wait.

Seconds became hours.

'It seemed like an eternity,' Pezzano said. 'We knew help was coming, but we also knew that the squad had to get through the crims before they got to us.'

Little did he know that Dave Farrell was standing outside the locked jail. And he was fuming.

'My superior wouldn't let us go in,' Farrell said. 'We were ready, but he thought it was still too dangerous. The guards inside contacted us on the intercom and we knew exactly where they were. My biggest fear was that they'd be moved. It they were taken elsewhere, we wouldn't have been able to find them. They could've been killed.'

So Farrell stood up to his superior.

'We're going in!' he screamed, as the squad smashed open the door.

Canisters were thrown into the jail, releasing tear gas and allowing the guards to push their way through the barricades.

Pezzano heard the screams.

'The noise was already deafening,' he recalled. 'But all of a sudden it became unbearable. That's how I knew the gas had gone in.'

Pezzano lifted himself from the floor, went to the door and looked out the tiny window.

'I saw one of my mates through the gas clouds,' Pezzano said. 'He was coming towards us. I can't tell you what a relief it was to finally see him, and to know that help had arrived.'

But this didn't mean that Pezzano and the rookie guards were in the clear.

'We could see the shit that was chucked at the poor buggers as they came in,' Pezzano said. 'There were bars, beds and buckets of water being hurled. The inmates threw everything at them. The squad had to overpower them, hand-to-hand, before getting to us.'

Finally the cell door was cracked.

'A guard rushed in,' Pezzano said. 'Then another and another. Dave Farrell was one of them, and it was only then that we knew we were safe. The squad had got in and restored calm, locking the rioters back into their cells. I can't even begin to describe what I felt when they came in. I've told Dave many times that he saved my life.'

When Pezzano surveyed the mess, the broken bottles and blood, he wondered how he was still alive.

'The place was destroyed,' he said. 'And who knows what else could've happened if the squad hadn't reached us in time.'

To this day, Pezzano can never forget the horror. He wonders whether it could have been stopped.

'This wasn't a normal riot,' he said. 'The inmates weren't demanding anything. Usually prisoners riot because they want better food or improved conditions. This was a strange one.

'There was a bit going on in the jail system at that time. We were managing the Comancheros in Long Bay and Parklea had the Bandidos. There was a bit of a power struggle with the Comancheros. Lots of them were in the remand centre and pretty well established, but these up-and-coming fellas came in, challenging them. I think the riot all stemmed from that. Information might've been passed and things went a little haywire.

'To cut a long story short, we knew something was happening. You could say that the atmosphere wasn't right, there wasn't a lot of talk from the inmates as usual, and we could sense something in the air.'

But Pezzano never expected he would be locked in a cell, trapped with two other officers, and fearing for his life.

'This wasn't something you could prepare for,' he said. 'This was a maximum security jail full of hard men, not like the young punks today. I had no doubt the bravery of the guards saved my life. I ended up staying in the job, but the other two, well, for whatever reason they never came back.'

Race Wars

'It was just brutal. They just ran at each other and punched, kicked, belted and stabbed.'
Long Bay guard

The inmate walked straight towards the prison officer. The guard nodded, acknowledging the model prisoner, who was always polite and well-behaved. But the inmate didn't respond; his gaze trained at the floor. He continued towards the officer, and when he was near enough –

Whooooosh!

The inmate charged – hard – into the guard's shoulder.

'Sorry, boss,' he said, as the other prisoners headed out to the yard for lunch. 'Thought you were someone else.'

'Right,' said the guard as he grabbed the inmate and spun him round before jamming his hand into his back. 'You're gone. No playtime for you today.' The guard marched the inmate across the landing before shoving him into the open cell. He slammed the door shut and twisted the key.

'Enjoy your lunch,' the guard said.

The prisoner smiled. 'I will now. Only knuckle sandwiches out there.'

Those eight words were the first indication of the blood that was about to be shed. Of the punches, kicks, stabs, and of the men carried out, bleeding and bent. There wouldn't even be time to arm up or send for gas.

'I went up there that day and all seemed okay,' said one of the first responding officers. 'But when I was about to leave, another officer said it might be a good idea to stick around. A crim had just shouldered an officer and was punished by being put in his cell. But instead of kicking and screaming to get out, the bloke was happy to be there. Straight after that, other inmates started acting out. It was only a moment after the first guy pushed into the guard that we knew shit was about to go down. They were all trying to get locked up.'

The guard in the tower surveyed the yard. There were 200 inmates jammed inside the barbwire-surrounded concrete 'play area'. They were quiet. Too quiet. In fact, the silence was almost deafening. The guard watched on for about ten minutes, rifle held firmly in his hands. He was sure something was about to start because today the inmates weren't playing cards. They weren't using the phone either, and no one was playing ball. Most were standing in groups, staring silently across the yard. Others, the loners, pinned themselves against the fence.

Then a booming voice erupted from one of the groups.

The war had begun.

The guard steadied his gun as two of the groups merged, forming a tsunami of green that thundered across the yard. But the other prisoners in its path didn't move. Instead of running away from the looming wave of destruction, they too formed a cyclonic green sea of their own and stormed right back.

'It was just brutal,' said a guard. 'They just ran at each other and punched, kicked, belted and stabbed.'

The ensuing riot, which occurred in November 2009, was dubbed the worst incident in Long Bay in 25 years. It began with a scream, followed by a flying punch and ended when shots were fired.

'I went in and grabbed the first injured bloke I saw,' the guard said. 'He was the first we got out; a big Aboriginal guy who was cut up pretty bad.'

'What do you want?' the guard screamed at the rioting masses as he rushed away from the storm.

'They don't want nothing, bruz,' came the reply. 'Nothing from youse, anyway.'

The guard ran back into the fray to pull another hurt inmate to safety.

'We were dragging injured blokes out one after the other,' the guard continued. 'They were dropping everywhere.'

But, strangely, no one attacked the guards.

'They weren't going after us,' the guard explained. 'I've been involved in riots where I've practically shat myself. But there wasn't one stage during this riot where I thought it was a big thing, as far as we, the guards, were concerned. We were going in and pulling blokes out, and they never once said anything to try to threaten us. They didn't throw things or issue demands.

'We didn't have time to grab the riot gear, but in the end there was no need for shields or batons because it wasn't about us but them. The crims were chasing each other down and unleashing on anyone they could find. As per usual, it wasn't one-on-one, it was ten-on-ten.'

Bang, bang . . . Bang, bang.

Two thunderous cracks rang out from the rifle, the bullets thumping into the ground. The armed guard in the tower paused to see if his shots had any effect, but the mass fighting continued. He sent another two down, this time closer, the bullets spitting dirt into the inmates' legs.

'It lasted about 15 minutes,' said the guard. 'And only ended because four shots were fired. The guys in the towers always fire into the ground. They can't fire into the walls because it ricochets. They can't get too close to the crims either, unless they're left with no option but to kill them. The shots went into the safe area, but they were close enough to make the inmates stop fighting.'

Their knives hit the floor as their hands reached for the sky.

It was finally over.

The surrender was swift, so much so that those who were bloodied and broken and unable to move were the only ones who couldn't lock themselves up.

The eight instigators were identified, rounded up and taken to the Metropolitan Medical Transient Centre.

'We threw them in segregation and that's where they stayed for three days,' said the guard. 'We quizzed them and they told us it was between them. This was a race war, not so much a riot. It was Abos versus Islanders, Lebos versus everyone. And all of them spilt blood.'

'Authorities hushed up a prison riot at Long Bay Jail last week in which wardens were forced to fire shots to quell the "worst incident in 25 years",' the newspaper headline screamed.

'Up to 80 prison guards were needed to stop the fighting last Tuesday when violence erupted between up to 40 Middle Eastern and Aboriginal prisoners.

'The prisoners, some maximum security, used gym weights to savagely beat each other and officers, during the melee which lasted up to half an hour. At least three prison officers, including a female guard, were injured in the attack and needed medical treatment.'

The riot was far from the worst incident in Long Bay Jail in 25 years, according to some prison officers.

'It wasn't as bad as they made it out to be,' commented a guard. 'Not when it came to us, anyway. Unlike most riots where they want something and attack the guards, this one wasn't directed at us, but at each other. The crims went off and it was a racial thing. When I say it wasn't much, that's not quite right because the inmates were going to town on each other. There was a whole yard of them brawling, just trying to kill whoever they could find. But when it comes to Long Bay, well, it was nothing.'

The riot was grossly exaggerated by the prison officers' union after officials dismissed the riot as an 'incident'. The inmate-on-inmate feud and the blood they spilled was turned into a game of political football.

'A stink kicked off afterwards and it was portrayed as a massive riot because the bosses put it down as an "incident",' the guard continued. 'Our union blew up because it was bigger than that; a yard full of crims stabbing each other, and they went to the press and blew it up.'

15

ESCAPING

Code Name: Operation Street
'*When you lock a man up and leave him with nothing to do,
except look around and think about how to get out of there,
eventually he will get out.*'
Former Long Bay inmate Ian Hall Saxon

Long Bay Jail's most mysterious inmate was quietly released
from prison in 2008. And once again he vanished . . .

Ian Hall Saxon is the Long Bay enigma, a reclusive
man who disappeared from the jail in 1993, in what would
become the most talked-about and speculated escape in
this nation's history. He was recaptured two years later,
but to this day nobody really knows how he got out. They
certainly don't know that he was stabbed three times
after he was found, was denied medical treatment after

having a stroke and spent two years in solitary confinement with police informers and Dogs. Nor do they know about the German shepherds sniffing his 'nuts', or his friendship with Ivan Milat.

Saxon has never spoken about his escape or his time in prison.

Until now . . .

'Mr Big', the rock promoter turned drug importer turned Long Bay's most famous inmate, had just returned to his home in Auckland, following a Shaggy concert. A two-hour set from 'Mr Boombastic' had him cracking a joke.

'It was about as painful as being in Long Bay,' Saxon said.

The 71-year-old had been working in Rotorua for the past three days, helping plan everything from logistics to sound production for the concert, much like he did 40 years ago when he'd assisted during Frank Sinatra's tour in Australia.

'I'm back to doing what I do best,' Saxon said. 'I've been in Auckland since I've been out. I didn't have much choice because I didn't think I was very welcome in Australia. It's suited me fine up until this point and, to be honest, it's nice to have got the chance to go through the old country again. You have to remember I've been away from the place for 44 years.'

Saxon, a Kiwi by birth even though he speaks with a refined Australian accent, then talked about New Zealand's majestic South Island. He also dropped the name of the biggest band in the world.

'I've only been down to the South Island once when I was helping Chuggy [concert-tour entrepreneur Michael Chugg] with some promotional stuff for Coldplay. But I'm pretty much retired now – by the time I got back here, I was already of pension age. I'm 71. I don't do a whole lot. When the boys have the concerts, I will pitch in and do what I know best. But come winter, the music scene is pretty barren. I'll escape at least a month of the Kiwi winter and head to Thailand.'

It's ironic Saxon chose to use the word 'escape' when talking about his Thai trips. After all, that's what he's most famous for and what has, essentially, defined his life.

The alarm sounded at 2.15pm on 2 March 1993.

The prisoner had 'vanished'. Long Bay Jail was now closed. And the search that would last for 750 days had begun.

Ian Hall Saxon was officially reported missing at 12.10pm, when a guard told the jail's governor, Ian Schubert, that Mr Big could not be found.

Saxon had not reported for muster, and a 30-minute search of the jail turned up nothing. Not even a clue. His cell was empty; bed made, personal belongings stacked neatly on a shelf. He was not in the showers, nor in the yard, nor in any of the buildings the small army of guards had frantically searched. The first port of call was the Assistant Super-intendent of Industries (ASI) office, where Saxon worked as a clerk. He should have arrived to begin his duties, which included filing paperwork, at 9.30am. He hadn't.

ASI officer Wayne Hammond noticed that Saxon hadn't

turned up for work but thought nothing off it, because the intelligent prisoner also worked in the library.

'I didn't check on inmate Saxon because he was working in between the library and the ASI's office,' said Hammond. 'It wasn't unusual for him to be in either of those areas.'

But Saxon was in neither. By 2.15pm, prison authorities came to the conclusion that Saxon had left the Metropolitan Remand Centre (MRC). They didn't know when or how.

The interviews began and the mystery grew. The guards only muddied the waters they should have made clear.

The initial report into the escape, a two-page report compiled by Director of Security and Investigations Donald Rogers, suggested Saxon had escaped in a delivery van sometime in the early morning. The truth is, he didn't have a clue.

'This is the most possible scenario,' Rogers wrote in the report. 'The other alternative is he may have escaped through the visiting section. Although this has not been entirely dismissed, it would seem very unlikely as he would have had to pass through three manned posts.'

Four days later a more comprehensive report was produced.

'At this stage it is not known how inmate Ian Saxon executed his escape from the remand centre,' the report said. 'There are a number of theories that are being investigated by a joint operation consisting of the NSW Federal Police, and the National Crime Authority – code name: Operation Street. The popular belief is that Ian Saxon left the jail in the stores delivery van. This is supported by the fact that this vehicle left the institution between the hours of 10.56am and 11.14am on the day in question. This is confirmed by the entry made in the Vehicle Log Book.'

Not only was Saxon's escape a genuine mystery, it was also highly embarrassing. Before he disappeared, the former rock 'n' roll roadie was the jail's prized inmate and one of the most famous criminals in the NSW prison system. His tale had already captivated the country.

Police searched the Eastern Suburbs unit Ian Hall Saxon shared with his brother, but found nothing. Despite the police being informed that Saxon had imported a large quantity of hash, there was no incriminating evidence to prove that this man was the Mr Big of Australian drugs.

Then an officer on the scene picked up a crumpled piece of paper. He pulled back the creases, smoothing the note back to its original form. He almost fell over when the type became clear.

He was holding the clue that would end an illegal empire. The piece of paper was a receipt for a nearby storage unit containing the 'mother lode': $5.3 million in cash, three gold bars and 40 South African gold Krugerrand coins.

Saxon had his very own Aladdin's cave, thanks to the sale of 10 tonnes of hashish resin worth an estimated $77 million.

Ian Hall Saxon began his life in Auckland, New Zealand, as an aspiring musician. He loved everything rock 'n' roll and looked to be on the path to fulfilling his dream of becoming a star.

A singer and saxophone player, Saxon released a single in 1965 called 'I'm Getting Better'. He moved to Australia in 1968 with his band, Ian Saxon and the Sound, but they soon split in 1972. During his four years with the band, he met some key players in the music industry, whom he'd impressed with his intellect and knowledge of the road. Saxon ended up working for emerging music giant Frontier Touring as tour manager. He travelled the world, organising gigs and hanging out with rockstars.

It was these trips overseas that opened his eyes to the potential money on offer from drug dealing. He met people who had connections that could get him 'whatever he wanted'. His first drug bust came in 1977, when he was arrested in California for possession of cannabis. He only had a small amount of 'grass' and was let off with a fine. In 1980 he was jailed in Tahiti for importing 2 kilograms of cocaine. Saxon was well on the way to becoming Sydney's Mr Big in the drug business.

Saxon led a rockstar lifestyle of cash, women and fast cars during the early 90s, thanks to his involvement in an international drug syndicate that acted in the US, Pakistan and the United Arab Emirates. All that ended on 26 January 1990, when he entered Long Bay Jail. There, among the hard sandstone and cold steel, he was now Mr Not So Big.

Four years after his release from prison, Saxon was ready to talk about his experience in Long Bay – to reveal the horrors that forced him to escape.

'Long Bay was just bloody horrible,' Saxon said. 'I saw people killed; I saw the worst of everything. If anyone had to be in there for two years, let alone 17, it is just ludicrous. A fucking nightmare.'

Saxon was given the standard treatment when he was refused bail and sent to the Metropolitan Remand Centre at Long Bay. He was no longer a rockstar, not with his pants around his ankles and a prison guard threatening to shove a gloved hand up his arse. On the outside, he was infamous; a nation was intrigued. On the inside, he was a curiosity; his notoriety would only get him so far.

'What I was caught for was pretty big,' Saxon said. 'Yes, they called me Mr Big; I got all that shit. But I was no refined gentleman when I went in. I wasn't a white-collar type who was caught with his fingers in the till. I was into some big things and I knew what would happen if I got caught. My best friends were gangsters and they'd been in and out of prisons for years. It's not like I didn't know what I was in for.

'I didn't have a network when I went in, nothing like that, but when you get arrested for a crime of that nature you are a bit of a celebrity. But that fades very fast, let me tell you.

'I got the usual shit when I went in. They took everything away from me, stripped me naked and gave me the once-over. I think I was put in a two-out cell, at least initially. To be honest that wasn't a bad thing, as you find out about solitary later, but sure, it was still horrifying.'

Saxon would call the remand centre home for the next three years; not convicted but refused bail. His days in court became almost as horrible as his new home. Saxon doesn't speak highly of his lawyers. In fact everything that follows, at least in Saxon's mind, can be traced back to them.

'The lawyers were supposed to be my friends,' Saxon said. 'But they weren't. If we'd approached this whole thing right from the beginning, I should have gone in, quietly pleaded guilty and saved the state and everybody the great farce of taking the thing to trial. In all likelihood I would have gotten about ten years on the bottom. That would have been a fair sentence for what I'd done. If I had pleaded guilty, I would have served my time and I would have been out by 2000. For 11 months I was going to this fucking circus of a committal hearing full of people objecting to everything and anything.'

Saxon had had enough. So he tried to escape.

The details of Saxon's first bid for freedom have never been revealed. There had been speculation he'd tried to escape in 1990, but those rumours were unconfirmed. That is, until the NSW Crime Commission interviewed him in 1998.

'Now, coming back to this escape, this alleged escape in 1990, you deny, do you, that what you and these other two men were doing was in preparation for an attempted escape?' the Commission asked.

'Yes,' Saxon said. 'I do.'

He was further grilled.

'What's the truth?' Saxon continued. 'Well, the truth is I don't really want to discuss it. It's past history.'

But, at age 71 and enjoying his freedom, Saxon has finally come clean.

'I was caught trying to make an escape,' he admitted. 'From the oval at the back of the remand centre. I was caught with two other guys. I was going to go over the wall. We had made a grappling hook and knotted a rope out of sheets. A car was waiting for us on the other side.

'I attempted to escape in October 1990. I was caught. That is the truth of the matter.'

The reason for this, according to Saxon, was that he was sick and tired of his trial. He knew he was going to be found guilty, but he did not know when. He couldn't stand another day at Long Bay.

'The chance came up to escape,' Saxon said. 'And I took it, albeit unsuccessfully.'

And that's when prison life became harder, the failed attempt at freedom making life hell.

'Ron Woodham's storm troopers made my life unbearable,' Saxon said of the former boss of Corrective Services NSW. 'Because I'd tried to escape, he constantly harassed me, and his squad came after me almost every night. They would come in at 2am, quietly open my cell and get me naked in the hall with their German shepherd two inches away from my nuts. Three or four of them would go into my cell and trash it. I would go back in and all my sheets and clothing would be piled up on the floor, my toothpaste squeezed all over the wall. The dog would walk in and piss over everything. It was an absolute living hell.'

Saxon, once again, decided to escape. But this time he would bide his time. He vowed he would not fail.

'I just had to get out,' he said. 'But I knew I couldn't. Not yet. I had to lay low and make them think that I wasn't a risk. I had to wait until I was no longer a target.'

That opportunity finally came two years later. And this time there were no faults or failures, prison sirens or nut-sniffing dogs.

'When you lock a man up and leave him with nothing to do, except look around and think about how to get out of there, eventually he will get out,' said Saxon. 'I had nothing to lose and just went for it. I was just another criminal with nothing left to lose.'

Saxon began planning his next escape as soon as he was caught for his first.

'A few inmates and I conspired to exploit a flaw in the system that had been discovered by another prisoner. This prisoner had in fact been released some weeks prior to March, but even before this he was allowed outside the jail on certain occasions to perform certain duties.

'He noticed that every Tuesday morning the laundry would be collected from both wings at the remand centre. On most occasions, whichever officer was driving the laundry van was in the habit of driving further down the complex to the cafeteria, instead of taking laundry directly to the Metro-politan Remand Prison (MRP). The reason the officer would drive to the cafeteria was to pick up a bacon and egg roll.

He would then get out of the van and go into the cafeteria on his own, leaving him, the inmate, sitting in the van, otherwise unattended.

'The inmate told us that he believed he had found a flaw, which could enable an escape. At this stage we had developed a good rapport and he knew I was looking at a very serious sentence, so he asked me if I was interested in getting out by the way he'd discovered. I agreed.'

Saxon agreed to pay the fellow prisoner $40,000. The prisoner later claimed the amount was as much as $350,000. Saxon said the claim was not true.

On the morning of the planned escape, Saxon woke up at about 6am and dressed in his 'civilian clothes' – the same ones he used for court – which he had obtained from another prisoner who worked at the reception. Saxon most likely paid this prisoner too. He grabbed a clipboard, as a prop for later purposes, and sat on a sheet on the floor. He rolled himself into a ball: knees tucked into his chest, arms tightly gripping his bent legs. An inmate brought the four corners of the sheet together and knotted them, making a cotton escape hatch. Saxon, now disguised as dirty laundry, was hoisted onto a cart and wheeled to the laundry truck. After an hour or so, when the guard wasn't looking – presumably munching on bacon and egg – Saxon was lifted onto the truck. He would soon be free.

'I've heard all the rumours,' Saxon said. 'Like the one where I was helicoptered to freedom before leaving the country in a Learjet. But, unfortunately, it was all pretty basic – I went out in a laundry bag.'

Saxon was hauled off the truck by the inmate and unwrapped. Decked in his civilian clothes and holding the clipboard – 'looking official', as he later put it – he walked straight past the boom gate and onto the street. Saxon said several prison employees walking into work distracted the guard by the gate.

A car had been waiting for him, and 'Australia's most wanted man', who would soon have a record bounty of $250,000 on his head, was free.

'I had no idea that we would pull it off,' Saxon said. 'But we did. I didn't care if I was caught because I had had enough. But I wasn't. I was out.'

Saxon became an enigma – a code nobody could crack and a man nobody could catch. Some said he was in Asia, sitting on a beach with a bag of cash. Others said he was dead. But nobody knew where he was or how he had got out. Embarrassed officials applied the blowtorch, politicians promised rewards, police hunted, and the Crime Commission grilled. And slowly the Saxon enigma cracked.

With an enormous reward for his capture, and former friends giving him up, Saxon was found 750 days after his escape. With the help of the FBI, Saxon was handcuffed and thrown into a police van in San Diego, USA, on 22 April 1995. He was captured alongside Colombian drug lord Fabio Garcia, the father of 'Tap Dog' and Australian actor Adam Garcia. There was no escaping the mighty clutches of the FBI, and Saxon was deported to Australia, where he would stand trial for both his original drug-related charges plus a new one . . . escaping lawful custody.

But the Saxon saga was far from over. What he did next would lead to a hung jury, a lonely cell and a new beast threatening to bite his balls – the corruption watchdog, the Independent Commission Against Corruption (ICAC).

On 27 September 1995, Ian Hall Saxon pleaded not guilty to his escape charge. He refused to reveal why he was contesting the charge. What? they screamed. How could someone be forced from jail? There were so many questions but not one answer.

The mystery would last a year.

On 3 September 1996, Saxon's lawyer informed the Director of Public Prosecutions that Saxon 'was removed from the MRC against his will and taken to Newtown.'

Yes, that's right, Saxon was claiming he'd been kidnapped. Snatched up and smuggled out of Long Bay Jail, against his will. Who in their right mind would want to leave that place?

And once again Mr Big was big news.

In early 1997, Saxon was secretly moved to Maitland Jail to give evidence to the Crime Commission. Finally he would explain.

A robotic Saxon looked his inquisitors straight in the face and told them he'd been taken from his cell by prison guards. They took him in the dead of the night, whacked a bag on his head, and removed him from jail. Next thing he knew he was in a house and they were standing over him. The feared men of the Malabar Emergency Unit were demanding cash, the fortune they said he had stashed in the ground. Then they left him alone, probably went home to their wives for tea, and Saxon escaped.

The former rock 'n' roll man had a vivid recollection of the event. He spewed out intimate details of the house: no curtains, no furniture and a 'For Sale' sign in the front yard. The story was dramatic but plausible. So much so that only one member of the jury did not believe him when his trial was brought to court.

The hung jury forced a retrial, but the case was never heard. Suddenly Saxon claimed he was guilty, quietly copping two years for his escape. He was never prompted to explain how he'd got out or why he'd changed his plea after almost beating the charge.

So why did Saxon make up the story? And why did he then not stick to it?

'No one had any idea how I escaped. There were rumours here and there but no one had a clue. They had been bashing their heads together for a couple of years and I thought I would take advantage of that. Really, they had set themselves up for it. But eventually the gig was up. I wasn't going to get away with it again.'

Saxon went back to jail. And then he got stabbed.

Whack!

The right hook hit Saxon flush on the chin, the rock-hard knuckles sending a crack of lightning into his jaw and blackness to his brain.

Saxon was out; his legs gave way, his body thumped to the floor. When he eventually came to, he pulled himself up onto his knees.

Pop! Pop! Pop!

The shiv was jammed into him at an incredible speed.

'In 1998 I was stood over and stabbed three times,' Saxon said. 'There were fools who thought I still had money and they came after me. I didn't, of course, and the ridiculous thing about it was, even if I did still have money, I wasn't going to give it to them.

'These two young guys came at me in the morning, and one of them hit me on the chin. I was in the yard, and I went down on my knees and I felt whack, whack, whack. I thought I'd been kicked, but I hadn't – I'd been stabbed. Each time the blade hit bone and because of that they didn't pierce any vital functions. I guess that was a stroke of luck.'

Saxon reluctantly described the prison shiv that was rammed into his body; the attack having left him with three visibly red scars.

'They used what was the weapon of choice in prison,' Saxon said. 'Something that was easy to make, and easy to find.

'There used to be a little metal spindle, on the rollers, in the mop buckets in jail. They used to extract the spindle from the rollers and sharpen it down to a fine point. It looked like a spike – a steel spike. And that was what those two bastards used.'

Soon after the assault, Saxon was hauled before the ICAC to answer questions about his escape.

'There isn't much to talk about in prison,' said an inmate who asked not to be named. 'And that escape became a bit of a legend. Everyone had a story about it and claimed to know how he really got out. The common thread behind it all was that Saxon had paid. He was rich, and the guards don't mind a bribe. That's how we all reckon he did it.'

The ICAC swooped, dragging prisoners in. Three of them claimed to have information about payments Saxon made to guards. And so the investigation began. Saxon was moved into segregation and housed with former police and prized informers, amid fears he would be silenced by those he'd paid. But Saxon is adamant the only people he'd given money to were prisoners.

'When I finally buckled and went to the ICAC I told them the truth,' he said. 'But they didn't believe me. I'd gone so far down the track that they couldn't believe a word that came from my mouth.'

After a lengthy ordeal, the ICAC said they could find no proof of corruption and only a probable method of escape. They thought corruption was likely, but not certain.

So again plenty of questions, again no answers, and again Saxon disappeared . . .

'Could I please have Ian Hall Saxon's MIN (Master Index Number)?' the reporter asked as she called the prison. 'I'd like to send him a letter requesting a legal visit.'

The sound of the keyboard strokes went down the line. 'Mmmm,' came the reply following a brief silence. 'Sorry, we have no record of him.'

And then the line went dead.

Had Saxon been released? Was he dead? Or had he escaped again?

'No, I was in the Special Purposes Unit (SPU),' Saxon revealed. 'I didn't have a name in there; all I had was a number. People couldn't find me and I wasn't on records anywhere, so they'd call up and think that I'd vanished again. The only people I had contact with were my family, but that was rare and everything they sent in or I sent out was screened and sometimes not delivered.'

Saxon was alive but he didn't exist. Alone in his cell in the SPU he saw nobody, except for the occasional Dog.

'I should have never been there,' Saxon said. 'It's a place for Dogs and informants. The guy who was involved in my case, Mark Standen, he's probably still there. He was a Dog, but I wasn't. And that's what was so awful about it.

'They kept me in solitary confinement for two years. For two fucking years, and I didn't want protection or need it. I'm sure it was payback from a vengeful system. When they realised the media spotlight wasn't shining on me anymore, they went after me and made my life a living hell.'

Saxon claims he was left to rot in his cell. But he did the best he could, vowing not to be broken.

But the silence was deafening and the boredom numbed his brain. He spent most of the day in his cell, let out only for exercise, and he didn't talk to or see anyone, other than guards.

'I thought I was dealing with it all OK,' Saxon said. 'I told myself it wasn't so bad. I told myself I could spend some time on my own. But a couple of years into it, I had a stroke.'

By the time the convulsions racked his body, Saxon could barely raise the alarm. His body fast fading, he frantically dragged himself across the floor. With his last command from the captain's chair, Saxon smashed his hand on the emergency button. Help was on the way.

'But they didn't give me medical attention for a day,' Saxon said. 'I collapsed in my cell and hit the alarm button. I just got to the thing, I was that bad. They came in and I was a bit better, but still bad. They just told me if I didn't feel well in the morning to let them know. They said they'd call a doctor if I hadn't improved.'

Morning came and Saxon was the same.

'The doctor was horrified,' Saxon said. 'He took me down to the hospital and I was found to have had a stroke.

'Up until that point, I thought I was dealing with the confinement. After all, it was a comfortable cell and I didn't have to worry about being stabbed. But when they tried to get to the cause of my stroke, they could only bring it back to stress. And it was the stress of being treated like a fucking animal.'

The stroke was Saxon's ticket out of Long Bay and this one was stamped 'one way'.

'Thank goodness,' Saxon said. 'They moved me out of there, but not because they were being nice. After the stroke, the governor of the jail was scared I would die in his prison. He didn't want to take responsibility for my death and he moved me on. They sent me down to Cooma and I was in the Southern Highlands of New South Wales for about three years. It was better than Long Bay but still a place I'd rather not be. It was a less secure version of the Special Purpose Centre (SPC), full of police and informers. I thought I'd stay there but I got out. I was diagnosed with pancreatic cancer and moved back to Sydney.'

Saxon beat cancer, although he now has to have a camera ('stuck up the eye of my dick') once a year.

Saxon could see the finish line. Eligible for the pension, the one-time Mr Big was sent to Lithgow to see out his prison days. He would soon be out and this jail, about two hours from Long Bay, would be his final hell. But Saxon's remarkable prison story was not over yet. Before slipping out of prison, before leaving Australia and vanishing from the country for good, he would become a serial killer's friend.

'I shared some time with Ivan Milat,' Saxon said. 'And I really didn't mind him at all. He was friendly and we got on well. Whether or not he was guilty of all that stuff he was in for, well, I don't know. People tell me he was, but in jail he was just a perfect guy, someone who was great to be around. He was polite, not a big-noter, and he didn't cause any trouble.'

Textas and Laxatives

'The coppers got calls from people all over the shopping centre saying a man with a limp and a texta'd-on beard was acting suspiciously.'
Long Bay guard

The police officers followed the man across Bronte Lane and into Bondi Junction's Oxford Street Mall. The Saturday morning shoppers scurried past, oblivious to the limping man and the two police officers who were trailing him.

At 10.15am the men in blue made their move, confronting the man, who was all skin and bone, in Grosvenor Lane.

'Excuse me,' one of the officers said. 'We have reason to believe you are Robert Cole, an escaped prisoner from Long Bay Jail.'

The man shrugged. 'Why would you think that?' he asked.

The officer tried not to laugh. 'Your disguise for one thing,' he said.

Robert Cole was standing in the middle of the bustling street mall with texta scribbled all over his face. He had grabbed a thick permanent marker and made himself an instant beard.

'Mate, it was hilarious,' said a Long Bay prison guard, who saw Cole right after he was taken into custody. 'The coppers got calls from people all over the shopping centre saying a man with a limp and a texta'd-on beard was acting suspiciously. I don't think he was very hard to find.'

Though Cole's disguise was dumb, his escape was genius . . .

Robert Cole was an average small-time criminal. He was sent to Long Bay after being convicted for armed robbery and an attempt to abduct with intent to commit carnal knowledge. Cole was not tough. He knew he couldn't protect himself.

'I was there when he came in,' said a former prison guard who wished to remain unnamed. 'He was smack – do you know what that means? He wanted to go into protection because he was scared. He was a little fellow, maybe 5 feet 9 inches (1.73 metres), not the type of bloke who fancied himself in a blue.'

Cole also claimed to be mentally ill. He was imprisoned in 13 Wing in the Metropolitan Medical Transient Centre and housed alongside infamous Cobby killer Gary Murphy.

'For whatever reason, he ended up down in the hospital,' the guard continued. 'He seemed like a normal bloke and was a mad punter. He may have tricked them into thinking he was nuts.'

Cole also loved to walk.

'He was always doing laps around the A Ward yard,' the guard said. 'The prisoners are allowed a lot of time in the yard and Cole would always be out there, doing lap after lap after lap. He also enquired about getting some training tips and a fitness program. He was already skinny but seemed obsessed with his weight. The area he walked was about 60 metres by 30 metres, around a tennis court and then some grass. Cole would be there for most of the day, walking around in circles.'

Towards the end of 2005, Cole began to diet, progressively eating less and less. His weight plummeted until he was nothing but bone.

'I remember looking at him and saying, "God, you have lost some weight,"' said the guard. 'He hadn't been eating, sometimes days at a time. Everybody noticed. He was down to about 55 kilograms, probably. But no one suspected a thing. The patients in that ward are on a lot of medication, and some of them can make you get a gut. People thought he was just conscious of appearance, and doing all that he could to make sure he didn't get fat. No one could have guessed what he would do next.'

It was 6.50am on 18 January 2006 when the prison guard walked into Cole's cell. 'Wake up,' he said.

But Cole didn't move.

The guard shouted again. Nothing. Then he pulled back the sheet.

Cole wasn't there. Instead, his sheets and blankets were crumpled and his pillow stuffed, to make it look as though he was sleeping in his bed.

The guard scratched his head. *Where the fuck is he?* he thought.

'The door was shut,' recalled the guard. 'It had been locked all night. And nothing else seemed disturbed. The bars in the window were intact, no holes in the wall. He'd just vanished.'

The alarm was raised and the prison guards searched all the cells and the entire perimeter of the yard. But Cole was nowhere to be found.

'Soon they saw that some of the brickwork beside the bars of his window had been chipped away,' the guard said. 'It was an old hospital, that one, and at the old-style bars is an open brick window. He was able to chip away the brickwork that sloped away.'

And then it clicked.

'He had lost a lot of weight,' said a prison spokeswoman on the day of the escape. 'He is a very narrow person, so he squeezed his way through the gap in the brick wall.'

Cole's achievement was quickly dubbed the 'Dieting Escape'. Genius.

'He'd measured up the width of the gap and knew what weight he had to get down to,' a guard said. 'He'd been able to chip away enough before that night so that he was able to squeeze out the bars.'

But getting through the bars was only job part-done. He still had to avoid motion detectors and scale two fences.

'One of those fences is big,' the guard said. 'And I mean big. He picked the spot where there was no barbwire, and it was only a tiny part where the wire didn't go all the way around.'

Cole was over and out, in an ingenious escape that left Long Bay Jail officials red-faced. An investigation was launched and the attacks began.

'There are some serious questions that need to be answered,' said Shadow Minister for Justice Andrew Humpherson. 'What we have confirmed is there must have been some serious lapse of security, both human and technology. Either the electronic system failed, or whoever was on duty and supposed to be watching had not been there or had missed it. It is a major security failure.'

In truth, the escape can be blamed on prison policy . . . and a sleepy guard.

'That spot is not manned at night,' said a guard of the watchtowers in hospital prison. 'There are men in the towers at the MMTC, but they can't see that far. They have guards in the towers in the hospital during the day but not during the evening. It wouldn't have happened if they weren't trying to save money on guards.'

Still, the solo guard in the wing should have been more vigilant.

'On the night shift you go into the little office, and you're supposed to do checks every 15 minutes,' the guard continued. 'But obviously you go down there and have a bit of a snooze. The nurses do it, too.

'Even then, no one could have predicted Cole would have got through the bars. But he knew what he was doing and off he went. It was a massive effort. First, to be skinny enough to go through the window, and then to be strong enough to get over the fence.'

And as for the second part – escape via texta?

'Well, that was fucking dumb, but he was pretty clever in the way he got out of jail.'

Half a Hacksaw

'The yard is far too small and it's not possible to see out of it. It would make an enormous difference if it had a window. I miss very much seeing things like cars, roads, trees and flowers.'
Former Katingal prisoner Russell 'Mad-Dog' Cox

Long Bay prisoner Russell Cox surprised the guard.

'Left my shoes out in the yard, chief,' he fired, matter-of-fact, at PO Johnson. 'Can you buzz me through so I can get them?'

Bzzzzzert!

The gate slowly shuddered open after the guard approved his request by pushing a button.

Cox nodded before walking through.

PO Johnson did not know Cox was hiding a table tennis bat under his shirt.

Nor did he know Cox had used half a hacksaw blade to cut through the iron bars.

Or that Cox would be on the run for 11 years after he stuck the bat into a crack in the ten-foot wall, making a ledge to reach the bars he had cut with his hacksaw.

And PO Johnson certainly did not know that simply by having pushed that button he had just helped Cox become the first man to escape Australia's first inescapable prison.

The $1.5 million monstrosity was almost razed before it was completed.

Boom!

The bomb went off. Concrete and steel flew in all directions.

'Someone tried to blow it up before it was even finished,' said former Long Bay PO Dave Farrell. 'That's how controversial it was. Activists were already up in arms over what it would become and the amount of press and hype surrounding it was extraordinary. Sure the building got wrecked a bit, but that didn't stop them from building it. I remember watching the police escort the ready-mix concrete trucks in after that.'

'S Block' survived two bomb attacks while it was still in construction. The first caused considerable damage and the second would have destroyed the most controversial prison in Australian history before it had even been built if the bomb hadn't been defused and destroyed in time.

'The bombers were never found,' said a former guard who asked not to be named. 'We suspect it was one of the prisoner action groups because they'd all been carrying on about how inhumane this prison would be. They had a few radicals involved and it wouldn't have been hard for them to reach out to a crim with some expertise in the field of making things go bang.'

The nightmare of 'Katingal' – as S Block would later be called – began in 1968 when NSW Corrective Services Commissioner Walter McGeechan decided he needed to follow in the footsteps of the United Kingdom, Germany and the US and build Australia's first 'super max'.

'The worst inmates were all up in Grafton,' said a guard who worked with the former commissioner. 'That's where they had held the "tracs" (intractables) since 1943. But the riots in Bathurst and in Grafton had begun to expose prisoner bashings that had happened. The screws just laid it into them up there, and it was getting out into the public, so we needed to get on top of it and find another solution to stop these blokes from acting out.

'This class of prisoners was seriously bad. They were either deranged or old-school tough blokes who did not give a shit anymore. They were really hard, violent men. And there was nothing we could do to keep them from raising hell. The only way you could stop these crims was through violence because that was all they knew. In the end it became pretty obvious that the only solution was to segregate them away from everyone, including the guards.'

The Grafton Correctional Centre was later exposed by the Nagle Royal Commission (1976–1978) as a 'brutal regime' where 'the majority of guards, if not all, would have taken part in the illegal assaults on prisoners.'

There was little doubt McGeechan was aware the guards were 'routinely bashing' the inmates at Grafton before the Nagle Commission shed light on the rough treatment in 1978. And he would later admit one of the reasons for approving the new Long Bay prison was because of his dissatisfaction about the 'physical repression' in Grafton Jail. The other reason he gave for the secretive S Block project was that Grafton was too far away from Sydney. McGeechan said most prison guards were based in Sydney and it was unfair for them to move.

The justifications for the establishment of the $1.5 million jail that would 'potentially contain dangerous prisoners for the protection of the community and of prison officers in particular', as the commissioner wrote to the Department of Public Works between 1968 and 1972, were never satisfactorily explained. The prison could have been built to protect those inmates who could not shield themselves from danger by way of segregation. It could have been built to help rehabilitate the worst prisoners in New South Wales without Grafton-style abuse, instead using behavioural reformation through world-leading programs. Or it could have been built to keep such prisoners out of sight and out of mind by literally locking them away from the world. In truth ... it was all of the above.

S Block was renamed Katingal, a far less fearsome name, after prison official Ian Saunders consulted Sydney University professor of anthropology Adolphus Peter Elkin. The renowned scholar, who began his studies in Aboriginal culture in 1927, recommended the controversial prison be named Katingal. An Aboriginal word, Katingal means rigorous initiation undertaken by tribal Aborigines who have broken their laws. After this initiation, which involves separation from all social contact, the offenders are reunited with their tribes.

Katingal opened in October 1975 and was part of the Long Bay Prison Complex at Malabar. It was built on an old oval behind the hospital and next to the remand centre.

'My first impression of Katingal was bad,' said former Katingal prisoner Paul Simson. 'All we could see was cement and no windows. I was taken through an electronically opened door, which clanged loudly. I was placed in a cell on my own. The cell contained a cement bed with a mattress, a cement table, a steel toilet ... there were two fluorescent lights at the back of the cell with heavy glass in front of them. There was a spy hole in the back wall. Meals were passed in through a steel trap at the back of the cell. There was no work of any kind at Katingal. Whilst at Katingal, I suffered hallucinations and nervous spasms.'

The first two prisoners admitted into this new block were both rapists and murderers. Allan Baker and Kevin Crump were sent to Katingal for their own protection. They had raped and murdered a pregnant woman in 1973 and they would have been raped and murdered too had it not been for the strict protection provided by the NSW prison system. They would have been eaten alive, apt considering both prisoners were rumoured to also be cannibals.

Fred Harbecke was the first non-protection prisoner to be admitted to the jail. He was serving a life sentence and was deemed to be one of the most dangerous prisoners in New South Wales following two violent escape attempts. Next was Earl Heatley, a 'remorseless killer' and then armed robber Bernie Matthews. They would soon be joined by the 'worst one percent' of criminals in the state, which included Archie 'Mad Dog' McCafferty, Ray Denning, Warrick Jones, Marko Motric, Allan McDougall, Billy Baldry, Peter Schneidas and, of course, Russell Cox.

The prisoner was immediately disorientated.

'It all looks the same,' he said, looking at the white walls, glass and identical cells. He turned to stare at the other side of the room. Now he was completely confused. 'Is that a mirror or another five cells?'

There were only 40 cells in Katingal and they were exactly the same. They each measured 84 square feet (7.8 square metres). They had concrete beds and tables, and stainless steel toilets with drinking taps just inches from the bowl. They were all devoid of natural light and air.

And, on top of this, each cell had a little 'peep hole' at

the back for the guards to secretly watch the inmates' every move.

'Katingal was done in such a way that you didn't have to come in contact with the prisoners,' said former Long Bay governor Michael Vita. 'It was called the electronic zoo because everything was activated via a massive control panel. Cells, doors – everything – was opened with the press of a button.

'There were pathways and landings under the cells. The building was white and massive. There was zero natural sunlight in the building and the cell doors were solid iron with no bars. Each cell had a small window where the prisoner could look out but they could see very little. The crooks were locked up most of the time with their food delivered through a hatch in the door. And when they were out of their cells, they could not get to the prison officers because there was a void separating them from the guards.'

The new prisoner sat in his cell, still baffled. He looked through his tiny window and saw the electronic clock. This would eventually stop him from going mad, the changing digits the only way he could tell if it was day or night. He would only catch sight of the sky – and that is all he would see of the outside world because of the towering solid concrete walls – for an hour a day in one of the two exercise yards. He would spend most of his time locked away, and he would be accompanied by three guards on those few occasions he was let out.

Inmate Russell Cox spoke about the prison that was supposed to end the brutality of Grafton, before he helped close it. According to his statement made to the Nagle Commission:

> There are constant complaints about the air conditioning, which is the only source of oxygen outside of the exercise yard. Inside the cells the foam mattresses become wet with condensation. All the cells are supposedly ventilated by air seeping through the quarter-inch crack under the door and the stale air is sucked out through the suction device incorporated into the toilet. It is a dismal failure in practice. What gets me down is the lack of peace and quiet in here. There is a constant banging of the electronic doors and of people walking up and down the corridors. I find that I am losing my memory. I repeat myself, and I can't concentrate. I can't read and I become short tempered. The fact that I am dependent on the jail weighs me down too. Everything is at the whim of the officers and every effort of the individual is crushed. The only difference is what is on television. I am very depressed that I can't see any part of the outside world. In the cells and in the shop it is not possible to tell whether it is day or night. The yard is far too small and it is not possible to see out of it and it would make an enormous difference if it had a window. I miss very much seeing things like cars, roads, trees and flowers.

But Cox would soon be reunited with the things he missed, thanks to half a hacksaw blade . . .

*

Even the guards hated Katingal. The first men who worked in the jail found themselves getting lost. They would open the cell door, ready to take the prisoner to a visit, and find a completely different inmate sitting on the floor.

'Oh, wrong cell,' they would say.

So the floors were painted differently, colour-coded so that the officers could identify which of the eight sections they were in.

'The layout of that place was horrible,' said former PO Dave Farrell. 'It was very badly designed. The officers hated it. It was a bunker-type thing and the noises inside echoed around. When the prisoners played up, the officers had to wear industrial earmuffs. It was that loud. The physical construction of the landings was such that the prisoners were on one landing or above the offices. They used to piss in jars and throw it on them.

'It was a very difficult time for all right from the start. Katingal was certainly before its time but I think people didn't realise that putting up too many physical barriers was a bad thing. The more physical barriers you put between people the more problems you have. People just become more aggressive.'

Few felt sorry for the guards when the horrors endured by the prisoners were exposed.

'I think Katingal has affected me in the following ways: boredom, depression, humiliation, dulling of the mind,' a prisoner would tell the Commission during the Nagle investigation. 'The boredom is caused through the same routine every day, with no variation seven days a week. I have nothing to look forward to and am confined to the same small area with the same few prisoners, month after month. TV is inviting to pass the time but soon drives me to boredom.

'Depression is caused through the amount of food and the consequential hunger, having to ask for anything I wish, no matter how trivial, knowing that most requests will not be met, that reports are continually made on me, knowing that I am classified as being amongst the worst one percent of prisoners in the state when I believe I am not the person I am made out to be.

'Humiliation is caused through lack of privacy and regimentation. There is no individuality and I may as well be a piece of machinery. I am not given a chance to do anything creative.

'Dulling of the mind is caused through depression, humiliation and boredom. No fresh people or experience, no creative activity, being over-familiar with the attitude of the prison officers and knowing they have complete control of my existence.'

Inmates were handed a document when they arrived at the Malabar prison. The 'Information for Inmates' hinted at what was to come. The paper told them how they should behave, that their privileges would be determined by the program they were on. An incentive scheme in Katingal saw the 'best' prisoners on program three and the 'worst' on program one. Being good meant you got a wall draping, a bedspread, a daily newspaper and a parcel containing Minties and potato chips.

The bad were not allowed to watch TV, listen to the radio or read a paper. They would have zero contact with the outside world.

Regardless of the program they had achieved, prisoners in Katingal were given a limited amount of toilet paper to use each day, and their soap, toothpaste and razors were given to them before they showered and taken back from them as soon as they had finished.

Letters sent to or from the prisoners were heavily censored, visits could be denied, and education and work were limited. Housing an inmate in Katingal cost a staggering $86.35 a day.

Katingal prisoner Russell Cox was walking back to his cell, steeling himself for 21 hours of boredom, when he heard a faint groan come from behind one of the iron doors.

Mmmmmm . . .

A little louder this time.

Cox, who was accompanied by three guards, looked through the small window and into the cell. He jumped back when he saw the blood.

Prisoner Allan McDougall was spread on the floor, blood pooling on the concrete around his hands. The inmate had slashed his wrists. He could not take Katingal anymore.

'One prisoner from our yard eventually broke under the strain and was taken to Morriset,' Cox said. 'I'd known Allan McDougall for two years and he seemed quite normal and happy. In Katingal he gradually deteriorated until he refused to come out of his cell at all. One night in December in 1976, at about 10pm, when I was going into my cell, I looked into his and saw him on the floor with his wrists slashed.'

That's when Cox knew he had to get out of Katingal ... before he tried to kill himself too.

Cut. Cut. Cut.

The teeth of the broken blade sent a fine silver dust into the air as a 2-millimetre groove was ripped into the iron bar. Cox tried to be quiet, slowly pulling the hacksaw blade backwards and forwards. He did not want a guard walking into the yard and finding him 3 metres in the air. He sawed with his right hand as his left held onto the other bar. Prison officials would never know how he obtained the blade, though they had no doubt in their minds as to how he was able to do this so high up from the ground.

'He was an extremely strong man,' said Michael Vita. 'One of the fittest men I had ever seen. Cox was always exercising. He would constantly be doing push-ups, chin-ups and running, walking – whatever he could. I don't think it was too much of a surprise that he was able to hold himself up that high for long enough to cut through the bar. Not too many other prisoners would have been strong enough to do it. But Cox certainly was.'

Even fellow Katingal inmate Bernie Matthews spoke about Cox's fitness regime as that of Spartan quality, where Cox would exercise religiously and lived on a high protein diet.

Matthews also claimed to have known how Cox got the hacksaw blade and who he'd sourced it from. The armed robber and former Grafton 'trac' said the blade was given to him by another inmate who was also plotting an escape. Matthews said eight prisoners, originally from Maitland Jail on their way to Katingal – including Raymond Denning, Steve Shipley, Roy Pollitt, Dick Lynott, Terry Humphries, Freddy Owens and William Sutton – were planning to cut through their handcuffs with a hacksaw blade they had brought in, and they'd escape while being taken to court. So they gave Cox the blade to break through the bars as a back-up plan.

Despite Katingal's strict security, it was still possible to deliver clandestine messages out of the building. The high concentration of uric acid produced by the body overnight allowed prisoners to write messages using a crude quill dipped into urine, which soaked into the page and was invisible to the naked eye. The application of heat by the letter's recipient produced the hidden message. Within weeks, a hacksaw blade securely wrapped in carbon paper to avoid the metal detectors, was smuggled into Katingal. Russell Cox was given half the blade and he employed it to good effect, cutting the bars of the caged canopy over the exercise yard.

Cox shoved the table tennis bat into a crack in the wall at about 6.30pm on 4 November 1977 and used it to launch himself towards the bars. He didn't know if the guard was looking, but he didn't care. It was now or never.

The Maitland crew had left the day before but had not escaped. They'd been caught attempting to cut through the roof of the escort van and were being held in Maitland Jail while the failed escape was being investigated. Cox was forced to make a hasty decision. Would he wait for them to come back? Or would he go now? Cox didn't know when, or even if, the prisoners would return – and so he took his chances.

After hacking his way through the bars, the athletic prisoner pulled himself up and onto the canopy before scaling down the wall. Cox ran across the yard and threw himself against the next barrier, a 4.5-metre-high cyclone fence topped with barbwire.

'Stop!' screamed the screw who'd spotted the climbing Cox. But, realising just how far away the inmate was, he hopelessly yelled: *'Escaaappe!'*

Cox was over and out by the time the official alarm was raised. He had done the impossible. He had escaped from the inescapable. And then he vanished.

The largest manhunt in history was launched at the request of embarrassed prison officials. But they could not find 'Cox the Fox'. The criminals who hid him, fed him and helped him establish a new life were the only ones who knew of his secret location. And this is where the twist comes in – Cox might never have been found if it hadn't been for the inmate who became known as Raymond 'Dog' Denning, one of the Maitland crew who'd organised the blade that he'd used to escape. The infamous criminal never forgave Cox and gave him up in an elaborate hoax escape, according to former detective-sergeant Roger Rogerson, and could have played a big role in his recapture.

'They got Denning out and he used the same criminal network that helped Cox escape to help him,' Rogerson said. 'And he used them to find Cox and set him up.'

Cox was recaptured 11 years after his escape from Katingal, when he and Denning shot at police in Doncaster, Victoria, in 1988. The pair linked up shortly after Denning fled from the minimum-security wing of Goulburn Jail in the same year and they committed a series of armed robberies together before being arrested. There is no proof or previous suggestion that Denning had set up Cox, but it is without doubt that Denning became a police informer following the arrest, with the two-time escapee giving up every criminal he had information on in return for a reduced sentence. Denning died of a drug overdose in 1993 shortly after being released.

'It was a hotshot,' said Rogerson. 'He was killed for being a Dog.'

Katingal was closed eight months after Cox escaped. The Nagle Commission recommended the jail be shut in a scathing report delivered in 1978. Corrective Services ignored the recommendation at first, but eventually shut the prison after months of public outcry. Cox's escape helped close the house of horrors by casting a burning bright spotlight on the jail. The concrete bunker stood as a reminder of one of the greatest failings in Australian penal history until the building, subsequently used for storage and training, was finally demolished in 2006.

Not a tear was shed.

Australia's Most Forgettable Escape

'I could have used this to get out too, but I don't need to because I'm dead inside already.'
Convicted killer Anthony Lanigan

Anthony Lanigan walked up to PO Roy Foxwell and handed him a broken hacksaw blade.

'Here,' he said. 'I didn't mean to kill her and I'm no longer a risk. I'm done. I don't care and I'm happy to die here.'

Foxwell looked at the blade. The inmate had lied to Foxwell before, so seeing the contraband presented before him made the prison officer think that, this time, Lanigan was being for real.

'Cox?' he said.

Lanigan nodded. 'It was given to me after the escape. I could have used this to get out too, but I don't need to because I'm dead inside already.'

Foxwell was indirectly responsible for what would have been Australia's greatest escape had Lanigan not been caught.

'A fellow PO, Edgar Brown, came up to me one day and said, "Tony Lanigan wants to talk to you,"' Foxwell said. 'So I went to see him in Long Bay. Lanigan was in tears. He looked at me and said, "I didn't mean to kill that woman. I was just waving the gun and it went off."

'I said, "Tony, that is bullshit. You shot her in the back of the fucking head. Give me something if you want me to believe you."

'That's when he turned around and gave me the hacksaw blade. He told me that it was the one Cox used to escape from Katingal. I really don't know how he got it, but he was there with Cox and he was always highly respected by the other inmates. Lanigan gave it up to prove that he was genuine about finally being ready to toe the line.'

Digging in the Dark

'I like this one, it has a big hole.'
Long Bay inmate Michael Murphy

The prisoner walked through the yard. He was desperate to share some exciting news. Soon he was at the front of the line, the phone receiver in his hand and the number dialled.

Ring. Ring.

'Hello,' answered the woman.

'Hi,' Michael Murphy, one of five men who would go on to rape and murder Anita Cobby, replied. 'I'm getting out this weekend. I'll see you Sunday.'

Click.

But Murphy was wrong.

This is the untold story of how a call from an infamous killer prompted the search that would stop Lanigan from pulling off Australia's very own Shawshank Redemption-style escape that had been 18 months in the making.

Tony Lanigan approached PO Foxwell, asking for a transfer to Parramatta Jail.

'I can't stand it in here, boss,' professed the convicted killer. 'I still have nightmares about this place and I was comfortable at Parramatta. Do you reckon you could get me back there?'

Foxwell knew his claim was legitimate.

'I'd known Tony for some time,' Foxwell said. 'He'd always been polite and straight up and down with me.

He'd been at Parramatta for a while but was at Long Bay on a medical escort. He wanted to return to his old cell, so I rang Harry Duff, the governor at Parramatta, and told him that Lanigan wanted to go back there. Duffy said yes.'

But Foxwell's good rapport with the bearded crim did not stop the prison officer from being suspicious.

'I told Duff to be careful of Lanigan because he was a cunning bugger,' he added. 'He could be up to something.'

And so Lanigan returned to Parramatta, but not necessarily to his old cell – well, not straight away. Someone else was there: Michael Murphy.

'Lanigan was put elsewhere, but he was desperate to go back into the one he had before,' Foxwell explained.

So eager was Lanigan that he confronted Murphy and demanded he move to another cell.

'Why would I do that?' the killer said. 'I like this one, it has a big hole.'

Murphy had found the tunnel, now a year in the making and half-done. Lanigan eventually convinced him to relocate into another cell, but he was no longer getting out of jail on his own.

'Lanigan had been spooked by the move to Long Bay and he knew he was fast running out of time,' Foxwell said. 'So he didn't mind including Murphy because he needed all the help he could get. He told Murphy he could go with him if he helped him dig the last half.'

The Parramatta prison guards were suspicious of the cell change.

'Duff rang up and told me Lanigan had settled back into

his old cell,' Foxwell said. 'I asked him if he'd searched it, because Lanigan was smarter than he looked and he could have wanted the cell for a reason. He told me that it was thoroughly searched and nothing was found.'

The guards looked everywhere – well, everywhere but under the cupboard fixed to the wall.

Lanigan became nervous, the cell search making him paranoid. They did not find the tunnel, not this time, but what about next? He needed to escape. And now.

So he formed his very own chain gang, a murderous group of 'lifers', which consisted of killers, rapists and a paedophile. Lanigan identified those most desperate to get out of jail, and recruited five prisoners serving life sentences for their shocking crimes. Among those believed to be in his chain gang were rapist and murderer Bill Munday, armed robber Stephen Shipley (a fellow Katingal survivor) and Leslie Walker. Somehow – and still nobody knows how – Lanigan stole, was given, or cut six keys to his cell and gave them to Murphy, now his foreman and second-in-charge. Murphy distributed the keys to the other inmates and they went about digging the most extraordinary tunnel in Australian penal history.

'Lanigan would work the nightshift because it was his cell,' Foxwell said. 'He would tunnel all night, only having an hour or so of sleep. During the day, each of the six would go down for a couple of hours one at a time so they wouldn't be missed.

'They had seven separate shifts going in the tunnel. It was quite something.'

Following months of digging and clandestine trips into the ground, the job was almost done. Beginning with a 3-foot (1-metre) hole in the one wing cell floor, the tunnel ended just 30 centimetres below the turf of the linen company next door. Lanigan gathered the troops.

'We're breaking out Saturday night,' he said. 'We'll go down after lights out and break through in the dark. You'll be home for breakfast on Sunday.'

Murphy shook with excitement. This was the day he'd been dreaming about ever since he'd found the hole in the cupboard, a piece of furniture that featured only in that cell and not in any of the others. So he grabbed a fistful of silver coins, jammed them into his pocket and ran to the phone to share the news with his grandma.

'And the truth is they almost got out,' Foxwell said. 'I got word that something wasn't quite right at Parramatta, so I rang Duff and told him he should search the cells. He told me that it was funny I said that because he just got a phone call from Murphy's grandmother. She had rung the jail and asked what time he was being released and told Duff that he'd called to say he was getting out. Duffy thought, *What's all this about?* and checked out Murphy's cell.'

What the guards found were six keys to Lanigan's cell. Murphy quickly cracked, the prospect of being beaten by three prison guards making him sing.

'They were going to escape on the Saturday night and Murphy called home to say he was getting out,' Foxwell said. 'The idiot ruined it.'

The guards walked back into the cell they'd searched just months before. But this time they ripped off the cupboard, which was firmly fixed to the wall.

'There was the tunnel directly underneath,' Foxwell said. 'It was bloody amazing.'

The guards locked down the prison, and called for torches and police. They found the tunnel on the morning of Saturday 8 September 1979, the day of the scheduled escape.

Working for the Establishments Division, Foxwell was called in to investigate the attempted escape. He then went to see Lanigan, his old mate.

'He filled me in on all the details,' Foxwell, now retired, said. 'He told me everything. Lanigan reckons they were digging for 18 months all up. He did most of it, but brought the rest in at the end. They used everything and anything to dig – screwdrivers, knives, a shovel they pinched from the maintenance shop. They improvised and used whatever they could. They even knocked off wood from the stores to make support beams, electric lights and extension cords. They took bits and pieces from all over the jail.

'All the flooring in Parramatta Jail was sandstone, same as any old building in those days. It was soft enough for him to get through. And once he was in, he didn't have to dig the whole way, because there were tunnels in the foundations.

But still he had to get through three or four walls, and over a moat before getting under the main wall.

'The tunnel was almost finished and they would've come out at the Parramatta Linen Service, which we owned and operated. Crims worked there and it was quite secure, but they would've been able to get out. No doubt about it.'

Tony Lanigan was sent back to Long Bay Jail after he was given another five years for the attempted escape. And, once again, he walked up to PO Foxwell.

'I'm screwed, Mr Foxwell,' Lanigan admitted. 'That has destroyed me. You won't have any trouble from me again. It's just shattered me. I really thought I could do it and I came so close.'

Foxwell didn't believe him, not until he produced the half hacksaw blade.

And Lanigan stuck to his word and never caused trouble. A shadow of his former self, he quietly grew old.

'I saw him later on in Grafton,' Foxwell said. 'He pretended he was mad. He used to dance around with these funny steps. He was totally in La La land. The psychiatrist said he was gone. They said it was because of the guilt of murdering the woman that had done it to him.'

Lanigan always claimed his second murder was an accident. After being released in 1977 for killing a man during a robbery in 1969, Lanigan shot dead Narelle Grogan, 33 days after leaving jail, as he attempted to rob the Cronulla home of her opal-dealing father, Jack Anderson.

'Lanigan was in tears when he came back in for that,' Foxwell said. 'He told me he didn't mean to kill the woman.

He said he'd ordered them to the floor after unlocking the safe and he was just waving the gun around and it went off. Either way, the innocent girl was shot in the back of the head.'

Lanigan might have never have been caught for the murder had it not been for an informer. Former senior detective-sergeant Roger Rogerson said he arrested Lanigan after a Long Bay inmate passed on the details.

'It was Bobby Chapman,' Rogerson said. 'He was desperate to get out on bail. I told him he had to give me something, but it had better be super good. He went and spoke to Neddy Smith and he gave him the information. Bobby came back and said he had never Dogged in his life but he would tell me who murdered that girl at Cronulla. He said it was Lanigan and that he had gone into the opal dealer's house to rob him and things went wrong.'

Then in 1995, 16 years after his failed bid for freedom, Lanigan finally escaped. There was no digging this time, no tunnels or trenches, no cohorts and their phone calls. Lanigan, now 47 and a minimum-security prisoner, simply turned his back on the Long Bay farm, a place where low-risk inmates worked, and walked through a hole in the fence. A search was launched but he was never found.

'He was tending to the growing plants, and he just disappeared,' Foxwell said. 'He was heading out towards Prince Henry Hospital on the far side. There have been no sightings of him and no one ever found his body, not even one sign. Some people said that he may have been so guilty that he jumped into the ocean, which wasn't far away. They said he could've chucked himself off the rocks.

'Lanigan had strong connections with the Painters and Dockers gang in Melbourne, and they could've arranged something for him. But in those days no one was visiting him or writing to him, which makes it highly unlikely that he had any help.

'Sometimes I imagine him sitting in a cabin somewhere, maybe by a fire, saying, "I finally fooled you, Roy."'

Unofficially, Lanigan is considered dead. Two years earlier, the man once desperate to escape had sabotaged his parole because he was so scared of being released. About to be freed with his sentence to expire, he absconded from work release before handing himself in the next day. He got an extra two years for the 'escape' and was due to be released again in 1995, when he disappeared – for good.

As for Michael Murphy, he escaped from Silverwater Jail in 1985, after also being given an extended sentence for his role in the escape. But he was back behind bars the following year after being arrested for the rape and murder of Anita Cobby with his brothers, Les and Gary, John Travers and Michael Murdoch.

16

FAILING

Not all escapes are successful, no matter how clever or original they are. Sometimes the most brilliant bids for freedom are foiled by complex investigations and crafty cunning. But most of the time, it's just dumb luck.

Let's take a look at Long Bay's Best of the Busted.

Banging Boots

'He'd come up with a pretty ingenious plan to escape.'
Long Bay guard

The guard at reception placed the jacket, the shirt and the tie on the counter.

The inmate looked at him. 'What about me shoes?' he asked.

'Yeah, right. I forgot about them,' said the guard. He picked up a pair of black boots from the locker and brought them to the prisoner. 'Here they are,' he said, slapping the soles of the boots together before putting them on the counter.

The inmate dived to the floor.

'What the hell are you doing?' said the guard, looking down at the prisoner, who was crouched with his hands over his head.

Eric Heuston, the inmate picking up his clothes for a morning court appearance, wiped the dumb look from his face and picked himself up from the ground.

'Jeez, chief,' he said. 'I thought you were going to throw them at me.'

But Heuston didn't think his boots were about to be thrown from the air. He thought they were going to explode . . .

Heuston went back to his cell. He dumped his clothes on the end of the bed and sat for a while, wondering if his plan would work.

So far so good, he thought.

He held a boot in each hand; his right was holding a bomb, his left a detonator.

'Eric had his clothes brought in by a friend before his court appearance,' said a former guard. 'Part of the normal jail process is that you pick up your civilian clothes the night before your court appearance. The crims would shower

278

before they went to bed and get up early and change so that they'd be ready for their escort.'

But Heuston was not planning on getting on a bus in the morning. He was going to get out tonight.

'He'd come up with a pretty ingenious plan to escape,' the guard said. 'He'd got his friends to make some special boots for him. The big chunky heels were hollowed out, and gelignite was put in one and a detonator in the other.'

With his 'banging boots', Heuston was ready to go. He walked out of his cell, across the landing and down the stairs to ground floor. He walked right up to the end of the remand centre, to the wall made of glass brick. Heuston assumed it was the weakest point of the building and was now ready to blast his way out. Taking the boot that held the explosive, he placed it at the bottom of the wall. Grabbing the other, he made his way down the hall until he was close enough to detonate the bomb, but far enough not to explode himself. He took one more look at the wall to make sure nobody was in harm's way then –

Boom!

The shoe exploded. Glass, leather and wood flew into the air. The noise shattered the evening silence and the inmates roared. The smoke slowly cleared and Heuston was primed for his getaway. He was thinking about the snipers in the towers as he ran towards the smashed wall. Well, at least he thought it was smashed . . .

'The blast was big,' the guard said. 'It made a hell of a noise and a huge mess, but it wasn't powerful enough to blast through completely.'

So Heuston was left standing there, detonator in hand and nowhere to go. He ended up in court the next morning, presumably without shoes, and would have to go back again soon to face another charge – attempted escape.

Cutting Keys

'You can never underestimate how crafty an inmate can be.'
Former PO Roy Foxwell

The prisoner thought he was a genius. The wood stolen from the workshop, the copper torn from a gutter and the lead chipped from the Long Bay boiler was about to get him, and whoever had the money, out. Yep, he was fucking Houdini. The best bit was they wouldn't – *they couldn't* – suspect a thing. How could they? The prison had just upgraded to a new state-of-the-art key. No one could cut a Lockwood.

Nobody except him.

'The old handcuff key used to be like a hairpin,' said former PO Foxwell. 'It was just a round, straight bit of metal with a notch on the end. The crims could pick them faster than you can open them with the key. All the shifty buggers would escape as soon as they were taken off to a court appearance or moved from jail to jail. They would pick the lock, remove the handcuffs and bolt from the van.'

Thanks to the new Saf-lok handcuffs and keys introduced

to the jail, picked locks, kicked out windows and prisoner absenteeism from court would be a thing of the past. Or so the authorities thought.

'It was a smaller version of a regular Lockwood key, the type you would see today,' said Foxwell. 'And it was supposed to stop all the escort escapes. But you can never underestimate how crafty an inmate can be. They sit there all day thinking about getting out, and they often do what we reckon is impossible.'

Jingle!

The prisoner jumped to attention – this was the noise he'd been waiting to hear. The guard had pulled the keys from his belt, ready to open the gate. The inmate walked towards him and stopped when he was close enough to focus on the small key, which swung and sung as it slapped against other metal, a chorus line of copper dancing on the heavy chain.

The inmate wasn't interested in the big one being turned into the lock by the guard. No, he was staring at the new, tiny one – the one that could get him out.

Width, breadth and height of each metal tooth stored in his head, he went back to his cell and pulled out the wood and the lead. The wood pushed and pressed the soft lead, chipped and cut. Soon he had a mirror image mould.

Later, when all was quiet, he broke the plastic covering the powerpoint and reefed the wire from the wall. He put the razor, which he'd pulled out earlier from his plastic shaver, on the floor and sat the copper on top of the steel. The twin cable, now separated, turned the razor into a hotplate when the electrical current met in the middle after being jammed into either end. The copper sparked and spat before turning into ooze, the molten metal pouring into the mould.

When the inmate woke up the next morning, he slapped the mould against the cell floor, releasing the newly forged handcuff key on the ground.

In total, he had made and sold six. Soon he would escape, and so would the others, if the guard hadn't discovered the forged key he had stuck in his shaving brush.

'We found it,' said Foxwell. 'The key, the mould – everything. We couldn't believe it because it was only months after the new keys and locks had been introduced. I took the gear straight down to Maroubra police station so I could warn the police. If the inmates were making copies inside, God knows what they were doing outside.'

Foxwell was the investigating prison officer. He rightfully suspected the mould had produced more than the one key they had found.

'I eventually got this bloke's confidence,' he continued. 'I pressed him and he told me he'd made six keys. He'd kept the original for himself and passed on another five. At first he wouldn't tell me who they went to and where they were, but I eventually got it out of him.'

Stunningly, the keys had travelled all over the state.

'There was one at a little prison on Milson Island,' Foxwell said. 'He told me I would find it in the edging of a cardboard box that contained a stereo player inside. I went up there and, sure enough, I found it exactly where he said it would be. There was another hidden in a brick at Long Bay. We ended up getting them all – except for one.'

Foxwell knew who had it. But he didn't know where he was hiding it.

'The crim who had it had just had a son,' Foxwell said. 'He was absolutely mad about his boy, and the visits were the only thing that got him through the rest of the week in jail. I found this out and called him into my office. I'd faked a letter from the Commissioner, forged the signature and everything, saying that if he didn't give me the key he would be shipped off to Grafton the very next day. I told him he needed to give me the key or he'd be on a bus and on his way.'

The inmate was not fazed. He looked straight at Foxwell. 'So what?' he said.

Foxwell smiled. 'Well, you won't get to see your family. It's a long way from here.'

The inmate laughed. 'My missus will move straight there. Do your best, chief. I'm not giving up shit.'

Foxwell had counted on this response. 'Then we'll wait until she settles right on down, finds a house, and maybe even a job, before we move you to Maitland. And when she does that all over again there, we'll move you to Bathurst.'

The inmate no longer looked sure.

'You have two choices,' Foxwell continued. 'Be here in an hour with the key or with a packed bag. Because if you don't have the key to me by then, the bus heading to Grafton will be waiting for you.'

The inmate walked out. He returned 40 minutes later. 'I have nothing further to say,' he said, turning his back and leaving as fast as he'd arrived.

'Well, where's your bag?' Foxwell screamed.

The prisoner turned again, winking as he nodded towards the floor.

'Sure enough it was there,' Foxwell said. 'The key was on the floor.'

Foxwell grinned before waving the inmate out. He had every key now. He had just foiled six escapes.

Trapped Rats

'There were plenty of diggers in Long Bay, and the way you would deal with them was to send them up a floor. If you found a tunneller, or you suspected one, you would just put them in the top landing. At least, if they had a desire to dig, you would find them in the cell below.'
Former PO Dave 'Emu' Farrell

'I can't sleep,' whined the prisoner. 'The chewing, the banging, the clawing . . . It's right under my bloody cell! It's driving me mad. These rats must be as big as dogs.'

The guard who was working the night shift in the remand centre nodded. He walked towards his colleague. 'Fucking rats again,' he said.

'I've been hearing them too. We better get maintenance to go down with some traps.'

So down went the maintenance man . . .

'Dog-sized rats, my arse,' fumed the maintenance man, his torch cutting through dark and dirt. He'd brought the traps – *his biggest traps* – and poisoned pellets.

'Here, Lassie,' he joked, knowing he had more chance of finding Scooby Dooby Doo than a rat, whether it be the size of a pitbull or a pug.

Crack!

He jumped, his torchlight slicing through the dungeon-like dark.

The trap he'd laid last week sprung, the unhinged metal missing his foot by a millimetre, slapping cheese and wood instead of flesh and bone.

'Rats!' he fumed again, much louder this time. He kicked at the deactivated trap, then stumbled on something that brought him crashing to the ground.

Thud!

Pushing himself up, he took his flashlight, pointed it at his feet and saw the electrical cord.

'He found an extension cord that led to a light,' said a guard. 'And then next to the light he found a shovel. And next to the shovel he found a crowbar. And then he found the big hole in the roof.'

The maintenance man rushed from the dark and towards the guard. 'We don't have a rat,' he said. 'We have a runner!'

The guard needed no further explanation. 'Lock down!' he screamed.

The prison officers, armed with torches, headed underneath the remand centre and uncovered the digging equipment. They didn't have to do much to find out who had been digging. All they had to do was follow the tunnel.

Crack!

Metal slammed against concrete as the cell door was thrown open. Jerry O'Holia, an inmate of African descent known for always carrying a shiv, jumped from his bed.

'What is the meaning of this?' he asked.

Tap. Tap.

'Yep,' yelled the guard standing in the prisoner's cell. 'Clear.'

The guard smashed the tiles with his sledgehammer.

'There was a huge hole right at the back of his toilet,' said the guard. 'He had dug all the way to the bottom landing and underneath the wing, and all he had left to go was the external wall.

'You could see how this bloke got the gear to do it because he worked in maintenance. He had the necessary tools to pull apart his toilet and then the walls and the floor. He did it at night because no one else was around.

'O'Holia was absolutely shattered when his tunnel got found. He thought he was going to get out. And maybe he was even more shattered because of the way he got caught. He was going down there every night, God knows how long he was at it. And the thing that brought him undone was rats.'

According to former guard Paul Rush, O'Holia was a mischievous prisoner who was always up to no good. He was also a loner, which was probably why no one knew about the tunnel before the maintenance man stumbled across all his hard work.

'He was a funny bloke, that one,' said Rush. 'Not sure what he was in prison for, but while he was there he was into everything and anything. He was always hanging around the inmates that ran his jail and he was in the middle of everything. Whether he was running, setting up a deal, or dealing, he was involved in something. He ended up getting the shit kicked out of him on a couple of occasions by some Maori enforcers. But no one took him lightly because he was a big, fit bloke who always had a shank.'

The guards scratched their heads. *What do we do with this one?* they thought.

This digger was already on the first floor.

'There were plenty of diggers in Long Bay,' said former guard Dave Farrell. 'And the way you would deal with them was to send them up a floor. If you found a tunneller, or you suspected they were one, you'd put them in the top landing. At least if I had a desire to dig, you would find them in the cell below.'

The Long Bay walls and floors were like sirens to the shipwrecked.

'There were always plenty of tunnels about,' said Farrell. 'The floor out there was sandy soft and it was quite easy to get through. Inmates could use anything to have a go and they tunnelled everywhere.'

Sure, digging was easy, but they were all on a hole to nowhere.

'They were wasting their time because like Parramatta Jail, there were no structures underneath that could mini- mise digging. They were all separate jails and the only place you would come out was in the yard of another jail. Not that it stopped them.

'We busted a heap of them the late 70s. I reckon we had at least five attempts in 3 Wing. There was a boiler beside that jail and some crims thought they could get into it and out that way. Maybe they could have? But we found the tunnels before they had a chance.'

Infamous Sydney criminal Jockey Smith – a hard nut despite his name – was one of the many who tried. But like the rest, he failed. Smith's reputation and status among the criminals gave him access to the unimaginable.

'He built a tunnel all the way under the walls,' said former inmate John Elias. 'I could hear the jackhammer. He was making noise every day and no one would dare say a word. He turned up the volume on all the TVs and radios, and whacked away. He started from behind his sink and got a tunnel that went all the way to the wall. He probably would've been the bloke who got the closest to getting out because he'd bought – or someone had given him – the plans to the jail.'

A veteran Long Bay guard knows of at least two other genuine tunnel attempts. He still works at the prison, and has been with NSW Corrective Services for over 30 years.

'In the Metropolitan Remand Prison (MRP) they found a massive tunnel that led from the activities room all the way to the boiler house,' said the guard. 'That escape was foiled last-minute, like all the rest. To be honest, we caught most of them out of sheer dumb luck. And if we didn't stumble across the tunnels, it would be because someone who knew about it would get nervous and Dog. Many years ago in the Central Industrial Prison (CIP), they had another one that went all the way out to the external wall. Needless to say, that was also foiled.

'The one next door in the MRP was better. It was during the early 80s, and they were caught just before they got out. The tunnel would have been 40 or 50 feet and that's a bloody long way.'

Rush revealed that the biggest of all the Long Bay escape tunnels was quickly covered up, the men at the top quickly sending in cement trucks to fill a very embarrassing and large hole.

'In 1991 we found a huge tunnel in the Reception and Induction Prison (RIP), as it was called at the time,' Rush said. 'It was the most hardcore jail in Sydney during the early 90s. There were four or five inmates involved and it almost led to a mass escape. But the incident was hushed up quickly and quietly, the trucks coming in and filling it all with concrete.

'The tunnel started under the activity centre in the RIP, which is where the sex offenders unit currently is. The inmates involved worked in the maintenance department, where they not only had access to relevant machinery, but also to the site they needed to get rid of the huge amounts of dirt they were pulling out, which was the industrial dump area. Without this area, they would've had nowhere to get rid of all the dirt and they wouldn't have been able to dig the tunnel. Like most of these escape attempts, they were caught only weeks before they would've been able to get out.'

17

GANGING

'This was just a statement. There was no reason for it, other than for the new mob to tell the rest of them that they were here.'
Former NSW Corrective Services Intelligence Officer and Long Bay PO Paul Rush

The four giants, all tattoos and muscle, convinced the guard to open the gate.

'Yeah, bro, we have to go do that job for the chief,' said one of the men.

Errrrrrrk!

The gate opened and the 500-kilo four-man train of destruction steamed through the yard and into the wing.

'There he is,' one whispered. 'That's the bloke we have to get.'

The men dumped the steam for stealth and became four beastly ballerinas tiptoeing towards his cell.

He never saw it coming.

Whack!

The man stayed on his feet. But he was stunned.

Uffff! Crack!

He was too wounded to retaliate; the next blow went smashing into his body, the one after that into his head. He was done. The victim could have stood a chance against the four – he was just as tough and as big – but the king hit had denied him a fighting chance.

Thud!

Finally he went to ground. And that's when the posse really went to town.

'The belting he got was just vicious,' said former Long Bay guard and NSW Corrective Services Intelligence Officer Paul Rush. 'He ended up in hospital with ruptured kidneys, a bruised liver and many broken bones. They were just stomping the shit out of him by the time we got in.'

This was the start of a famous feud that would see blood spilt on the streets. The man, now under heavy guard in hospital, was the sergeant-at-arms of the world-famous Hell's Angels. And that is exactly why the four men belted him until he was black and blue, bloody and broke.

'This started a massive fight between the two gangs,' said Rush. 'And it's still going on. There was always an unwritten law in jail that anyone of seniority in an MCG (motorcycle gang) was not to be touched. But Michael and Sam Ibrahim didn't care about the rules. They left the Nomads and created their own MCG called Notorious, deciding that they were going to do what they wanted.

'They formed an MCG, even though it wasn't officially recognised as an MCG. They flew their colours in jail and their members were all Lebanese and Polynesian. They were intent on stirring up the establishment.

'Then the Hell's Angels sergeant-at-arms came into Long Bay. He was a very big, tough man, and by law of the jungle he should not have been touched. But on this occasion, the new MCG didn't want to abide by rules set by other MCGs. They had their own charter and no agreements with anyone else.

'So four of them were sent to bash the Hell's Angels sergeant-at-arms. They managed to talk their way into the wing he was being held in. They snuck in and, boy, did they get him good. We were there 45 seconds after the alarm was raised, but it was too late. The four guys were booting into him on the ground when we got there. These weren't little boys that got him either. One of them was an ex-Tongan heavyweight boxer, who I believe fought in the Commonwealth Games.'

Until this moment, all gang fights were almost exclusively over who controlled the prison's drug trade.

'This was just a statement,' Rush said of the attack on the Hell's Angels member. 'There was no reason for it, other than for the new mob to tell the rest of them that they were here.'

And then suddenly they were all fighting each other.

'The Lebanese were hitting Lebanese,' said a guard. 'The Polynesians were hitting Polynesians, and the Anglos . . . well, they were still being hit by everyone.'

In an instant, those who were once allies became enemies and those who were once enemies became allies.

'In 2003, the entire gang culture was turned on its head,' said Rush. 'Before then the gangs all operated by race. They were what we called "jail-developed" gangs. They were based on culture and ethnic background. The Kooris would stick together and go up against the Asians or the Polynesians. And then you would have the Lebanese, who were always the most powerful, going up against anyone and everyone. They were the prison gangs.

'You also had your outside influences – gangs that are called the High Density Gangs (HDGs). HDGs operate outside of jail, and historically never have much influence in prison. So, for example, a Lebanese inmate who was in the Nomads on the outside would enter jail and become part of a Lebanese gang that would include a number of Lebanese men from rival MCGs. They would mix in jail and forget whatever their HDG differences were on the outside.

'It was always racially based, no matter what your affiliation was on the outside. When you came to jail you stuck to your culture.'

That age-old system changed in 2003 when the outlaw motorcycle gangs decided they wanted no more.

'They rewrote their charters and made a statement to their members, saying anyone who went to jail must stick to their own gang,' said Rush. 'And that's predominantly what the gangs are now. The same gangs that operate outside run the jails. Yes, you still have the Asian gangs and things like that, but if you're in a gang on the outside, then you cannot join another gang in jail. And we're not just talking MCGs. It extends to gangs like the Syrian Kings and Brothers for Life.'

This declaration saw Long Bay become a battlefield.

'There were a lot of problems during the transition period,' said Rush. 'We had a stable environment, and suddenly those who previously held the power are fighting each other. We went from having Lebs running the jail to the Nomads taking control. It was a brutal time.'

But before the future came the past . . .

The inmate stood in the yard. He was old, hard and had a reputation, both inside and out. In the 1990s that was usually enough. This Sydney standover man did not need to be in a gang to survive. But he had to be on the lookout all the same.

The sun belted down on the yard, the concrete unusually warm for this winter's day. He was ribbing his mate about the football when the Polynesian prisoner grabbed him.

'Unc,' he said, softly and quickly. 'Shit's about to go down. You blokes should get out of here. Go to the corner. It has nothing to do with you, but you could get hurt.'

Respect afforded this non-gang-affiliated white fella a warning.

'A Polynesian leader called Moses was given an absolute flogging down in Goulburn during the days of the killing fields,' said that very same inmate, now out of jail. 'The place was a nightmare and they had to segregate the races into wings. The Lebs had somehow gotten to Moses and they bashed the shit out of him. It had nothing to do with Long Bay.'

But it soon would.

'I was standing in the yard, talking about football, when this big Fijian kid came over,' the inmate continued. 'He was a huge bloke, very fit and solid, but also very polite. I always found the Polynesians to be respectful when it came to their elders. This guy, and most of them, would call me "Unc". So this bloke told us they'd got Moses in Goulburn and they'd been sent the word to put it in here. He walked off and we retreated to the corner of the yard.'

Ahhhhh!

The Lebanese man screamed as the shiv was jammed into his back.

Nnnngggh!

The next one went in before he even had a chance to hit the ground. And then it was on.

'The Lebs were getting stabbed left, right and centre,' said the former inmate, who was watching on from a safe distance. 'All of a sudden the Islanders were holding shivs and they were jamming it into any Lebo they could find. There was a king hit and it was on. There were 40 or 50 going at it – it was fucking brutal. They were dropping like flies and then the squad came in and fired the tear gas before bashing everyone. It happened in 10 Wing and it was the worst gang fight I ever saw. In the end they carried about five or six out on stretchers. Most of them went to hospital, but there were at least five who never came back.'

The Long Bay gangs were always vicious, and if you weren't in one, you'd be in a bad position.

'There were Lebo gangs, Indigenous gangs, Islander gangs and Asian gangs,' said former inmate John Elias. 'They stood over the weak for money. If you weren't in a gang you were fucked. And it was the poor Anglo-Saxons who were fucked. They were always the minority in jail, and they'd come in for, say, stealing a car in Campbelltown and they wouldn't know anybody. The only white blokes who were sweet were those who came in with a reputation. The others would be targeted straight away. They would be stood over and made to be shit-kickers for whatever gang got to them first. They'd be forced to smuggle drugs into the jail up their arses and other dirty jobs like that. It made me sick, to be honest. The Asian gangs were the quietest. They all stood in a circle in the yard and would never turn their backs on anyone for a moment.'

Former PO Turner agreed the young white offenders were the most vulnerable in jail.

'So if you put all 150 prisoners in the yard at the same time, you'll see the gangs quite clearly,' he said. 'You'll have ten different groups that are all racially divided. Then you'd see some walking around alone and you'd know they were the targets. They were mostly Anglo guys, and they'd have their shoes stolen in a second. If you're on your own and you have possessions, someone will just take them off you. Shoes, socks, hats, anything that isn't prison issue will go. They'll bash you if you don't hand over whatever they want from you. If you stand up to them, you might earn a little bit of respect, but you'll also cop a hiding every time they come up to you. You have to affiliate yourself with somebody.'

The most superior gang in the wing managed all the contraband.

'They're the ones doing the deals,' said Turner. 'It's a lucrative trade and the strongest gang controls everything. All gang-related problems are over drugs, with one group trying to bring down the other for control of the wing. And in Long Bay the power shifts from day to day. Five Lebanese prisoners might be admitted to the jail and all of a sudden they have the numbers. You also have circumstances where a single bloke will be sent in to fight a group of five or six. That bloke would end up being belted, but he would have won the wing for his gang because the others would be sent to other jails. With the five or six of them gone, his gang would have the numbers.'

The emergence of high density gangs saw an unprecedented spike in gang violence. As a result, this new wave of in-house terror and brutality saw the rise of the first Australian prison gang unit.

'I was one of the intelligence officers,' said Rush. 'In the first 18 months we responded to a dozen or so major incidents around the state as the HDGs infiltrated the jails. The highly specialised gang unit was formed in 2003 to deal with the problem. We studied and monitored the gangs and tried to prevent the violence, and we also reacted to it when it happened.'

The information gathered by the unit was stunning. They learned inmates were operating HDGs from within prison. In 2006 they joined forces with the NSW Police, working alongside crime squads like MEOC (Middle Eastern Organised Command).

'We identified gang members from inside jail as well as gang-affiliated members,' Rush explained. 'Everything we uncovered we passed on to the police and it was one of their best sources of intel.'

Surprisingly, legal listening devices obtained most of the information. Rush estimates there were at least 100 listening devices secretly recording the conversations of prisoners in each jail in New South Wales.

'They were put in by the NSW Police under statutory law,' Rush adds. 'I can assure you now that every high-profile inmate in a NSW jail will have a listening device somewhere in their cell.'

Mobile phones were first smuggled into prison in 2001 and became an extremely dangerous contraband. It has been alleged prisoners have operated criminal empires from within jail by using an illegal phone, although PO Rush believes otherwise.

'Mobile phones came into the scene in about 2001,' Rush said. 'That's when they were finally small enough to be smuggled in. Mobiles are always a security issue, but I don't think they're the major problem they've been made out to be. Most of the guys would only use them to speak to their girlfriends. I'll be surprised if, even today, gang members are talking business on their mobile phones from prison. There would be no high form of criminal activity discussed over phones given today's technology in tracking and listening. It's people on the outside who would make the calls for them. We have a very significant database and you'd be surprised what the police know and what we know.'

With escalating violence both inside and out, the gangs forced vulnerable men to join their gangs.

'Recruitment in jail became very high and very significant,' Rush said.

'In that environment you had the baddest of the bad and the toughest of the tough, so it was a perfect recruitment ground. Men would join because they thought they were tough and wanted to be in a gang, or because they weren't tough and needed to be in a gang because they couldn't look after themselves.

'The young Anglos had an especially hard time. Back in the day, the older guys with reputations would take some of these guys under their wing and protect them. But when the MCGs kicked in, the young guys were forced to join gangs and were then ruthlessly exploited. They'd be approached and asked to join, and they'd be left with no choice. What these young Anglos didn't realise was the impact their gang affiliation would have on them personally and also their family. A lot of these guys just thought they could do whatever in jail and they'd be sweet. But that wasn't the case. The MCGs would get their home numbers and ring their parents, demanding $1000 in membership fees. They'd tell the family to pay up, or their son would be flogged.'

Racial gangs continued to operate despite the rise of high density gangs. A 2009 riot was caused by a dispute between two racially aligned gangs.

'The inmates went to town on each other because of a race issue,' said a guard who wished to remain unnamed. 'It was reported as a particularly bad riot, but it wasn't so much a riot because it wasn't directed at the guards. It was a dispute exclusively between the inmates. Like usual, it was ten blokes giving it to one. I grabbed a big Aboriginal bloke who was cut up pretty bad, and he told us it was a race thing.'

The gang-sparked violence became a political issue when Corrective Services told the press the riot was a mere disturbance, angering the Prison Officers' Union.

'A stink kicked off afterwards and it was portrayed as a massive riot because the bosses put it down as an incident,' the guard said. 'Our union blew up because it was bigger than that, a yard full of crims stabbing each other, and they went to the press and blew it up. It was highly exaggerated in the media, with guards being injured and it being called the worst riot ever, but it was still pretty bad as far as gang fights go.'

18

GUARDING

John Mewburn

'The noises coming out of him . . . well, the only thing I could relate it to was the sound of a dying animal.'
Former Long Bay superintendent Dave Farrell

The cars rushed on by, one after the other, finally out of the stop-start of peak hour and nearing home.

Zoom. Zoom. Zoom.

The drivers stare straight ahead, thinking only about dinner and sitcoms, and certainly not hammers smashing brain. Some glance at the prison to the side of the road, the sandstone walls topped with barbwire, and they hope those maniacs inside never get out. But they don't acknowledge the little cottage that sits on the corner, now darkened by the creeping shadows of towers and walls.

The John Mewburn Child Care Centre is the anonymous building that sits on the intersection of Austral Street, Ireton Street and Anzac Parade in Malabar, New South Wales. The cars continue to whizz on by, the drivers rarely noticing the house, let alone its name. And sadly, most of the prison guards next door in Long Bay don't recognise its title either.

But they should, because John Mewburn's fate is what gives them cold sweats at night.

PO John Mewburn turned away from the prisoner, key in hand, and hunched over to unlock the reinforced steel door.

Thud!

The hammer smashed into his head, the force of the impact throwing him against the wall. His skull had been shattered, and the blood spurted from his wound as he slid to the floor.

The prisoner smiled as he watched the red slowly pooling on the white floor before walking off. He did not say a word. He waltzed into the next wing, about 50 metres or so from the body. He entered the bathroom and carefully washed the blood from his hands. He returned to the corridor. A prison guard was walking past.

'You should check on Mewburn,' the prisoner said, casually. 'I think he could be sick.'

The nurse heard the moans; a horrible sound. She headed towards the door, and then she screamed.

The guard, John Mewburn, was covered in blood, which gushed from the gaping hole in his head. Pieces of skull were scattered across the floor. His eyes were open but vacant. He couldn't talk, couldn't move. The only sign of life was that terrible noise. *Mmnwhhhhhh*. The nurse, shocked to the core and now as white as the hospital walls, raised the alarm.

'We were among the first on the scene,' said founding Malabar Emergency Unit officer Dave Farrell, now retired and living in Queensland. 'I went in there and saw blood everywhere. I was a young fella, fresh from the bush, and the noises coming out of him . . . well, the only thing I could relate it to was the sound of a dying animal. It was the sound of death. The scene has never left me and will haunt me for the rest of my life.'

The prison was swiftly shut down. The guards did not know what had happened, but with sirens blaring, they locked the inmates in their cells. Roy Foxwell, who was one of the guards working at that time, heard the nurse's cries and went straight to her.

'I was in the office when we heard the commotion,' Foxwell said. 'We raced over and when I got there, they were carrying out the body. Mewburn was on the stretcher and half his bloody brain was hanging out. I was in shock. I walked in to see if there was anything I could do and I ended up in the middle of the crime scene. It was just horrendous. Later, I found a piece of his skull on my shoe.'

With guards now swarming and Mewburn being rushed to hospital, Farrell saw the nurse shaking in the corner.

'She was just absolutely shattered,' Farrell said. 'She'd tried everything to save the poor bugger's life. She was covered in blood and as white as a ghost. I tried to console her, but really there was nothing I could do that could take those disgusting images away.'

Mewburn never stood a chance and was pronounced dead, the news hitting the prison like an earthquake.

'There was so much tension in the air,' Farrell said. 'You could feel it. It was everywhere. Everyone in that prison wanted to find the bloke who did it. And rip his head off.'

The guard came forward.

'I saw Peter Schneidas leave the bathroom, rubbing his hands,' he said. 'He told me that Mewburn should be checked on because he might be sick.'

Schneidas, a prisoner known as an 'intractable', one of the most difficult inmates to deal with, was soon standing in front of the guards. They were a furious mob, snarling and snorting, screaming in his face.

'We took him out to the yard and we all looked at him,' Farrell said. 'I never felt so much hatred in my life.'

The former Katingal prisoner smiled. He did not deny the crime, and he almost stood proudly, staring them right back in the face.

'He was being a smartarse,' Farrell said. 'We strip-searched him and found a five-dollar note in one shoe. Why he had that, why I remember that, I don't know. Kenny Sharp, the old sweeper, was that angry he pulled Schneidas' pants off and tore them apart in front of his nose. He did it with his bare hands, in an incredible display of strength. I think he was giving him a message. But Schneidas was as calm as anything. The arrogance was just dripping from the pores of his skin. He was as guilty as sin and he didn't care.

'Everyone knew he'd done it. He was very close to being bashed – I suppose only the risk of losing our job stopped us from laying in.'

PO John Mewburn did not see it coming.

He didn't see the weapon Schneidas was holding, or the anger in his eyes. The inmate's right arm was out of view as he approached the gate, tucked behind his back, hand armed with hammer.

'There was absolutely no reason for Mewburn to fear the attack,' said former Long Bay governor Michael Vita. 'He was an innocent victim who'd done nothing wrong to Schneidas at all.

'The attack happened in the Observation (OBS), which was a unit for people with mental health issues. Schneidas was originally sent to jail for cheque fraud, but prison turned him into an animal. He was out for blood that day. So he got himself a hammer and decided he was going to get the first person he saw.'

Farrell also described the crime as senseless.

'Mewburn was opening the gate when he was attacked from behind,' he said. 'He had no chance at all. I can still picture his body lying there, up against the side of the wall, in a corner, spread out. There was claret everywhere and a deathly silence. Numbness, that's what it was, just echoing around the room.'

It later emerged that Schneidas had killed the guard in a bloody protest to a looming jail transfer. From the relative comfort of the hospital prison, the thought of being moved stoked Schneidas's murderous rage.

'He didn't want to be escorted out the next day,' Vita said. 'He'd been told he was going to Goulburn Jail. He objected but his request was refused.'

It remains officially unknown how this man, who'd already received a ten-year prison sentence for an earlier attack on a prison guard, got his hands on a hammer.

'I'm fairly certain it was the hammer we used to check on the bars,' Farrell said. 'Every wing had them. He probably lifted it from the office.'

Foxwell, too, supports this reasoning.

'There were two trains of thought on where he got the hammer,' he said. 'One was that he might've got it from the maintenance shed in the OBS. But more likely he got it from the office – every day an officer in the unit would take the hammer into the rooms and bang on the bars to see if they'd been sawn through.'

The attack sparked industrial unrest – every prison guard in New South Wales was shocked and appalled by the attack. They immediately went on strike, demanding that the closed Long Bay Jail supermax prison, Katingal, be reopened for Schneidas. He deserved nothing less.

*

It was clear that Schneidas was now a marked man – Long Bay Enemy No. 1.

'He was hated by the prisoners as much as by the guards,' Farrell said 'They just fucked with his mind.'

Schneidas attempted to explain his crime to a psychiatrist, claiming he was provoked by the system.

'I'm 20 years old,' he said. 'I've been through Katingal, Grafton, Maitland and OBS. I've been beaten and given the reputation for violence. I've never been given a go; I've never had a decent job in jail. I admit I've hit back, but I've never been violent outside of jail – only inside, in response to the way I've been treated. I've tried to behave myself, but it gets me nowhere. They won't give me a chance. I'm not looking for trouble; I try to avoid it. I have a bad reputation and things just go from bad to worse in jail.'

Schneidas believed the prison system was responsible for his crime.

Bernie Matthews, an armed robber who served time with Schneidas at both Grafton and Katingal, echoed the same sentiment, hinting that the prison system played a role in the guard's death in his book, *Intractable*.

Schneidas spent five years in solitary confinement. Guards claimed he was never bashed in retaliation for his crime. Though Schneidas was given a life sentence for the crime, the ruling was re-determined by the Supreme Court in 1993 and Long Bay's most hated man walked free in 1997. Ten months later, he died from a heroin overdose.

Mewburn's name lives on through the little cottage at Malabar. The man described as a 'true gentleman who gave crims biscuits' should never be forgotten. And he won't be. His untimely death embodies the fear every guard feels as they walk through the gates of Long Bay before a new day of work.

The Brave One

'He never complained. Not once. He used what time he had left to help others. He was a true gentleman.'
Former Long Bay PO Michael Vita on PO Geoffrey Pearce

No amount of colour could bring the cold, hard cement of the prison quadrangle to life. The wall, splashed with several shades of green, was still hellish, the paint nothing but a band-aid for the ugly brick building that kept the criminals locked away.

But the mural, one of five painted by an inmate, in the school-like quad called 'The Circle', was one thing that kept PO Geoffrey Pearce from getting bored. Aside from the paintings, there was only barbwire, a basketball ring, and two fellow guards saving it from complete desertion.

The door slammed shut as the prisoner shuffled onto the concrete. The guard wasn't the slightest bit concerned; besides, this inmate was probably on his way or was just coming back from an appointment.

'Coming through, chief,' the inmate said as he stood before him. 'Just heading to the hospital. Can you let me pass?'

Pearce nodded, pulled the key from his belt and turned

towards the locked gate. Bending over, he placed the key in the lock. 'Ouch!' he suddenly yelled, jumping backwards. Pearce looked behind him to see what had caused him to jolt.

And that's when he saw it. The most feared and horrible weapon in the prison world: a blood-filled syringe, the tip jammed into the flesh of his bum.

The prisoner smiled and Pearce turned white.

Questions flooded the guard's mind: *Why? Who is he? What have I done to him?*

Pearce couldn't answer any of the above because he had never seen this inmate, Graham Farlow, up until now. He'd only been a prison guard for a month.

A fellow officer saw the crim hovering over Pearce and charged. He was about to shout out, when he saw the needle. He was at an immediate loss for words.

While the prisoner was returned to his cell, Pearce was lying in a hospital bed, waiting for another needle to be stuck into his skin for a blood sample to be taken. The nurse walked over, holding a syringe.

'The worst-case scenario is that you're infected with HIV,' she said. 'We don't know for sure, but even if you are, the chances of him infecting you with a jab is more than 400–1 against.'

Geoffrey Pearce was stabbed with an HIV-positive blood-filled syringe on 22 July 1990. A month later he was diagnosed with the virus, eight months later he had AIDS, and seven years later he was dead, aged 28.

Prisoner Graham Farlow had been given a death sentence, and he was filthy on the world. He wanted someone else to feel the humiliation, self-pity and pain, which was now making him lose his mind. So the inmate grabbed a syringe, most likely obtained from a left-wing prison 'needle exchange' program, and he pushed it deep into his most prominent vein. Then he drew back on the plunger, the rushing blood turning the clear vial red. Armed and very dangerous, Farlow walked out into the yard and stabbed the first person he saw. Just like what had happened to Mewburn many years before, the attack was senseless. PO Pearce was at the wrong place, at the wrong time.

Up until 1990, there had been no known accounts of anyone contracting AIDS after being intentionally pricked by a blood-filled syringe. And so Farlow became the first person to make such an urban legend real when he infected Pearce with HIV, which soon developed into full-blown AIDS. Despite thousands of horror stories of people being casually injected with HIV-positive blood – syringes left needle up on cinema seats, random jabs on crowded streets and parting gifts from one-night stands – Long Bay Jail made headlines worldwide when Pearce became the sole documented incident of a pinprick attack leading to the deliberate transmission of HIV.

The attack rocked the jail and sparked a new round of AIDS hysteria. Both guards and prisoners were shocked and saddened by the attack. But most of all they were scared.

If they can get him, each one of them thought, reflecting on the 21-year-old guard who had been completely innocent, inoffensive and now infected, *they can get me.*

Those with targets on their backs were no longer worried

about shivs, metal poles and lumber bats. The most harmful weapon in the prison didn't have to be sharpened on the walls, ripped from a bed, or stolen from a woodwork class. No, this one was far more frightening because it killed slowly, painfully and resolutely.

'HIV became a deadly weapon,' said Michael Vita, who would go on to head the first official prison unit to educate people infected with HIV/AIDS. 'And no one in the prison liked it at all. The Government, officials and health care professionals were all about education and prevention. They handed out needles and condoms. We protested. Give them condoms? That's a good idea. Give them condoms so they can fill them with HIV cum and throw them at us. And needles? Why did they want to hand them weapons?

'We became paranoid of AIDS, and so did our union. We suddenly had strict policies and were given infection control pouches containing bleach, gloves and a little mirror. We were told to treat everyone as though they were HIV-positive. The days of searching an inmate without taking precautions were over. We wore proper prick-proof gloves whenever we touched anything and we used mirrors for checking behind every cornice.

'I wasn't too worried back then; I thought it was all overkill. But later, when I ran the Lifestyles Unit, I realised what happened to Pearce could happen to anyone. It dawned on me that any of these guys could wake up one day and think, "Fuck it. I'm sick, I'm not well and I'm going to die." Shitty at the world, just like Farlow, they could grab a syringe and shove it into anyone. I thought about it a lot when I worked there because I was walking past infected prisoners every day. One of them could have had the shits with me over something as simple as a visit. They all had syringes in their drawer. All they needed to do was pull the needle out, draw some blood and then stick me. They already had a death sentence, so there was nothing to lose. It was a risk, a real risk, and sadly Geoff paid the price.'

When the detective opened the door, the pitch-black cell was flooded with light. Farlow was momentarily blinded. The most-hated man in Long Bay – a bounty was already out on his head – had been tackled, cuffed and thrown straight into Long Bay's loneliest cell. His two escorts, hardened guards who never took a backward step, had snarled in his ear as they'd slammed the cell door. The bigger guard had vented his frustration by smashing at the switch on the outer wall, turning off the only light in the windowless cell. Farlow had been left alone in the dark with nothing but a piss bucket and a piece of foam to sleep on.

The detective was already standing by his bed by the time his eyes stopped stinging, the blinding brightness now gone. Farlow looked at the man holding the notepad and smiled. The detective had arrested and charged the prisoner without asking a single question.

Farlow was undeniably guilty and frighteningly proud. But this murderer would never be found guilty of assault, even though he should have been charged with murder. The disease that killed Pearce also killed Farlow before he could be tried and convicted of his unprecedented crime. There was no doubt he would have been found guilty. And he would have been facing more charges had he not died.

Moved to Goulburn Jail after stabbing Pearce for his own safety, Farlow cut his own arm with a shiv and tried to spray prison guards with his infected blood. This man, who was saved from a life sentence by death, should be forgotten. But the man he killed should be remembered, celebrated and praised for not just everything he stood for, but for the way he lived his last remaining days . . .

Geoffrey Pearce knew he was going to die the moment he was born, like every living thing brought into this world. Following the attack, he figured the only difference between him and everybody else was his death would come sooner rather than later. But unlike most, he knew his time was limited, and he decided to cherish what he had, rather than dwell over what he'd lost.

So Pearce returned to the job that had cost him his life.

'He was back at work straight away,' said Vita. 'That shows you what type of man he was. We all spoke to him afterwards, asked him how he was. But we danced around it a bit, conscious not to make it such a big deal. Not that he acted as though it was. Pearce was quiet, unassuming and sensible. Even after what had happened, he was never full of anger or rage. He never said, "Fuck you, world."'

Pearce became an advocate for HIV and AIDS sufferers. He told them his life wasn't over, and neither was theirs.

He took aim at the bigots, refusing to be ruled by their fear. He continued to relish all that he enjoyed in life, despite the repercussions his HIV diagnosis had brought.

'He loved football and he was a good player in our team,' Vita said. 'But we put him in the side not because he was good but because we wanted to include him and make him feel like part of the gang. It almost backfired, though. Some thought he might give them HIV. I think Pearce knew that, but he kept on playing. He was a very strong character, a proud young man and he became an advocate for his cause and did a lot of good.'

I Was a Long Bay Guard

This is the personal account of life as a prison guard by former Metropolitan Security Unit Prison Officer Grant Turner.

I joined the DCS in 2000 and received 11 weeks of very basic training at the correctional academy at Eastwood, Sydney. I started work in the Long Bay Hospital on Christmas Day of that year.

It was a real eye-opener dealing with inmates who'd been deemed unfit for society but unable to be found guilty of their crimes due to mental illness. One such inmate was Paul Olliers. Paul was about 5 feet 5 inches (1.65 metres), with a thick and strong build. He was covered in scars. He was convicted of manslaughter decades before I joined the DCS. He had passed his sentencing release date but was still incarcerated because a court ruled he was too dangerous to rejoin society.

Paul was a special kind of human. He would do anything for a cigarette or a chocolate, and when I say anything . . . I mean *anything*. He would eat his own shit if you gave him a drag or a bite. Officers were constantly dragging him back into his cell or a holding yard because he refused to behave. Paul had no common sense and he would attack anyone who had something he wanted. And he always wanted cigarettes, food and sex. I had to use force on Paul a number of times. He wasn't the only unruly inmate there, but he was always bashing someone or being bashed by somebody. He didn't mind if he was flogging or being flogged – he just lived to fight.

I walked into Long Bay Hospital (LBH) for my first shift. A senior prison guard shook my hand. He then gave me his only advice.

'Stay away from this fucking idiot,' he said, pointing straight at Paul.

So I did.

Later that day Paul walked past me with his lunch.

'Fucking bullshit,' he muttered. 'Hot. Fucking hot bullshit.'

I then watched him walk to the toilet and dunk his lunch container into the unflushed filth. Most inmates allowed their food to cool, but Paul couldn't wait, so he shoved his food in the shitter.

One day I had to drag him into time-out after he tried to bite an officer who wouldn't make him a cup of coffee.

He attempted to kick me, screaming, as I forced him into his cell.

I ended up forming a rapport with Paul after three years. Paul and I eventually conversed, basic talk but a break-through all the same. He wasn't a strong communicator and started every conversation with 'Gimme-a-moke-ya-cunt.' He considered me a friend and constantly held out his hand for a shake, but I always refused because I didn't know if he had been slurping down toilet water soup. Three years later, after I'd left LBH for the Metropolitan Security Unit, I was assigned back to LBH to assist with Christmas brew searches.

Whack!

While I was chatting to the officer in charge of the area, Paul crept up behind me and hit me in the neck. It hurt. I turned around and 'subdued' him instinctively. As he hit the ground he laughed. I looked at his smiling face and realised that this was his fucked-up way of greeting me. I got him to his feet and looked him up and down. He wasn't the crazy person I remembered but an old, developmentally delayed senior citizen. He had taken to banging his forehead on the wall and had a large calcified lump above his eyebrow from continual self-abuse. I let him go and he walked off. I watched him as he shuffled around the yard.

'Give-us-a-moke-ya-cunts,' he said over and over again, talking to nobody, just looking at the ground.

People fear going to jail, and rightly so. If you come to prison and meet Paul, or someone like him, he will want something from you. He will walk straight up to you and demand it. How you respond will determine how you will spend your days in Long Bay.

He will take everything you have if you give it to him. He will own you. You will become his bitch if he pushes and you don't push back. But if you give him a shove, if you tell him to get fucked, you better be able to fight. Paul, and those like him, are scared of nothing. Say no to them and they will fight. They might even kill.

Ten years after first meeting Paul I saw a nurse pushing him in a wheelchair through the Prince of Wales Hospital. He had been released to a state-run care facility. I said hello and he stuck his hand out to shake mine.

'Gimme-a-moke-ya-cunt,' he said.

I ignored his hand (again thinking about the shitter) and he thought it was hilarious. The nurse gave me a dirty look. She thought I was a mean bastard. But I wonder if she would have given me the eye had she known about all the innocent boys this man had violently and sexually assaulted. Would she have even raised an eyelid had she known about the ruined lives and tortured souls?

I found out Paul had a melanoma on his face and would soon die. I did not feel sorry for him. I never felt sorry for a prisoner, because that wasn't my job. Most inmates want to serve their sentences as quickly and as anonymously as possible. And so do some officers. I've met blokes who hate the job and are just in it until they find something better. But most officers look at the job as a career and want to work in the DCS for many years. They set personal goals and go about climbing the corporate ladder. Others are idealists and want to improve the inmates. They think they can reform them and go about doing just that.

Most of the time, it's boring, repetitive and tedious work with limited personal reward. There is constant abuse from wannabe gangsters, and sometimes it feels the administration cares more for them than you.

I enjoyed my time regardless; not because it was a good job, but because I worked with good people. I met some of the hardest, funniest, kindest and best people of my life while working in jails. I walked with my back turned to killers but I was never afraid. I knew my colleague would risk his life to protect me.

But don't think anyone will protect you if you go into Long Bay as an inmate. Paul might be dead now, but I can guarantee someone just like him will be waiting to meet you as soon as you are left, all alone, in your cell. No one can guarantee your safety in Long Bay. You might be bashed, you might be raped and you might be killed. What is certain is that you will meet a psychopath just like Paul. Trust me when I say you don't want to end up in Long Bay. This is Australia's hardest prison.

SELECT BIBLIOGRAPHY

Age, 'Rapist out of sight but not out of mind', 2 August 2003

Australian Associated Press, 'Cole's Houdini-style jail escape one of the best', *Australian Associated Press*, 20 January 2006

Chipperfield, M., 'Behind the wire', *Sydney Morning Herald*, 30 August 2007

Coroners Court of New South Wales 2010, *Coronial inquest into the death of Anthony Behr*, Coroners Court of New South Wales

Corrective Services Academy 1997, *Long Bay Correctional Complex Conservation Plan, Commissioned by the Department of Public Works for the Department of Corrective Services*, Department of Corrective Services, Sydney

Fife-Yeomans, J., 'Sex change killer to be free as a bird, *Daily Telegraph*, 3 April 2010

Independent Commission Against Corruption 2000, *Investigation into the Department of Corrective Services: Fifth Report: Two Escapes*, ICAC

Independent Commission Against Corruption 2013, *Investigation into the smuggling of contraband into the Metropolitan Special Programs Centre at the Long Bay Correctional Complex*, ICAC

Kass, T., *Long Bay Complex 1896-1994: A History*, Department of Public Works and Services, Sydney, 1995

Kennedy, L., 'Triple killer slain in jail', *Daily Telegraph Mirror*, 22 March 1994

Matthews, B., *Intractable: Hell Has a Name, Katingal: Life Inside Australia's First Super-max Prison*, Pan Macmillan, Sydney, 2006

McClymont, K. and Baker, J., 'Stockbroker Rene Rivkin found dead', *Sydney Morning Herald*, 2 May 2005

Morri, M., 'Gates shut on a criminal era as parts of Long Bay Jail close', *Daily Telegraph*, 17 January 2013

Morton, J., *Maximum Security: The Inside Story of Australia's Toughest Gaols*, Pan Macmillan, Sydney, 2011

O'Toole, S., *The History of Australian Corrections*, UNSW Press, 2006

Parliament of New South Wales 2013, *Issues Backgrounder*, NSW Parliament, No. 2, February

Parliament of New South Wales 2013, *Crimes (Serious Sex Offenders) Amendment Act*, No. 4

Perry, M., 'Driver warned of jail's sexual gorillas', *Reuters*, 6 January 2009

Smith, N. and Noble, T., *Catch and Kill Your Own*, Ironbark, Sydney, 1995

Smith, N. and Noble, T., *Neddy: The Life and Crimes of Arthur Stanley Smith*, KERR, Sydney, 1993

SELECT BIBLIOGRAPHY

Sydney Morning Herald, 'Rivkin to spend weekend at Long Bay', 7 February 2004

Sydney Morning Herald, 'Rivkin still under suicide watch at Long Bay', 8 February 2004

7.30 Report, 'Hepatitis C thrives in jail', Australian Broadcasting Corporation, 14 June 2001

ACKNOWLEDGEMENTS

Long Bay's secrets could not have been revealed without the 52 people who contributed their stories, records and pictures to this book. Many of you have asked to remain anonymous and so you will. Your thanks will be my eternal gratitude.

This project was born over a beer with former PO Grant Turner. Grant opened the gate and gave me a fully guided tour of Long Bay. This book would not have happened without you. Thanks, mate.

Former detective-sergeant Roger Rogerson became my very own personal investigator after I called him for an interview. Not content with just giving his words, the 'Dodger' spent countless hours conducting unpaid research and also gave me safe passage into the Sydney underworld.

Roger was charged with murder shortly after this project was completed. I am shocked by his alleged involvement in the crime, and will be disgusted with him should he be convicted. Until that time, I will not judge and can only be grateful for the help he gave me. I really hope Roger is the man I found him to be, and if not, he deserves to be locked up in a place like Long Bay.

Roger also put me in touch with Roy Foxwell, a tough old bugger who also asked for nothing and gave me everything. The former high-ranking guard gave me his stories, his photos and his friendship.

Former governor Michael Vita was the first guard I formally interviewed for this book. He gave me an honest and no-holds-barred account of his working life and set the benchmark for every interview to come.

Dave 'Emu' Farrell, widely accepted as the toughest bastard to have ever worked at Long Bay, would have given me the shirt off his back if I'd asked. He didn't only just give me his stories, Emu sent me photos, reports and put me in contact with many current and former guards.

I'm also lucky to have a mate called John Elias. Johnny is a former rugby league player, a former World Cup coach, a cancer survivor and a two-time Long Bay inmate. John is endlessly generous to his family and friends. John has always had my back, and I thank him for it.

Ian Mathie is another fearsome man, whose toughness is only outweighed by his generosity. Ian was my mate before I knew he was a two-time inmate. He gave me his stories, his protection and his friendship.

Award-winning crime reporter Adam Walters also proved journalists can be friends with my former *Daily Telegraph* colleague unselfishly handing me his contact book.

I would also like to thank the following people for agreeing, albeit reluctantly in some cases, to being interviewed or helping arrange interviews for this book: John Heffernan, Mick Pezzano, Paul Cafe, 'Former Legend', 'Scary Eyes', 'Kostya', Graham 'Abo' Henry, Tom Domican, Rodney Adler, Ian Hall Saxon, Nat Wood, Jamie Partlic, Paul Rush, 'Nemo', NSW Police, Mick Cumberland, Jaclyn Bates, Jess and Trent White, Shami, and my brother Andrew Phelps, who always does everything and anything he can to help.

I would also like to acknowledge the outstanding crime writing of Stephen Gibbs and Janet Fife-Yeomans. I became very familiar with both your bylines and standout journalism during my research.

A big thanks to Mick Carroll and Tim Morrissey for allowing me to neglect the *Sunday Telegraph* while working on this book and for supporting me endlessly. And of course to my one and only publisher Alison 'what are we going to do next' Urquhart and my two-time editor Cristina Briones. I can't wait to do it all again.

And last but not least I thank my wife, Catherine, and my boys, Riley-James, Harley-Jaz and Jax-Hendrix. I won't ignore you until I start the next one.

ABOUT THE AUTHOR

James Phelps is an award-winning senior reporter for the *Daily* and *Sunday Telegraph* in Sydney. He began as on overnight police rounds reporter before moving into sport, where he became one of Australia's best news-breaking rugby league reporters.

James became News Australia's Chief National Motorsports writer and travelled the world chasing F1 stories, as well as becoming Australia's No. 1 V8 Supercar reporter. James is also a senior feature writer for the *Sunday Telegraph*.

Following the bestselling *Dick Johnson: The Autobiography of a True-Blue Aussie Sporting Legend*, James has returned to his roots to delve into the criminal underworld with *Australia's Hardest Prison: Inside the Walls of Long Bay Jail*, *Australia's Most Murderous Prison: Behind the Walls of Goulburn Jail* and *Australia's Toughest Prisons: Inmates* (August 2016). James is a twice V8 Supercar media award-winner and a former News Awards 'Young Journalist of the Year' and 'Sport Reporter of the Year'.

AUSTRALIA'S MOST MURDEROUS PRISON: BEHIND THE WALLS OF GOULBURN JAIL

An unprecedented spate of murders in the 1990s – seven in just three years – earned Goulburn Jail the ominous name of the 'Killing Fields'. Inmates who were sentenced or transferred to the 130-year-old towering sandstone menace declared they had been given a death sentence.

Gang alliances, power plays, contracted hits, the ice trade, the colour of your skin – even mistaken identity – any number of things could seal your fate.

The worst race war in the history of Australian prisons saw several groups – Aboriginal, Lebanese, Asian, Islander and Anglo – wage a vicious and uncontrollable battle for power. Every day there were stabbings. Every day there were bashings. And then there were murders.

A controversial policy known as 'racial clustering' might have put an end to the Killing Fields, but soon something far scarier would arise, something called Supermax . . . Within the stark white walls, clinical halls and solitary confinement, it is where Australia's most evil men are locked away. It is home to serial killer Ivan Milat; the 'Terror Five' militants who plotted attacks across Sydney in 2005; Brothers 4 Life founder Bassam Hamzy and gang rapist Bilal Skaf, to name a few.

Murderers, terrorists, serial killers, gangsters and rapists – you will meet them all inside Australia's most murderous prison.

Out now!

AUSTRALIA'S TOUGHEST PRISONS: INMATES

These are the true and uncensored stories about Australia's hardest inmates, from Australia's hardest inmates.

Australia's worst serial killer, Martin Bryant – the man who murdered 35 people and injured another 23 at Port Arthur in 1996 – is now a 160kg slob who trades Mars bars for protection in Risdon Prison. Nineteen years after the massacre, his blond hair is gone, and so is his self-righteous smirk . . . but he is as evil as ever. Bryant has attacked several jail workers and still shows no remorse for the crimes that shook the nation. He is just one of the killers you will meet in *Australia's Toughest Prisons: Inmates*.

You will hear from the inmate who almost escaped from Silverwater Jail in a stolen helicopter, from the Rugby League player who almost became a drug mule, from the bikie boss who ran a million-dollar jail drug trade, from the founding Brothers 4 Life members on how the violent gang ran a crime empire from the inside, and from the men who watched as Carl Williams was beaten to death inside Victoria's most secure jail.

The secret lives of Australia's most evil men will be revealed for the first time, with inmates going on the record to talk about killers like Bryant, Ivan Milat, Neddy Smith, Carl Williams, Mark 'Chopper' Read, Michael Kanaan and Lindsay Robert Rose.

Award-winning author and journalist James Phelps reveals the horror of life inside Australia's most notorious jails, including Grafton, Pentridge, Minda, Risdon, Silverwater, Bathurst and Lithgow.

Out August 2016!